An Essay in Religious Understanding

GAUTAMA THE BUDDHA

Richard Henry Drummond

William B. Eerdmans Grand Rapids, Michigan

Printed in the United States of America

Library of Congress Cataloging in Publication Data

Drummond, Richard Henry.
Gautama the Buddha.

Bibliography: p. 219.
1. Gautama Buddha—Teachings. 2. Christianity and other religions—Buddhism.
BQ4132.D78 294.3 73-22281
ISBN 0-8028-3444-2

GAUTAMA THE BUDDHA

Also by Richard Drummond

A History of Christianity in Japan

To Pearl, with whom I have walked
the way to this understanding.

Abbreviations Used in the Notes

BD	*The Book of the Discipline (Vinaya-Piṭaka)*
BGS	*The Book of the Gradual Sayings* (*Anguttara-Nikāya*)
BKS	*The Book of the Kindred Sayings* (*Sanyutta-Nikāya*)
DB	*Dialogues of the Buddha (Dīgha-Nikāya)*
MA	*The Minor Anthologies of the Pali Canon* (*Udāna*, etc.)
MLS	*The Collection of the Middle Length Sayings* (*Majjhima-Nikāya*)
MQ	*Milinda's Questions* (*Milindapañha*)
PEB	*Psalms of the Early Buddhists (Therī-gāthā, Thera-gāthā)*
SBE	*Sacred Books of the East*
WCEB	*Woven Cadences of Early Buddhists* (*Sutta-Nipāta*)

CONTENTS

List of Abbreviations 6
Preface 9
Guide to Pronunciation 16

I. The Religious and Intellectual Environment 17
II. The Life of the Buddha 25
1. The Nature of the Biographical Materials 25
2. The Time and Place 27
3. Birth and Early Years 30
4. The Period of Seeking and the Enlightenment 34
5. The Public Ministry 44
6. The Daily Life of the Buddha 67
7. The End of the Buddha's Life 77
III. The Teaching of the Buddha 84
IV. Nirvana 113

V. Dharma 128
VI. Non-Self 138
VII. Toward Theological Interpretation 153
1. Developments in the History of the Church 160
2. Biblical Perspectives 174
3. Clarification of Criteria 182
4. Basic Evaluations 185
5. Foci of Understanding 189
6. The Problem of Personalism 192
7. Self and the "Critical" Role of the Buddha 194
8. An Oriental Summation 200
9. Concluding Postscript 205
Appendix I—Problems of Text and Canon 209
Appendix II—Defining History and Religion 214
Bibliography 219
Index 229

PREFACE

This book represents an attempt to contribute to religious understanding through the correlation of two scholarly disciplines. These are history of religions and theology (Christian or other). As an historian of religions I try to deal responsibly, that is, according to the best scientific methodologies of the discipline, with the historical data related to the life and teaching of the Buddha. I do not write primarily for professional buddhologists, but I trust that my treatment of the materials will be of interest and profit also to these specialists. As an historian, however, whose personal orientation of faith is Christian, I venture to cross the formal boundaries of the discipline in my quest for understanding. That is, in the process of interpretation and evaluation of the data I make use also of theological categories derived from Christian faith. I believe of course that adherents of other religious traditions are entitled to do the same from their own vantage point of faith. Indeed, there seems to be a growing concern among men and women of every religious commitment in our day to perceive their faith not as an isolated phenomenon but as a meaningful part of a larger whole. I trust therefore that this study will be of interest and help not only to intelligent Christian laymen but to all persons seeking some correlation of the religious history of mankind.

This kind of interdisciplinary work is increasingly felt to be necessary and legitimate by specialists in both history of religions and theology. Historians of religions have long reflected on the nature and scope of their discipline, and we may note certain changes in general orientation over the past century and a half or more of its development. There has always been a consensus that the proper methodological focus of the discipline is that of a social science dealing with historical data of a particular kind. But in what the late Joachim Wach designated as the first two periods of its history there was a pronounced concern to free the new discipline from what many felt to be the constricting influences of dogmatic theology, even to the extent of creating an antitheological bias.

In the period after the First World War, however, a number of scholars felt impelled to move beyond the pioneering emphasis upon philology, ethnology and other forms of technical expertise in order to seek integration of the materials, "to penetrate deeper into the nature of religious experience" and to explore "questions of an epistemological and ultimately metaphysical character." An important reason for this shift or broadening of interest was the emergence upon the scene of distinguished Christian theologians who became deeply interested in history of religions without abandoning their theological concerns. Friedrich Heiler, Rudolf Otto, Nathan Söderblom, Ernst Troeltsch and William Temple were outstanding representatives of this trend. Both Joachim Wach and Gerardus van der Leeuw, although better known as historians of religions, had similar theological concerns.

The development after World War I of crisis theology and in turn of the larger movement known as neo-orthodoxy was probably a major restrictive factor in inhibiting interest among Christian theologians in history of religions until perhaps the end of the 1950's. Historians of religion on their side generally continued to deal with questions of meaning and value, but most tended to refrain from the use of metaphysical or theological categories in their quest for understanding.

At present most historians of religion are still probably more concerned to relate their studies to the disciplines of anthropology, archaeology, psychology and sociology than to theology. Yet we note signs of a move in another direction. Certain notable historians of religion, such as C. J. Bleeker and Kees W. Bolle, are suggesting that the traditional limitations of the discipline need to be transcended if scholars are to be faithful to their responsibility to deal with the nature of the data of religion in their entirety. While historians of religion as such cannot submit to any particular theological orientation, the nature of religious data is such that they cannot be "understood" (which means also to be interpreted) merely with the use of empirical or "natural" categories. Religious symbols point to, and men in their religious practices look to, that which is "beyond" the realm of empirical experience.

An approach that is therefore being suggested is that while history of religions as a social and historical science must continue its focus upon the methodology of historical investigation, it can properly understand and interpret its data only if it enters into some kind of interdisciplinary cooperation with theology. The latter term of course is meant to specify not only Christian theology; the process becomes legitimate when approached from any posture of authentic faith and coherent theological reflection. But, as Kees Bolle has recently put it, "it is only a *specific theology* that can assist and reprimand the historian of religions in his own conflict situations." This book represents therefore an effort to make precisely this kind of interdisciplinary study, that is, to treat specific religious data from within the context of the discipline of history of religions and then to interpret and evaluate the data from a particular vantage point of faith. Concretely, I attempt to present the data of the life and teaching of Gautama the Buddha and to reflect upon their religious meaning and value from the standpoint of Christian faith.

A corresponding and proportionally more widely spread desire for this kind of interdisciplinary study has been emerging among Christian theologians, especially from the late 1950's, when the influence of Barthian theology began to wane. It is not without significance that British theologians were foremost among the early leaders; we may cite the Anglicans A. C. Bouquet and Max Warren and the Presbyterian H. H. Farmer. Something of the significance of the growing effects of this shift of perspective and interest, however, may be sensed from the statement made by Paul Tillich in the last public lecture he gave before his death in 1965. He asserted that if he were given the opportunity he would rewrite his entire *Systematic Theology* in the light of the history of religions. A similar aspiration is reported of the Ceylonese Christian D. T. Niles before his death in 1970.

The World Council of Churches in recent years has given increasing attention to study of the relationship of Christian faith and the primary events upon which it is based to the living faiths of mankind. Many parts of its constituency are currently engaged in serious dialogue with traditional or emerging religions as well as cultures. The election of M. M. Thomas, noted for his creative work in interpreting the Hindu tradition in the light of Christian faith, as chairman of the Central Committee of the WCC, the creation of the sub-unit, Dialogue with Men of Living Faiths and Ideologies, under the leadership of S. J. Samartha, and the focus of the 1971 Addis Ababa meeting of the Central Committee upon these issues are all indicative of the shift in perspective and concern of which I speak.

The "Declaration on the Relationship of the Church to Non-Christian Religions" was among the most significant documents of the Second Vatican Council in constituting a theological watershed for the Roman Catholic Church. It was subsequently noted that by the explicit recognition of the theological meaning and value of other religious traditions expressed in the Declaration, the Roman Catholic Church "has abandoned officially an exclusive claim to religious values for the first time in history." The understanding revealed in the Declaration constituted a focus of theological studies that had been carried on with increasing activity for several decades prior to the Council. In the years following even greater attention has been given to the problem with the result that it is now one of the major themes of contemporary theological concern in the Catholic Church.

Among the Roman Catholic theologians whose work significantly contributed to the results of the Council in this area may be cited the names of Maurice Blondel, Yves Congar, Jean Daniélou, Henri de Lubac, Raymond Panikkar and Karl Rahner. In subsequent years notable figures have been Gregory Baum, Ewart Cousins, Charles Davis, Hans Küng, Heinz Robert Schlette and, as men who are, or were, both theologians and historians of religions, Louis Gardet, Kishi Hideshi, Louis Massignon, Joseph J. Spae and Robert Charles Zaehner. Among Eastern Orthodox theologians Georges Khodr, Leonidas J. Philippidis and T. Paul Verghese are well known for their contributions in the area of the theological significance of the history of religions.

Protestants are almost too numerous to mention, but a perhaps arbitrary list would include, besides M. M. Thomas and S. J. Samartha, the Indians A. J. Appasamy, V. Chakkarai, P. Chenchiah, V. E. Devadutt, Paul D. Devanandan and D. G. Moses, the Ceylonese D. T. Niles, the Japanese Ariga Tetsutarō, Doi Masatoshi and Yagi Seiichi, and the African John S. Mbiti. In Europe and the Americas we may cite Ernst Benz, A. C. Bouquet, Kenneth Cragg, Nels F. S. Ferré, Carl F. Hallencreutz, Stephen Neill, Wolfhart Pannenberg, Wilfred C. Smith, John V. Taylor and Paul Tillich. Even though they do not write primarily as theologians, men such as the American philosopher William Ernest Hocking and the British historian Arnold Toynbee have contributed much to the discussion.[1]

There are of course considerable variations among the views of these men, but they almost all share certain basic perspectives or primary affirmations of faith with reference to our present area of concern. They affirm that God is sovereignly free within his creation, free, in particular, to manifest himself, his will and his saving grace outside as well as within the historic bounds and instrumentation of Israel and the Christian church. As Irenaeus put it, "Where the Spirit of God is, there is the church and all grace." These men understand with

[1] Note of course should be taken of Hendrik Kraemer, Arend Th. van Leeuwen, Edmund Perry, Georg F. Vicedom, and others of primarily Barthian theological orientation. While these men also have differences of view among themselves, in general they would not share, I believe, the basic perspectives mentioned in the following paragraph in the same sense as the others mentioned.

Georges Khodr that "All who are visited by the Spirit are the people of God." This is also to say that the great religions of mankind are, under God, potential "training schools of the divine mercy," that the living God, in his Son and through the Holy Spirit, is and always has been sovereignly and savingly present in the whole of his creation. As Raymond Panikkar has written, we have to do with a "universal economy of salvation and a certain mysterious presence of the Lord in a multitude of epiphanies."

This is not to say that these men, to use traditionally pejorative terms, have fallen into relativism or syncretism, in the sense of failing to distinguish between the living God and "idols" (penultimate symbols or realities as distinguished from the ultimate Center). Differently from most professional theologians of previous generations, they have relatively wide knowledge of the data of history of religions and feel impelled by the imperatives of their faith-understanding to include these data within the materials, in some cases even as "source" materials, for their theological work. These theologians, I believe, are all concerned to retain the specificity and authority of their Christian faith. But they sense an impelling need to enlarge the more traditional ranges of Christian theological material in the West to include evidences of the "wider work of God in the world." In other words, they wish to live "a universal life in the concrete," to universalize their faith without losing its specificity. They want to participate in the entire spiritual heritage of mankind, to correlate Christian faith with the whole, to the end that this faith may be enriched and enlarged, possibly corrected and reformed, without loss of authentic identity and continuity with the past.

A particular task that not a few of these theologians are laying upon those who as Christians are engaged in the study of the historical data of history of religions is to seek to identify all "Christic values" in other religious traditions as an important contribution to integrative syntheses and interpretation of the materials. They ask us to look for traces (*Spuren*) of the divine presence and work in the whole of human history, even though, as Karl Rahner has said, we have heretofore looked too ineptly and with too little love at other religious traditions to perceive these traces. This book then may be seen as an attempt, however inadequate, to respond to this imperative with reference to the specific phenomenon of Gautama the Buddha, whom Romano Guardini considered perhaps the "last" man adequately to be interpreted by Christian theology.

If I may speak of my personal background, a major specialty of my adult life has been Japanese studies. Even though the bulk of the historical section of the book is based upon a fresh examination of the original texts as found in the translations of the Pali Text Society, I must acknowledge that my approach to these materials has been influenced by the works and persons of noted Japanese buddhologists. Among these I should like to cite with particular appreciation the names of Abe Masao, Bandō Shōjun, Nakamura Hajime and Watanabe Shōkō. I wish also to mention gratefully as men by whom I have been greatly helped, the Japanese Roman Catholic scholar, Kishi Hideshi, now president of Eichi University in Amagasaki, and an American colleague-friend, Minoru Kiyota, Professor of Buddhist Studies in the Department of Indian Studies of the University of Wisconsin, Madison.

At this point I wish to offer functional definitions of two key terms used in this book, history and religion. I define history as the study and descriptive statement of the human past. Religion is that dimension of human life which refers to ultimate meaning, value and/or reality insofar as these are apprehended by the person or persons concerned. Further discussion of these definitions will be found in the second appendix.

I wish to express my sincere thanks to the following persons who read my manuscript and from whose criticisms I have greatly profited: Dr. Harmon H. Bro, visiting scholar, the Center for the Study of World Religions, Harvard University; Dr. Joseph M. Kitagawa, dean of the Divinity School of the University of Chicago; Dr. Minoru Kiyota, Professor of Buddhist Studies, the University of Wisconsin, Madison; and Dr. Raymond (Raimundo) Panikkar, Professor of Religious Studies, the University of California, Santa Barbara. I am gratefully indebted also to my wife Pearl and our son Donald Craig for similar help. None of these persons of course is in any way responsible for remaining errors of fact or judgment.

Richard H. Drummond

Guide to Pronunciation

The oldest source materials for the Buddhist tradition are found in two related Indian languages, Sanskrit and Pāli. Since, however, the Sanskritic forms are more familiar to English-speaking readers, I regularly use them with an occasional addition of the Pāli reading in brackets. Exact quotations may contain the Pāli form, as *Dhamma* for the Sanskrit *Dharma* or *Nibbāna* for *Nirvāṇa.*

The vowels of Sanskrit are generally pronounced as in Italian; the long *ā* in the English f*a*ther, *ē* like the *a* in ev*a*de and *ī* like the *i* in mach*i*ne. Short *a,* however, is a colorless sound comparable to the vowel of the English b*u*t or s*o*n. There is in Sanskrit an untrilled *r*-sound that is used as a vowel and transliterated sometimes as *ṛ*; I prefer, however, to transcribe this sound as *ri.* There is also an *ḷ* that may be pronounced as a vowel.

As for the consonants, *h* when it follows another consonant regularly effects an aspirated diphthong. *Bh* is pronounced somewhat as in the English clu*bh*ouse, but it issues as a single diphthong without pause between the parts. Palatal *c* is pronounced about like the *ch* in *ch*eese. *J* is approximately as in *j*udge. The nasal *ñ* is like the *ny* in ca*ny*on. The sibilant *ś* is similar to the English *sh* but pronounced more in the front of the mouth; *ṣ* is a variant of this sound uttered from farther in the back.

Ḥ is a final *h*-sound articulated from the position of the preceding vowel.

Ṁ, to be distinguished from the labial *m,* is a resonant semi-vocalic nasal pronounced with the mouth open.

Ṅ, to be distinguished from the dental *n* and the cerebral *ṇ*, is a guttural nasal pronounced like *ng* in si*ng*ing.

I

THE RELIGIOUS AND INTELLECTUAL ENVIRONMENT

Knowledge of at least the salient elements of the religious and intellectual environment of Gautama the Buddha is necessary to a proper understanding of his life and teaching. The focal area of that environment and also of the first generation of primitive Buddhism was northeastern India in the sixth century B.C. The Ganges river basin at the beginning of the sixth century manifested a burst of intellectual and spiritual activity that at some points resembles that of the Greek-speaking coast of Asia Minor during the same period. Thales, Anaximander and Anaximenes were all active in the first half of the sixth century; Pythagoras and Xenophanes were roughly contemporaries of the Buddha in the second half of the century. A spirit of critical inquiry, love of abstract speculation, remarkable skill in syllogistic and other forms of logical thought and, as the background suitable for this activity, a politico-social condition that greatly favored freedom of thought characterized both Ionia and northeastern India at this time.

The Ganges river basin was the area of religious and intellectual activity chiefly responsible for the creation of the *Upaniṣads.* These documents, which emerged over a period from around 800 B.C. to perhaps the lifetime of the Buddha or even later and were the religio-philosophical writings that formed the basis of almost all subsequent Hindu philosophical developments, gave literary expression to a radical reorientation of an important segment of Indian religious life from the cultic-sacrificial practices of Vedic-Brahmanism to the inner life and, at a certain stage, to man living apart from society. Like the Ionian Greek thinkers, the anonymous authors of the *Upaniṣads* were radical critics of certain of the accepted principles of thought and action in the land. Theirs, however, was not the only view to flourish. There were schools that advocated what we would call materialism, skepticism, sensualism and various other ideas. Almost all, however, shared to some extent in a critical stance toward the sacerdotalism of the older Vedic orthodoxy.

This was the period wherein a number of relatively independent city-states flourished along the Ganges, and none of the four major kingdoms of the area was able to conquer the others. This political situation, however, was to be but a temporary phenomenon. With the absorption of the city-states into larger political entities, the high degree of philosophical and religious freedom that accompanied their heyday died out. Differently from at least certain periods of classical Greek history or of Renaissance Italy, the Indian city-states found it impossible to form effective political confederations.[1] Most significantly, however, the life of Siddhārtha Gautama was lived at the height of the period of free intellectual activity.

We should not overstress the parallel between the Greek and Indian activities, because the former developed more in the direction of a study of physical nature while the Indian emphasis tended toward the spiritual and metaphysical. Psychologically, Indian thought has been largely introspective, and in relation to the phenomenal world it has primarily been concerned to seek Being that transcends nature. Yet the questions asked by the pre-Socratic Greek philosophers were similar to

[1] Nakamura Hajime, *The Ways of Thinking of Eastern Peoples*, pp. 112-113.

some of those asked by the Indians: What is everything made of?, How do things come into being, change and pass away?, What permanent substance or substances exist behind appearances?[2] Profoundly suggestive, however, is also the fact that Socrates, whose birth in 469 B.C. occurred but a dozen years after the Buddha's death, was, like the Buddha, primarily concerned for the ethical life of man.

We learn from an old Buddhist Scripture, the *Brahmajāla-Sūtra,* what were some of the problems that exercised the minds of the Indian sages of this period. They asked: Is the world finite or infinite, eternal or not eternal? Is the self (*ātman*) eternal or not? Are the world and self caused by some other being or do they exist as uncaused phenomena? Can the human understanding attain sure knowledge, or is it the case that no opinion can be considered absolutely certain? Does the self remain in existence after death, and if it continues, does it have consciousness or not? Does it have form or is it without form? Is it finite or infinite? Is it conscious primarily of unity or of multiformity? Is it happy or unhappy? Or does the self disintegrate after death like the body? These questions the sages sought to answer in varied and often contradictory ways.

Other texts relate that, like the Ionian Greeks, men were earnestly concerned about the relationship in the universe of parts to the whole, about the nature of matter and above all about the nature of human thought. The main problem for Indian thinkers, however, was that of human destiny, especially its destiny after death.

We note among the schools that existed in the age of the Buddha the Eternalists, who proclaimed that both the soul and the world are eternal. The Non-Eternalists maintained that only Brahmā as Creator is eternal and immutable, but that human beings and all else are created and both impermanent and mutable. Among the Extensionists, one group affirmed the infinity, another the finiteness of the world. One group of Equivocators, who "wriggle like eels," refused to take responsibility for ethical decisions and equivocated as to whether there is appropriate fruit or consequences of good and bad actions.

[2] Cf. Rex Warner, *The Greek Philosophers,* p. 9.

There were Fortuitous Originists who maintained that the soul and world arise without a cause. With their speculations others tried to "reconstruct the past" and "arrange the future." Some contended for the conscious existence of the soul after death, others for its unconscious existence, others opted for a state neither conscious nor unconscious, others for its annihilation. In every case, when asked about them, the Buddha emphasized that these speculations cannot be relied on and in fact have a deleterious effect on the future condition of those who hold them. The truth of his own teaching he believed to be of another order, "profound, difficult to realize, hard to understand, tranquillizing, sweet, not to be grasped by mere logic, subtle, comprehensible only by the wise, which the Tathāgata, having himself realized and seen face to face, hath set forth."[3]

There were thus profound differences in both world view and style of life among the various schools of thought in India at this time. They shared, however, a common methodology that differed radically from that of the Ionian Greek thinkers. The latter made the first completely rationalistic attempts to describe the nature of the universe. Their cosmological speculation made use of traditional, nonscientific elements, but a primary aspect of their methodology was reliance upon sensory data, in particular the observation of external phenomena. All Indian thinkers after the Vedic period, however, appear to have regarded the experiences of Yoga, that is, of introspective or meditative practices, as the primary basis for their discovery of truth. In spite of disagreement as to which of these practices were better or more effective, agreement was apparently universal as to the validity of this method for realization of both truth and spiritual freedom.[4]

The land of the Sākyas in the foothills of the Himalayas in which the Buddha was born was on the frontier of Brahmanic-Vedic civilization. By the sixth century B.C., however, that civilization had come to be a significant cultural constituent of the larger Ganges basin, albeit in an altered form. The Brāhman or priestly caste formed the spiritual elite of this

[3] *Dīgha-Nikāya,* I, 12-46; DB, I, 26-55.

[4] Cf. Edward Conze, *Buddhist Thought in India,* pp. 17-30.

civilization; we shall see that a relatively large proportion of the monastic disciples of the Buddha came from this caste. The Brāhmans furnished many of the disciples of other religious movements of the time: the Jains, the Ājīvakas and other kinds of wandering recluses or *śramaṇa* (ascetic, generally celibate strivers after knowledge).

Brāhman orthodoxy, however, by this time evidently included a relatively wide range of accepted content in both thought and practice. The primary authority of the *Vedas* and dependence upon the sacrifices and other rites enjoined by these Scriptures were still central to Brahmanic practice. Brāhman priests alone could perform these rites, and it was widely believed that human destiny depended upon their punctiliously correct performance. But the radical reorientation and implied criticism of Vedic religion that the *Upaniṣads* constituted had, at least in part, been taken into the larger structure of Brahmanic orthodoxy. The fluidity of the situation is seen in the fact that Brāhmans were very much in evidence among those responsible for the *Upaniṣads*, those who became wandering ascetics, or those who in particular united with the early Buddhist movement, the Ājīvakas or the Jains.

One characteristic, however, of the great spiritual and intellectual activity of the sixth century was that men of all castes felt impelled to participate in it. No one but a Brāhman could perform the sacred rites, but the main *Drang* of the age was away from rites and traditional practices of every kind. It specifically included a strong desire to overcome Brahmanic religious monopolies. The Ganges river basin was not the original center of Aryan culture, and the fact that the Upanishadic literature developed here among people of partly non-Aryan stock implies a certain cultural bias in the attempt to qualify if not to undermine Brahmanic dominance.[5]

The wandering ascetics (*śramaṇa*) frequently mentioned in early Buddhist Scriptures were those who had abandoned the household life for the (presumably) complete spiritual freedom of the homeless, mendicant way, and in this state they

[5] Cf. Iwamoto Yutaka, *Bukkyō Nyūmon*, pp. 40-41; Heinrich Zimmer, *Philosophies of India*, p. 60.

strove to solve the problems of life as perceived by men of their day. They came out of every caste, although most numerously from the Kṣatriya and the Brāhmans. As we have seen, they represented almost every extreme of doctrine and ascetic practice. Sometimes they scandalized their contemporaries by their misdeeds and immoralities, for there were evidently not a few charlatans among them. But there were clearly also noble and sincere men who were especially honored by the populace, because supernatural powers were believed to accrue to the life of renunciation of worldly ties and pleasures. It was in this, for India, almost unique era of spiritual and social freedom that Siddhārtha Gautama was born.

Amidst this variety and fluidity of thought there were, however, certain presuppositions that almost all sects assumed to be among the givens of life. One was the concept of rebirth, the origin of which lies outside the mainstream of Vedic-Aryan thought, although it appears in its later forms, perhaps first in the early *Brihadāraṇyaka Upaniṣad.*[6] This concept refers to the process whereby the whole of phenomenal existence—that of gods, men, demons, animals, and all lower forms of life—is believed to be involved in a cycle of continued rebirth (reincarnation) either on earth or in other realms of this or different worlds. Rebirth in turn is part of a larger cyclical process of phenomenal change called *saṁsāra.* The Brāhmans and related circles of the laity generally regarded this process in relatively optimistic wise, believing that proper performance of or participation in Brahmanic rites would guarantee their rebirth in favorable circumstances.

Most of the ascetics, however, viewed more bleakly the prospect of an unending series of rebirths. Perhaps influenced at least in part by the non-Aryan elements of their background, they regarded the cultural achievements of civilization in the Ganges river basin with a critical eye and saw the prospect of rebirth into the vanities of even the best situation therein as no truly desirable goal. Among these circles the view developed that the true liberation of man lay in breaking the

[6] Zimmer, *op. cit.*, p. 252; *Brihadāraṇyaka,* IV, 4, 3-6; Swami Nikhilananda, *The Upanishads,* pp. 234-235. Cf. W. N. Brown, *Man in the Universe,* p. 7; Nels F. S. Ferre', *The Universal Word,* pp. 238-239, 246-253.

whole chain of samsaric process. We note the emergence of a more negative evaluation of phenomenal existence than characterized the main thrust of Vedic or Upanishadic teaching, and a higher appreciation of the radically ascetic life.

The *Vedas* do not lack ethical teaching, but it is obvious that the Brahmanic interpretative emphasis upon the correct performance of sacrificial rites and ceremonies as central to men's salvation tempted the less earnest to a relative neglect of ethical concerns. The authors of the *Upaniṣads*, however, and, apparently, the ascetics in larger compass tended to support the possibly pre-Aryan doctrine that the process of rebirth is to be understood primarily in ethical terms. That is, the form of rebirth is determined favorably or unfavorably by the ethical quality of men's deeds (*Karma*) in this life. This view took deep root and has remained a vital part of subsequent Indian life.

As regards the nature of man, various views were held, as we have seen, but the most widespread was that man consists of both impermanent and eternal elements. In the former category are material and mental aspects both of which disintegrate at death. The eternal element is that which is reborn. It was called the self (*ātman*), the vital principle (*prāna*), the individual soul (*jīva*), or person (*puruṣa*).[7] Use of the last term suggests that, for some, continuity of a personal element in the eternal "essence" was implied. The doctrine of the eternity of the "soul" was understood in at least two different ways: either as an infinity of separate souls as taught by the *Sāṅkhya* school and by the Jain, or as a part or manifestation of the one universal Soul, the central teaching of the *Upaniṣads.*[8]

Among the methods employed by the ascetics to achieve their goal of cutting the chain of the samsaric (karmically interpreted) process, the techniques of Yoga in its primary meaning of disciplined–often severely ascetic–meditation were most popular. Their goal was to break through the impermanent elements of man into contact with his eternal principle, which was usually regarded as at least an aspect of Ulti-

[7] André Bareau, *Die Religionen Indiens*, III, 9.

[8] Cf. Edward J. Thomas, *The Life of the Buddha as Legend and History*, p. 35; Zimmer, *op. cit.*, pp. 256, 315.

mate Reality and therefore as of the highest religious significance. The methods varied according to the teacher and school, but deep mental and spiritual concentration was apparently basic to all.

Interpretations varied also as to the nature of Ultimate Reality. Certain schools believed in the existence of what we may call a high God, immaterial and immortal, in some cases personal, in others suprapersonal if not impersonal. He was called Brahman, or Brahmā, by some, Īśvara (Lord) by others. The last term came to be used within later Hinduism as the appellative for a highly personal God or gods. In the period we are now considering, the schools that believed in the continuity of the personal element in man even after liberation may be understood as presuming an ultimate distinction of the self from the Lord and possibly an element of the personal in the Lord. On the other hand, the central teaching of the *Upaniṣads* was that liberation is achieved by a realization in depth of the identity of the essence of the self (*Ātman* as true Self) of man with Brahman. The materialist schools, however, and certain others, completely denied the existence of a high God or ultimate spiritual Reality. Then there is considerable evidence from later Indian history that among the common people belief in the old gods of Vedic religion and pre-Aryan Dravidian and other divinities still continued although with some changes in emphasis. The era, in short, was distinguished by the remarkable breadth of religious and intellectual options that it made available to all interested persons.

II

THE LIFE OF THE BUDDHA

1

THE NATURE OF THE BIOGRAPHICAL MATERIALS

In attempting to portray even the main lines of the life and teaching of Gautama the Buddha (the Enlightened One), we confront at once specific problems. There is no formal "life of the Buddha" to be found in the older texts, which contain only incidental or fragmentary references to the events of his life. His immediate disciples evidently had little concern for such matters; Indian society in general is noted for its relative lack of interest in historiography or even the chronicling of events.

The first instance of a formal biography of the Buddha is the Sanskrit *Buddhacarita* of Aśvaghoṣa composed toward the end of the first century after Christ. Probably originating in approximately the same period is the largely legendary biography *Lalita-vistara* (The Pleasurable Biography), composed in Sanskrit somewhat intermixed with popular speech. A later biography important for its subsequent influence is the

Nidāna-kathā, written probably by the great Ceylonese scholar Buddhaghosa in the fifth century after Christ, that is, approximately one thousand years after the lifetime of its subject.

Admittedly we must be careful not to make too deft or final a distinction in these materials between that which is "historical" and that which is "legendary." The range of experience and expectation of less perceptive men should not become the final criterion of that which is historical in the life of a man of the spiritual stature of the Buddha. But the extent of what we are compelled to call legendary or mythical material in all of these later "biographies" is such that we are able to use them only with the greatest discretion. We shall therefore generally employ for our primary materials the older texts, even though legendary matter is found, in lesser quantity, in the oldest strata.[1]

Even in the case of the older texts, however, we deal at all times with materials that have passed through many hands. Leaving further discussion to the first appendix, we may note here that all of the extant texts are the products of a process of transmission that bore the possibility of "interpretation" and revision to a greater or less degree. Most scholars hold that the early monastic communities instituted appreciable changes in the traditions, particularly in the form of additions. Since the historical-critical method has not been applied to Buddhist sacred texts to the extent, for example, of the Christian Bible, assured results are few. I believe, however, that by combining the methodology of scientific historical research with "religious understanding" we can delineate a portrait of the Buddha which is both coherent and essentially faithful to the historical data.

Material that is nonhistorical of course may inform our understanding of Buddhism as an historical movement or even possibly give insight into aspects of the life and teaching of the Buddha. One example is the *Jātakas,* or stories of the previous lives of the Buddha. A central theme is the steadfastness of purpose of the great Being who beginning as the youth Sumedha persevered through innumerable lives amidst every kind of

[1] Cf. Nakamura Hajime, *Gōtama Budda,* pp. 12-18.

trial and difficulty until he finally achieved enlightenment as the Buddha Gautama.[2] Stressing the ideal of service to others, abandonment of selfish desire and merciful conduct, the *Jātakas* succeeded in transmitting what appears to be the essence of the spirit if not the direct teaching of the Buddha.[3]

2

THE TIME AND PLACE

Various dates have been given for the birth of Gautama the Buddha. The process is that of calculation backwards from the relatively fixed date of the accession to the throne of the great Mauryan emperor Aśoka in 274 B.C. Uncertainties remain, however, and the most that can be said is that the consensus of modern scholarship points to a date near 560 B.C.[4] Tradition is unanimous that the Buddha lived to the age of 80; the date of his death will thus be close to 480 B.C.

The oldest accounts agree that the Buddha was born in the grove of Lumbinī near Kapilavastu, capital of the small aristocratic republic of the Śākyas, which lay in a rich irrigated plain between the foothills of Nepal and the Rapti River. Kapilavastu is in the district of modern Nepal called Terai or Tarai. The Buddha's personal name was Siddhārtha (Pāli: Siddhattha), meaning "he who has achieved his goal," and his father's name Śuddhodana, who as rāja ruled the district under a measure of suzerainty of the king of Kośala. The term "rule," however, may mean no more than to serve as the elected president of the assembly of nobles.[5] Kośala at this period was the largest of the four chief kingdoms of northern India, the

[2] Cf. I. B. Horner, *Ten Jātaka Stories*, pp. vii-x.

[3] Cf. Watanabe Shōkō, *Shin Shakuson Den*, pp. 15-27.

[4] In China and Japan a date long traditional was 1067 B.C. Modern Buddhists in Burma, Ceylon and India claim 623 B.C. as the proper date, those in Thailand, Cambodia and Laos 624 B.C. Cf. Iwamoto Yutaka, *Bukkyō Nyūmon*, p. 38; Edward J. Thomas, *The Life of the Buddha as Legend and History*, p. xix.

[5] Cf. Sir Charles Eliot, *Hinduism and Buddhism*, I, 131.

others being Avantī, Magadha and Vamsā. Kapilavastu, however, clearly enjoyed a considerable measure of local autonomy both politically and culturally.

Siddhārtha's mother Māyādevī died a few days after his birth, and the responsibility for his upbringing fell largely on his aunt on his mother's side, Mahāprajāpatī Gautamī, who perhaps was or became a wife of Śuddhodana.[6] The texts record that she later became the first Buddhist nun.

The tradition is strong that the Buddha was born into the Kṣatriya or warrior caste,[7] although Gautama is a Brāhman family name. Vedic caste distinctions, however, probably had less significance in this area than in the older centers of Vedic-Aryan culture in northwestern India. There is some evidence, such as the presence of certain non-Aryan customs and the non-Aryan etymology of the names of Śākyan villages, to suggest that at least part of the population about Kapilavastu was of Tibetan-Burman and therefore of Mongoloid racial origin.[8] On the basis of the total evidence we seem to be unable to speak with finality of the racial background of the Buddha.[9] The Scriptures, however, consistently refer to him as of Aryan race, and the term *Ārya* is frequently used in his discourses to denote that which is noble and good. He clearly shared with many or most of his hearers experience of Vedic-Aryan civilization and perhaps a knowledge of the post-Vedic *Upaniṣads.* Of no little significance, however, in understanding the life and teaching of the Buddha is the fact that he came to take a position of radical independence toward the developing form of Vedic-Aryan civilization that we may call Brahmanism. The place of his birth and the location of his entire ministry in northeastern India are important elements in the background of this fact. We should also note certain sociological factors operative in the situation.

Northeastern India in the middle of the sixth century before

[6] Later tradition gives the circumstances of the Buddha's birth as replete with miracles, including accounts of a virgin birth. Cf. *Buddhacarita,* I, 19-26; SBE, XLIX, 4-5.

[7] E.g. *Jātaka,* I, 49; Henry Clarke Warren, *Buddhism in Translations,* p. 41.

[8] Cf. Iwamoto, *op. cit.,* pp. 2-16.

[9] Heinrich Zimmer believed both the Buddha and Mahāvīra, the contemporary leader of the Jain movement, to have been of non-Aryan racial stock (*Philosophies of India,* pp. 60, 221).

Christ enjoyed, as we have seen, a notable cultural flowering. Commercial activity had developed especially along or near the Ganges River, and larger towns were being created. As a consequence a merchant class of increasing wealth and social power emerged that was composed not of Brāhmans but of Vaiśyas, the third caste according to Brahmanic distinctions. The older ruling groups of the rural areas, generally classified as of Kṣatriya caste, also shared in the growing wealth and cultural self-confidence of the time and place. These two groups were evidently significant elements in the emergence of various forms of critique of the Aryan-Vedic civilization that had become the dominant cultural expression of North India, first in the northwestern section and later throughout the whole of northern India.

An integral element of the participation in Vedic-Aryan civilization was formal acceptance of the Brāhman priestly caste as solely competent to perform the rites connected with birth, initiation into adulthood, marriage, death, etc. Basic to this acceptance was recognition of the authority of the *Vedas,* the sacred Scriptures in conformity with which the Brāhmans conducted their rites. One of the most important developments, however, in the religious history of India is reflected in the creation of the body of literature called the *Upaniṣads,* which follow the *Vedas* in point of time but, as we have noted, manifest distinctly different religious apprehensions and emphases. The *Upaniṣads* profess to be theological explanations of the *Vedas* but in fact constitute a basic reorientation from Vedic ritualism and "polytheism" to inwardly directed religious practices and generally monistic philosophical speculation. This literature developed largely under the patronage of royal courts in the northeastern part of India. Kings themselves evidently contributed seminal thought as well as financial support to the activity.

This movement can hardly be called a religious revolt, because there is no overt attack on the older ways. Likewise, neither the Buddha nor his great contemporary Mahāvīra, the Jain teacher, attacked Brahmanism as a system to be done away with or urged their followers to refrain from participating in its rites. But both Buddhism and Jainism, and somewhat later the Ājīvakas, shared with the authors of the *Upaniṣads* a critical stance toward certain basic intellectual and religious principles of Brahmanism. The nature of this critique we shall consider more in detail in subsequent chapters.

We may add that the converts to the Buddhist and Jain movements, both monastic and lay, were drawn to a considerable degree from the families of the urban merchants and rural landowners. Though with different emphases, both the Buddha and Mahāvīra offered not only a currently acceptable solution to the problem of man's destiny in the cosmos. They affirmed in a new way the spiritual and social significance of the Kṣatriya and Vaiśya castes.[10] Both of these religious traditions had their origin in northeastern India. The place and the time of the Buddha's birth, therefore, are of vital significance in evaluating the movement that issued from his life and teaching.

3

BIRTH AND EARLY YEARS

A tradition developed that is referred to in the very earliest extant literature to the effect that the Buddha came down from *Tuṣita* ("Satisfied") heaven to enter the womb of his mother. The one who as teacher and seer leads gods and men, the one who puts gloom to flight is said to have dwelt formerly in rapture above.[11] A seer (*riṣi*) Aṣita in noontime meditation saw in trance the rejoicing of the gods at the birth of the man supreme, who was born for the welfare and bliss of all the world. He thereupon went to the land of the Śākyans and the abode of Śuddhodana, where hẹ took up the child and in words no little reminiscent of Simeon with the child Jesus prophesied his great enlightenment, his work of cosmic scope for the welfare of man, the universal extent of the influence of his life.[12]

[10] Cf. W. Norman Brown, *Man in the Universe, Some Cultural Continuities in India,* p. 101. Note must also be taken, however, that an appreciable number of the Buddha's monastic followers came from the Brāhman caste.

[11] *Sutta-Nipāta* 955-956; WCEB, p. 139.

[12] *Sutta-Nipāta* 679-698; WCEB, pp. 102-104. Cf. Luke 2:22-35.

We have no external criteria by which either to accept or reject this account, but at least we may take it as revealing the cosmic significance early believers assigned to the person and work of the Buddha. The accounts of his childhood life, however, are more obviously legendary. In the sources that may be considered as containing earlier materials there is almost no information about this period. Later stories, however, that credit the boy with learning the knowledge and skills appropriate to a rāja's son and manifesting extraordinary mental and physical ability would seem to err chiefly in degree. In adult life the Buddha showed remarkable mental acumen and skill in argument; his long life and arduous missionary journeys suggest a sturdy physical constitution.

The later biographies, on the other hand, portray the life of the young Siddhārtha as one of extreme luxury and magnificence to heighten the contrasts of his later sacrificial renunciation. Rather than softly luxurious, however, it is more likely that he was trained according to the standards of a martial aristocracy with emphasis upon the active life.[13] Some accounts indicate that he learned to read and write, a fact, however, of not too great cultural significance since probably no more than tax records and the like were written down at this period. Religious teaching was considered too precious to be communicated other than by word of mouth. In general, for the place and time Siddhārtha's position was one of relative wealth and privilege. Some accounts suggest that he was a thoughtful youth and had begun at an early age to reflect on the inconsistencies and frailties of human life.[14]

Siddhārtha is said to have married at the age of sixteen or seventeen, according to varying accounts, a bride named Yaśōdharā. Some sources state that he had three wives, others that he had several concubines.[15] Yaśōdharā bore him a son, Rāhula (meaning "hindrance"), possibly after his leaving home and family.

At the age of twenty-nine Siddhārtha was driven by an inner compulsion to leave this externally most attractive situation

[13] Cf. *Anguttara-Nikāya,* I, 145; BGS, I, 128.

[14] *Buddhacarita,* V, 1-23; SBE, XLIX, 49-52. Cf. Nakamura, *op. cit.*, pp. 40-47; Watanabe, *op. cit.*, pp. 63-68, 93.

[15] *Buddhacarita,* II, 29-32; SBE, XLIX, 21-22.

for the homeless life. This act was evidently the consequence of yearning to seek a higher good that had long been in the process of development.[16] Buddhist legend makes much of the renunciation involved, but the act needs to be seen in the context of the India of his time. We have noted the shift to an inwardly oriented religious apprehension and concern that was manifesting itself in the creation of the Upanishadic literature and in the distinct emergence of the "homeless" life as a proper vehicle for earnest seekers after spiritual truth and reality. Apparently no early civilization of man outside of India had anything like this practice whereby relatively large numbers of young men left the normal life of the world—home, family, occupation and society as such—to seek spiritual liberation and peace either singly or in groups in secluded forests and caves.[17]

Siddhārtha's decision, therefore, was not an isolated one nor out of keeping with at least an important element of the religious ideals of his time and place. We note record of his father's early concern to keep him from any contact with the ills of life, but this account suggests more than personal overprotectiveness, namely that the son of a high-born family, in disillusionment with the ways of the world, might well enter into the homeless life as a live option of the time.[18]

The texts relate in a form legendary but probably at least symbolically true how the father's intentions were frustrated by Siddhārtha's visiting Lumbinī Park over a succession of days. Here he came upon a decrepit old man, a diseased man, a dead man and an ascetic.[19] The last, in spite of his poverty, is described in one account as "carefully and decently clad," apparently happy and expressive of spiritual victory. The tale suggests both awareness of the ills of human life and an intimation of the way of liberation therefrom.

Another account purports to relate the Buddha's reflection

[16] *Dīgha-Nikāya,* II, 157; DB, part II, p. 167. Cf. *Majjhima Nikāya,* I, 163; MLS, I, 207.

[17] Cf. Sukumar Dutt, *The Buddha and Five After-Centuries.* pp. 26-35.

[18] *Jātaka,* I, 56; Warren, *op. cit.,* p. 53. Cf. *Vinaya-Piṭaka, Mahāvagga,* I, 23, 1; BD, part IV, p. 52.

[19] *Jātaka,* I, 58-59; Warren, *op. cit.,* pp. 57-58. Cf. André Bareau, *Die Religionen Indiens,* III, 13.

on the experience as he told it to his disciples later in his life:

> Now I too am subject to old age and decay, not having passed beyond old age and decay. Were I to see another broken down with old age, I might be troubled, ashamed and disgusted. That would not be seemly in me. Thus, monks, as I considered the matter, all pride in my youth deserted me.[20]

Similar reaction is repeated in the text with reference to reflection on sickness and death, and in each case the "pride in my youth" is said to have utterly disappeared. A finely perceptive sense of human solidarity is revealed in the account, but a profound disenchantment with all the forms of ordinary human existence is perhaps its main theme. It is highly likely that some such disenchantment constituted a major element in Gautama's decision to enter into the homeless life.

Early Buddhist monasticism magnified this negative analysis of human life to the extent that the cultivation of loathing for everything physical came to be considered as one of the necessary steps in the progress of the spiritual life. This context of thought is most likely the matrix from which issued the account that relates how Gautama was entertained by dancing girls on the evening when he left the "palace," his home and family. He fell into a deep sleep and later woke to find the women asleep in various positions of disarray. Their bodies are described as being wet with trickling phlegm and spittle. Some were grinding their teeth, muttering and talking in their sleep. Some had their mouths open, the dress of others had fallen apart so as to show their loathsome nakedness. Not only did this scene increase, it is recorded, the Buddha's aversion to sensual pleasures, but the whole place seemed like a "cemetery filled with dead bodies impaled and left to rot," and all existence appeared like houses ablaze.[21]

We find frequent references in Buddhist literature to the foulness of the physical. The offensiveness of the various excretions of the human body is emphasized, and meditation

[20] *Aṅguttara-Nikāya,* I, 145; BGS, I, 129. In this context we may well recall Shakespeare's account of the seven ages of man (*As You Like It,* act II, scene VII, 139-166).

[21] *Jātaka,* I, 61; Warren, *op. cit.,* pp. 60-61.

thereon item by item is urged as an aid to attain the disengagement from phenomenal existence by nonattachment that is necessary to attain the peace of *Nirvāṇa.*[22] A late text states that the Buddha likened the human body to a sore.[23] We shall note below, however, that elements in the tradition point to more positive interpretations of human life and suggest qualifications to the more extreme of these negative views.

4

THE PERIOD OF SEEKING AND THE ENLIGHTENMENT

The texts record frankly the resentment and grief of Yaśōdharā at her husband's departure,[24] but as the accounts have it, escorted by various gods and supernal spirits Gautama resolutely proceeded south and eastward from Kapilavastu. The first place where he stayed for some time was evidently the prosperous city of Vaiśālī, north of the Ganges River and capital of Videha of the Licchavis, a cultural center noted for its religious teachings. From there he proceeded to the capital city of the then prosperous and populous kingdom of Magadha.[25] This city, Rājagriha (the present Rajgir), located south of the Ganges River in what is the modern state of Bihar, was a major economic and cultural center of northeastern India, and its king Bimbisāra was noted for his patronage of religious teachers. Considerable evidence suggests that Gautama not only visited but seriously endeavored to learn from some of these teachers. In later life, probably with reference to the central experience of his enlightenment and the main thrust of his teaching, he is said to have insisted that he had no teacher anywhere.[26] Very possibly, however, the

[22] E.g. *Visuddhi-Magga,* written by the great Ceylonese scholastic Buddhaghosa in the fourth century A.D., ch. I; Warren, *op. cit.,* pp. 297-300. Cf. pp. 6-8, 24, 61, 360.

[23] I. B. Horner, *Milinda's Questions,* I, 101. This work was composed in its present form perhaps in the first century A.D.

[24] Cf. Watanabe, *op. cit.,* pp. 82, 116.

[25] *Sutta-Nipāta* 407-408; WCEB, pp. 61-62.

[26] *Vinaya-Piṭaka, Mahāvagga,* I, 6, 8; BD, part IV, p. 11. Cf. *Majjhima-Nikāya,* I, 171; MLS, I, 215.

later threefold structure of the Buddhist movement—*Dharma* (Law, teaching), *Vinaya* (Discipline) and *Saṅgha* (Community)—was derived from teachers whom he met at this period of his life. Ārāda Kālāma of Vaiśālī and Udraka Rāmaputra of Magadha both apparently imparted a fixed body of teaching (*Dharma*) and their disciples lived under a religious discipline (*Vinaya*) as members of a permanent order (*Saṅgha*).[27] Furthermore, these two teachers, while differing somewhat, evidently conceived of their spiritual goal and methodology of attainment in a way closer to the later Buddhist understanding than did either the Upanishadic or Jain. They aimed at enlightenment through the cultivation of trances or deepening stages of mental awareness.

Gautama was therefore probably influenced by these teachers as indeed by the entire spiritual climate of northeastern India of the time in his apprehension of the nature of the problem-situation of human existence and of its solution. As we have seen, the central problem for the majority of religious thinkers was how to escape from what they saw as the appalling prospect of men bound by karmic law to an endless series of rebirths in the processes of phenomenal existence. A generally negative view of phenomenal existence was widespread, and various ascetic practices, some being of the severest kind, were among the methods recommended. Meditation, together with asceticism, was practiced with intent to attain various stages of consciousness or states of "trance" as well as to acquire certain psychic powers. The system that came to be called Yoga had already been developed to a considerable degree. We shall see below the role that these basic apprehensions played subsequently in the life and teaching of the Buddha. Gautama, however, even though he was to a measure influenced by at least some of these teachers, was not satisfied with any to the extent that he wished to become a permanent disciple.

The period between Gautama's departure into the homeless life and his enlightenment is commonly given as six or seven years. He evidently practiced for a time the stages of meditation according to the prescriptions of Kālāma and Rāmaputra but ceased after he became convinced that they did not lead to

[27] *Majjhima-Nikāya*, I, 163-166; MLS, I, 207-210.

the enlightenment he desired. The Buddhist canonical account relates that the two teachers' goals, respectively six and seven stages of awareness, did not reach the eighth level of a later Buddhist formula. But scholastic formulations apart, Gautama was evidently dissatisfied with the teachers' understanding of their goals and also with aspects of their methodology. He then began ascetic practices of an increasingly severe kind. In the course of this regimen he acquired five disciples evidently attracted by his sincerity and the heroic style of his austerities. The texts record that he settled for the sake of these practices at a beautiful spot named Uruvilvā not far from the modern Bodh-gayā in Bihar.[28]

This was clearly the critical period in the quest of Gautama for the Good. He exhausted certain of the techniques of extreme asceticism, fasting so that, as one account has it, when he touched the skin of his belly, he took hold of his backbone. If he stroked his limbs with his hand, the hair fell off, because he ate so little. His complexion became such that men argued whether the color was black, deep brown or sallow. Just as fire cannot be produced from rubbing wet wood together but only by dry, so he thought, the body must be purged of its natural forces to become an instrument fit for the mind to achieve illumination. He strove with teeth clenched, tongue pressed against the palate, so to subdue, restrain and dominate his mind that sweat poured from his armpits. Yet however energetic his efforts, even though he achieved mindfulness unperturbed, his body was disturbed and without calm.[29]

This regimen of severe austerity gave Gautama neither physical peace nor spiritual enlightenment. At this point of profound frustration he is recorded as reflecting on the futility of these methods and wondering whether there was another way to awakening, to reach the states of consciousness of "furthermen," the surpassing knowledge and vision proper to a true Aryan. It then occurred to him that while yet living at home he had once sat in the cool shade of a rose apple tree while his father was ploughing (perhaps a ritual function). Here as he meditated he had achieved unusual self-control, insight and

[28] *Majjhima-Nikāya,* I, 163-167; MLS, I, 206-212.
[29] *Majjhima-Nikāya,* I, 240-244; MLS, I, 295-299.

rapture. He determined therefore to try this method again, as the way to awakening and to the happiness that is apart from sensory pleasures. Gautama neither at this time nor later divorced meditation from strenuous intellectual and moral discipline, but his turning was specifically in the direction of "faith"—a term frequently used in the early texts—and openness to spiritual "help on the way." He recognized, however, that to do this he must have strength from food, and he ate some boiled rice and sour milk. Some accounts relate that he also shaved his head and beard and washed in a stream. His five disciples then left him in disgust that he had wavered in his ascetic striving and had reverted to an easy way. But for Gautama this was the decisive step into what was later to be called the "Middle Way" of moderation and balance, which he was to follow in all of his later practice and teaching.[30] It was also a step away from mere strenuous effort into an understanding of the religious life as properly focused upon a kind of spiritual "participation."

The texts relate that Gautama found a suitable spot under a large tree, and as he meditated the experience came to him that ever afterward was known as the Enlightenment and that Christmas Humphreys calls "the womb, the heart and *raison d'être* of Buddhism."[31] Its importance was such as to make direct or personal experience a primal element in the entire movement that the Buddha initiated.

Mention should be made in this context of the frequent references in the Scriptures to Gautama's temptation during his struggle for enlightenment by Māra, the Tempter, a spiritual figure who served variously as the personification of evil, transitory pleasure and death. Most of the sources confine this encounter to the period immediately preceding Gautama's enlightenment, but the oldest materials suggest that this kind of spiritual struggle characterized the whole of the seven-year period preceding, and indeed, as we shall see, his subsequent life as well. The essence of his early temptation was evidently

[30] *Majjhima-Nikāya,* I, 245-247; MLS, I, 301-302. Other accounts add that to cover his nakedness he stole the shroud of a young servant girl whose dead body had been left for cremation and washed it. A young woman named Sujātā is said to have cooked the rice gruel for him in a new pot.

[31] Christmas Humphreys, *Buddhism,* p. 16.

to give primary concern to physical life and health and to follow the Vedic-Brahmanic way of sacrificial rites. The nature of Gautama's response was in effect to give priority to the values of spiritual truth and ethical goodness and to commit himself unreservedly to this way. His contest with Māra is recounted in considerable detail in the early Scriptures, and his victory therein came to play an important role in the faith of the developing Buddhist community.[32]

The texts vary somewhat in their description of the experience of enlightenment, but the one most widely accepted by Buddhists is that given in terms of the four stages of awareness and the three of knowledge as these came to be known in Buddhist scholasticism.[33] It is possible, however, that something like this structure of experience goes back to the Buddha himself. The first stage of meditation is described as born of detachment and rapturous but accompanied yet by initial and discursive thought. The second stage is born of concentration and rapturous but freed of initial and discursive thought. From rapture Gautama moved into joyful equanimity that was yet mindfully conscious, the third stage. He then entered into the fourth stage, which is characterized by neither anguish nor joy, in which his former pleasures and sorrows had ceased; he had become completely purified by equanimity and mindfulness.

In this condition of mind, composed, purified, clarified, supple yet with concentration, Gautama directed his attention to the recollection of his former lives "in all their modes and detail" to the extent of a hundred thousand births. Thus in the first watch of the night was the first knowledge attained; thereby "ignorance was dispelled, knowledge arose, darkness was dispelled, light arose, even as I abided diligent, ardent, self-resolute."

In the middle watch of the night Gautama is said to have attained the purified divine (*deva*) vision exceeding that of men. He saw all sentient beings as they pass away and are

[32] *Sutta-Nipāta* 425-449; WCEB, pp. 63-65. Māra is also known as Namuci. Cf. *Dīgha-Nikāya,* III, 77; DB, part III, p. 76.

[33] Cf. *Dīgha-Nikāya,* XXII; DB, part II, pp. 327-346. The earliest strata of material, such as the poems of the *Sutta-Nipāta,* make no reference to the four stages.

reborn. He perceived that this process, the primary characteristic of phenomenal existence, functions in a precisely measured chain of cause and effect. All beings reap consequences of good or evil character and circumstance in their rebirth according to the ethical quality of their deeds—of body, speech and thought—in previous lives. The structures of experience of the present life occur not by chance nor may they be altered by the performance of religious rites; they arise solely in consequence of the moral quality of our anterior deeds in this or prior lives. The term *saṃskāra* was used in the early Buddhist community to denote predispositions or habitual tendencies of character which inhere and condition a given state of sentient beings as the result of past deeds and experiences.

Then in the last watch of the night Gautama attained to the third knowledge, to the knowledge of the destruction of the canker sores believed to be constitutive of phenomenal existence. This was the knowledge of the solution of the basic problem-situation of existence and involved perception of what later came to be known as the Four Noble Truths (*Ārya Satya*). Gautama came to understand the situation "as it really is." He perceived the nature of existence as suffering, a term the meaning of which we shall consider in some detail later, the cause of suffering, the possibility of its cessation and the way that leads to the cessation of suffering. By this perception and knowledge his mind was freed from the canker of sensory pleasures, of the process of becoming, of ignorance. He was in effect freed from himself and his past, from the personally deleterious consequences of the previous workings of the karmic-causal process. He achieved knowledge in freedom and was able to affirm, "I am freed; and I comprehended: Destroyed is birth, brought to a close is the Brahma-faring (the doing of what is Right), done is what was to be done, there is no more of being such or such . . . ignorance was dispelled, knowledge arose, darkness was dispelled, light arose even as I abided diligent, ardent, self-resolute."[34] Siddhārtha Gautama had become the Buddha, the Enlightened One.

[34] *Majjhima-Nikāya,* I, 4, 21-23; MLS, I, 27-29. We may note here that the great Alexandrian Christian scholar Origen (ca. 185-253/4) as a corollary of his concept of the pre-existence of souls had a view of the predispositions of human character

It is impossible of course to know precisely how much of the above account may be attributed to the Buddha himself, but the consensus of modern scholarship would seem to be that it gives us at least the main lines of his later reflection on the event. There can be no doubt that the experience was vitally real for him and decisive for his subsequent career and teaching. He seemed ever after utterly certain that he had found the truth of existence and the way out of the human dilemma to Ultimate Reality that was also the most effective and satisfying way of life on earth.

The later biographies of the Buddha interpret the experience in the highest cosmic terms. They portray Gautama as foreordained to become a Buddha as a result of the merit he had built up in his previous lives.[35] The earlier traditions also portray him as aided by the gods (*devas*) at significant points in his experience prior to the enlightenment. They seem to reflect belief in a kind of cosmically significant process at work.[36] There is no evidence that the Buddha himself interpreted the experience as vicariously significant, that is, as specifically constituting atoning merit effective for other beings. Yet his subsequent career and teaching lead us inescapably to the conclusion that he understood the enlightenment as having the highest cosmic significance in a direct way at least for himself.

The Buddha clearly believed, as we have noted, that he had correctly perceived the nature of the human dilemma and the way out of this dilemma. But the enlightenment was for him more than spiritual insight or understanding. It also constituted liberation, specifically liberation from the chains of attachment to the entire process of phenomenal existence and thereby from his subjection to this process. He had achieved

---

similar at some points to that of the Buddha. Origen held that souls, before they were born into human bodies, had contracted "some degree of guilt in their sensitive or emotional nature" as a result of which they were ordained to meet "conditions either good or evil" (*Origen on First Principles*, I, 7, 4; III, 3, 5; III, 5, 5, G. W. Butterworth, tr., pp. 62-63, 227-228, 241-242). Cf. Henry Chadwick, *Early Christian Thought and the Classical Tradition*, pp. 115-116.

[35] *Buddhacarita*, XIV, 72-76; SBE, XLIX, 155-156. Cf. Richard H. Robinson, *The Buddhist Religion*, pp. 19-20, who sees the ethical interpretation of the process of rebirth as a unique Buddhist contribution.

[36] Cf. Watanabe, *op. cit.*, pp. 158-174, 199-201.

his goal through a methodology that, as we shall see, was in essence both spiritual "participation" and ethical conduct—in thought and word as well as deed—leading to a radical disengagement from phenomenal existence by nonattachment.[37] This disengagement, however, was to the end of what we may call a breakthrough into a transforming relationship with another order of reality, *Nirvāṇa.* This Reality, in the thought of the Buddha, was specifically other than phenomenal existence but accessible to men within existence if the proper conditions were fulfilled.

We shall consider this problem more in detail later in connection with the teaching of the Buddha, but one or two aspects may properly be clarified at this point. One of the primary characteristics of his later teaching is the Buddha's refusal to discuss in intellective terms the nature of the Reality he called *Nirvāṇa.* Basic, however, to some understanding of its meaning for him as well as the meaning of the experience of the enlightenment is the role of ethical conduct in the methodology of achievement. The concept of nonattachment to phenomenal existence also plays an important role in the *Upaniṣads,* but the notion that ethical conduct is of primary importance in the way to the achievement thereof receives a unique emphasis with the Buddha.

This primary emphasis upon the ethical also suggests something of the "nature" of *Nirvāṇa* or of Ultimate Reality as the Buddha came to perceive it. As we shall see, he refrained from the use of language that would ascribe "personal" elements to this Reality, but he recognized a *Dharma,* or power of Right, at work within phenomenal existence and yet in some way radically distinct therefrom. Action in accord with this power, as differentiated from forces of other quality in existence, was the one way available to the refuge and bliss that is *Nirvāṇa.* Furthermore, the ethical living that accords with *Dharma* is to be maintained, the Buddha taught, also after one achieves the aspect of *Nirvāṇa* that is attainable on earth.

We shall discuss later the problem of the relationship between *Nirvāṇa* and *Dharma,* but we may note here the fact of

[37] One text implies that Gautama worked at fostering thoughts of benevolence (*mettā*) also during the seven years of ascetic striving (*Anguttara-Nikāya,* IV, 88-90; BGS, IV, 54-55).

some relationship. Upanishadic as well as later Buddhist thought sometimes described the state of liberation or *Nirvāṇa* as beyond the distinctions of good and evil. We do not seem to find, however, this kind of language in teaching that can be ascribed with any confidence to the Buddha himself. To the contrary, the intimate association between *Dharma* and *Nirvāṇa* in his thought requires us to affirm that however *Nirvāṇa* may be understood as a state transcending the categories of ordinary human existence, it is a transcendence that in some way constitutes a culmination of the highest ethical qualities known in human existence. We shall consider later the possibility that the experience of the enlightenment consisted at least in part in some kind of integration in depth of the conscious and unconscious selves of the Buddha.

We note also in connection with *Nirvāṇa* the language of religious ultimacy, of bliss and eternity. It clearly constituted Ultimate Reality for the Buddha and was cosmically "profitable" for all men. In spite of the Buddha's refusal to ascribe ultimate religious value to phenomenal existence as such, his conviction that *Nirvāṇa* "is" and is attainable even while in the body, indeed has been attained, shows a positive view of the destiny of man in this world, at least *in potentia.* This profound hope for man can be affirmed as an elemental basis for all of his subsequent missionary career.

One further point may be noted with regard to the cosmic significance for the Buddha himself of the liberation in his enlightenment. He had achieved liberation from his prior subjection to the process of birth and rebirth by nonattachment thereto. This liberation, as we have seen, constituted in turn a breakthrough into a transforming relationship with another mode of Reality that he called *Nirvāṇa.* This event can also be described as a profound spiritual reorientation with cosmic significance. That is, the radical change of Gautama's relationship to all phenomenal existence, including his own, involved a kind of translation from one mode of existence to another. He had in some truly authentic and ultimate sense "arrived" or attained and possessed the Real.[38] In later life the term the

[38] The distinction made in the later Scriptures between *Nirvāṇa* and *Parinirvāṇa,* which latter is attained only upon physical death, suggests a concept of a difference

Buddha evidently preferred above others in order to designate himself was Tathāgata. It was not an exclusive term and was employed also of other Buddhas, but it probably denoted one who had attained to the indescribable state, to the truly Real.[39] The affirmation is of spiritual and moral victory with ultimate cosmic consequences. That is, the Buddha experienced to a self-transforming degree liberation from the spiritually and morally constricting results of karmic process, including the "calming" of all his habitual tendencies or predispositions of character that were of evil or selfish quality. His basic life-orientation was in a new direction; his primary self-relationship was with a new Reality.

We read that after his enlightenment the Buddha was tempted by Māra to turn back to the ascetic way from his chosen and tested path of ethical conduct, mental concentration and spiritual insight.[40] Another temptation was not to share the truth-reality of his experience with others. Perhaps we may detect something of an aristocratic bias in the reasoning that he is recorded to have done in the period immediately after his enlightenment: "This *dhamma,* won to by me, is deep, difficult to see, difficult to understand . . . beyond dialectic, subtle, intelligible to the learned . . . for a creation rejoicing in sensual pleasure, this were a matter difficult to see, that is to say causal uprising by way of cause. This too were a matter very difficult to see, that is to say the calming of all the habitual tendencies, the renunciation of all attachment, the destruction of craving, dispassion, stopping, *nibbāna.* And so if I were to teach *dhamma* and others were not to understand me, this would be a weariness to me, this would be a vexation to me."[41] Notable in this connection is another statement recorded in the collection of sayings called the *Dhammapada:* "Few are there among men who arrive at the other shore (become *Arhats*); the other people here run up and down the

---

of kind, though evidently not of quality, in the state of spiritual attainment possible within phenomenal existence as compared with that which is beyond it.

[39] Cf. Zimmer, *op. cit.*, p. 133. The word may mean simply "truth-finder," or "wayfarer."

[40] *Sanyutta-Nikāya,* I, 103-110; BKS, part I, pp. 128-129, 134-135, 139.

[41] *Vinaya-Piṭaka, Mahāvagga,* I, 5, 2-4; BD, part IV, pp. 6-7.

shore."[42] We may properly compare this latter statement with that ascribed to Jesus: "For the gate is narrow and the way is hard, that leads to life, and those who find it are few."[43]

However we may interpret sayings of this kind it is clear that the Buddha rejected the temptation to keep to himself the truth he had attained. A Pāli account relates that a great divine being of Hindu mythology, Brahmā Sahampati, reflecting that the world would be lost and destroyed were the Buddha to refrain from teaching the *Dharma*, appeared before him. His appeal was that there are beings with little dust in their eyes who are decaying but who, if they heard and became learners of the *Dharma*, will grow. The Buddha in effect acquiesced.[44] Indeed, he devoted the rest of his life until he died at the age of eighty to the proclamation of this truth. He traveled extensively throughout the Ganges river basin, giving himself unstintingly to his self-imposed task of teaching men to gain release from their bondage unto the state of true enlightenment. We note that there is reason to believe that the sense of universal mission he evidently possessed had no parallel in the previous religious history of India.[45] No chronological account of these years of labor exists, but the Scriptures record sufficient data to give us a fairly good notion of the Buddha's way of life and the growth of the movement that was to ensue. We shall consider first the fact and manner of his gathering of disciples both monastic and lay.

5

THE PUBLIC MINISTRY

A Pāli account relates that the Buddha remained in contemplation for seven days after his enlightenment and then spent another seven days experiencing the bliss of freedom as he sat cross-legged at the foot of a banyan tree. Then followed

[42] *Dhammapada* 182; SBE, X, 50. Cf. *Dhammapada* 85; SBE, X, 24-25.
[43] Matt. 7:14; cf. Luke 13:24.
[44] *Vinaya-Piṭaka, Mahāvagga*, I, 5, 4-13; BD, part IV, pp. 7-10.
[45] Cf. Nakamura, *op. cit.*, p. 120.

another seven days of contemplation at the foot of a mucalinda tree during which there were cold winds and rain and the serpent king encircled him with his coils to protect him from cold, rain and insects. Reference is made to one or perhaps two more periods of seven days of meditation. We note also that the first human beings whom the Buddha met after his enlightenment were two merchants who were divinely guided to serve him with food and be themselves long blessed by the service. They became, according to this account, his first lay disciples, although he did not teach in any formal way at the time.[46]

The truth of this record is at least that the Buddha meditated long and deeply on the significance and probable consequences of his experience. Reflecting as to who might be the most suitable persons to whom he might communicate his newfound truth, he thought of the five ascetics who had formerly served him. The text relates that with his divine vision he saw the five men in the deer park at Isipatana near Benares and thereupon set out to meet them there.[47] The account of the Buddha's consciousness of this action is the famous quatrain:

> To turn the *dhamma*-wheel
> I go to Kasi's city,
> Beating the drum of deathlessness
> In a world that's blind become.

This is to say that the message is of "immortality" and in the proclamation of the *Dharma* a veritably cosmic process is initiated.

The five ascetics, it is said, on seeing the Buddha approach, agreed among themselves to receive him but coldly. As he came near, however, they were compelled by a force they did not understand to welcome him with more than usual respect. Thereupon the Buddha taught them what is known as his first sermon. This was in effect, as the Pāli accounts have it, the

[46] *Vinaya-Piṭaka, Mahāvagga,* I, 2-4; BD, part IV, pp. 3-6.

[47] A later Chinese Scripture records an incident on this journey wherein the Buddha, having been refused passage by a ferryman, flew across the Ganges River (Nakamura, *op. cit.*, pp. 127-128; Watanabe, *op. cit.*, pp. 213-214).

Four Noble Truths and the Eightfold Noble Path. The concern of the ascetics was as to how the Buddha could affirm complete enlightenment when he had not attained it by the practice of austerities. The Buddha's answer was that the Middle Way of the Eightfold Noble Path is the only truly effective course. And in spite of the apparently revolutionary nature of this proclamation in the context of the thought and practice of contemporary ascetics, the five are said to have been forthwith converted to become the nucleus of the community (*saṅgha*) of Buddhist monks (*bhikṣu*; Pāli: *bhikkhu*). We should note that the account cites the five as achieving enlightenment in precisely the same way as the Buddha, so that there were "six perfected ones in the world."[48]

In organizing into a separate monastic community those who were willing to follow him with full seriousness into the homeless life, the Buddha made use of a practice common in contemporary Indian life among those religiously in earnest. In the Vedic-Brahmanic tradition young men of good family often served as disciples of a teacher for a considerable period; in the *Chāndogya Upaniṣad* Śvetaketu is said to have studied thus for twelve years.[49] The presumption was, however, that after this period the young man would marry and raise a family even though he himself became a teacher of others. But in northeastern India of the sixth century B.C., as we have seen, a tradition of a more severe asceticism had emerged. Ascetics (*śramaṇa*) committed, although apparently not formally vowed, to lifelong celibacy and mendicant poverty became the ideal of religious living for many. It was common for teachers to gather disciples for corporate as well as individual living of the homeless, mendicant way, as we have noted in the case of the teachers Kālāma and Rāmaputra.

In terms of formal structure the Buddhist monastic order was thus in full accord with the religious ideals of the time and place. We shall see, however, that there were appreciable differences in tone and style of life. The Buddhist monk was expected to manifest a dignified and pleasing, albeit simple,

[48] *Vinaya-Piṭaka, Mahāvagga,* I, 6, 1-47; BD, part IV, pp. 10-21. For the *Dharma*-wheel cf. *Sutta-Nipāta* 693; WCEB, p. 104.

[49] *Chāndogya,* VI, 1, 2; Swami Nikhilananda, *The Upanishads,* p. 327.

exterior in contrast with naked or unkempt ascetics. The Jain monk, to cite one example, was expected to sweep the way before him with a little broom to avoid crushing any living thing. The Buddhist monk, on the other hand, was primarily to exercise watchfulness over the moral quality of his attitudes and intentions.[50]

The Buddha's procedure at this point in the beginning of his public ministry may reflect a well-considered purpose. Nakamura Hajime notes that the distance from Benares to Bodhgaya is at least one hundred and thirty miles, a walk of perhaps ten days. He suggests that going to Benares, already a holy city where religious teachers and students were wont to assemble, points to the Buddha's intent to proclaim his message first among the top religious professionals of his time.[51] Such an interpretation well accords with the sublime assurance the Buddha apparently manifested from the earliest period after his enlightenment.

A Pāli account relates of this early stay in Benares the conversion of Yasa, the son of a wealthy merchant, to the monastic life and of his father, mother and wife (the first female disciples) to the position of lay followers (*upāsaka*, women—*upāsikā*). The story tells of Yasa's first coming to the Buddha as the latter was walking up and down, having risen in the night near dawn. We note here what appears to have been the kind of message the Buddha was likely to give to laymen. He spoke of the giving of alms, of moral conduct, of heaven; "he explained the peril, the vanity, the depravity of pleasures of the senses, the advantage in renouncing them."[52] That is to say, for laymen, the renunciation of attachment or desire for such pleasures, not their complete abandonment. Those who would follow the Buddha most closely entered the homeless state and became members of the order of monks. Others followed him as laymen, not leaving their homes or occupations but committed themselves, as the practice later devel-

[50] Cf. Zimmer, *op. cit.*, p. 255.

[51] Nakamura, *op. cit.*, pp. 129-130; cf. Watanabe, *op. cit.*, pp. 211-212.

[52] *Vinaya-Piṭaka, Mahāvagga*, I, 7-10; BD, part IV, pp. 21-28. We may recall in this context the words recorded of Paul, who before the Roman governor Felix and his wife similarly "argued about justice and self-control and future judgment" (Acts 24:25).

oped, to the three refuges (*ratna*, jewel) of the Buddha, the *Dharma* and the *Saṅgha* and pledged themselves to follow the five prohibitions. A primary formal responsibility was to give alms to monks–food, clothing and medicine–but the Buddha's ethical teaching for laymen as well as monks clearly covered a wide range of humane concerns.

We note in the above account that four young friends of Yasa, also sons of merchants of greater or lesser substance in Benares, followed him into the homeless state. Subsequently fifty more of his friends, all of the finest families of the district, followed suit. We read of the grief and dismay of parents at what they felt was the loss of their sons and the Buddha's response to their complaints. We cannot of course be confident of the numbers cited, but the situation seems authentic. The Buddha's reply was to ask how Yasa, or the others, having perceived the truth and having been delivered from desire and attachment to pleasures of the senses, could turn back to their former low level of life.

The Buddha evidently had remarkable success in winning followers from the beginning of this period of his career. We note that while many were from families of wealthy merchants, as from the Brāhmans, they came from all castes and classes of society. Apparently, however, he did not allow slaves to become members of the monastic order unless their masters freed them.[53] We have no evidence that the Buddha tried to abolish caste as an institution within society, but it is clear that distinctions of caste had no formal meaning within the order of monks.

According to the order of events of one tradition, after the conversion of Yasa and his fifty friends and while still at Benares, the Buddha gave his initial command to the monks to enter on what was in effect a universal mission. They were told to go singly, not by twos, on the way, but their tour was to be "for the blessing of the manyfolk, for the happiness of the manyfolk, out of compassion for the world, for the welfare, the blessing, the happiness of *devas* and men." They were to teach the *Dharma*, which is "lovely at the beginning, lovely in the middle, lovely at the ending." They were to explain "with

[53] Cf. Bareau, *op. cit.*, III, 15.

the spirit and the letter" the religious life of complete fulfillment and entire purity.[54] We shall consider later the primary significance for both the life and the teaching of the Buddha of this understanding of the *Dharma* as "lovely."

We may legitimately doubt whether this "Great Commission" was given at this particular time and place, but the content is essentially in keeping with what we know of both the later practice and teaching of the Buddha. In the same passage we note again the existential analysis that there are beings "with little dust in their eyes," who not hearing the *Dharma* are retrogressing spiritually but who on hearing it would learn and grow. This saying, we should note, is not properly to be understood as an injunction to go only to the "best prospects" but as an appeal to hope, instruction that there are those who are spiritually prepared to receive the preachers of the truth, as if the fields were white unto the harvest. And at the same time the missionaries were to go to the "manyfolk."

The symbolic significance of the initial trip to Benares seems strengthened by the record that after staying there "for as long as he found suiting" the Buddha returned directly to Magadha to the park at Uruvilvā. We read that enroute he met a group of thirty young men of high social position who had come with their wives to enjoy a picnic in a forest grove. One, however, was without a wife and had brought a woman of low standing with him. She stole their belongings and ran away with them. As they were looking for her they came upon the Buddha sitting at the foot of a certain tree. He questioned them as to the object of their search and upon learning that they were looking for a woman, asked whether it were not better to seek for the self. They acquiesced, sat down to listen to his teaching and, "having seen *dhamma,* attained *dhamma,* known *dhamma,* plunged into *dhamma,*" asked and received permission to become monks.[55]

We cannot of course be certain as to the time and place of this incident, although the nature of the details suggests a high degree of probability as to its essential historicity. Far less

[54] *Vinaya-Piṭaka, Mahāvagga,* I, 11, 1; BD, part IV, p. 28.
[55] *Vinaya-Piṭaka, Mahāvagga,* I, 14; BD, part IV, pp. 31-32.

reliable is the account of events occurring after the Buddha's return to Uruvilvā. Here we read of wondrous manifestations of his psychic powers before three leaders, all brothers with the surname Kaśyapa, of different groups of matted hair ascetics, respectively five hundred, three hundred, and two hundred in number. As a consequence of these wonders all of the ascetics, teachers and disciples, were ordained into the order of the Buddha's monks and followed him when he then set out for a period of stay in Bodh-gayā. Here he is said to have delivered the famous Fire Sermon, the content of which we shall consider later.[56]

Assuredly we cannot take literally the details of these particular psychic power manifestations, such as surpassing the serpent king in blowing forth smoke, flame and heat without harming the serpent or burning down the hermitage, nor the precise numbers of the ascetics converted. Yet, while the Buddha was evidently not a worker of miracles such as healing the sick or raising the dead, the frequent references in the Scriptures to his psychic powers (*siddhis*) suggest more than usual gifts of this order. Leaving aside qualities that seem obviously legendary, we may note the power to read the minds of others and to perceive events occurring at a great distance. It seems reasonable to believe that the Buddha in fact possessed considerable powers of this kind. We may even doubt whether in the context of the Indian religious tradition it would have been possible for him to have gained substantial numbers of followers without noteworthy achievements in this area. Two of his chief disciples, Mahākaśyapa (Kaśyapa the

[56] *Vinaya-Piṭaka, Mahāvagga,* I, 13-21; BD, part IV, pp. 32-46. We should note that this passage includes an account of the Buddha's causing water to recede at a time of flood. A somewhat similar account is given of miracles, which included also an act of self-levitation, performed by the disciple Sāgata at the Buddha's request in the presence of "eighty thousand village overseers." The explicitly stated conclusion of the overseers is that if the disciple is capable of such feats, of what must the teacher be (*Vinaya-Piṭaka, Mahāvagga,* V, 4-8; BD, part IV, pp. 236-238)? We need not discuss here the accounts in later works of miracles like the multiplication of a cake provided by a guildmaster and his wife for the Buddha and five hundred monks. Cf. Thomas, *op. cit.*, pp. 238-246. Actually the Buddha is said on several occasions during time of famine to have been able to eat only a handful of rice a day of the kind used for horse fodder. For a rationale of the Buddha's restraint in performing miracles see *Dīgha-Nikāya,* I, 211-223; DB, part I, pp. 276-284.

Great) and Maudgalyāyana, were also noted for their psychic gifts.[57]

One other element of the account of the psychic manifestations deserves special attention. As a sign of their intent to become disciples of the Buddha, the five hundred ascetics of Kaśyapa of Uruvilvā let their hair (after having shaved their heads), their braids, their implements for fire-worship according to Vedic-Brahmanic practice and all the belongings proper to their former religious way of life be washed away in the flood that had arisen. In what may be one of the older poetic recensions we note a polarized account of the two ways. Kaśyapa is described as having abandoned extreme asceticism and the ancient rites of fire, for the Buddha delighted not in sacrifice or burnt offerings but in the peaceful path of purity and nonattachment that leads to liberation.[58]

From Bodh-gayā the Buddha is recorded as having proceeded to Rājagriha, the capital city of Magadha, taking with him his monastic disciples now numbering well over a thousand. Here he stayed in a shrine located in the Palm Grove pleasure garden. The winning of the Kaśyapa brothers and their ascetic disciples of the matted hair evidently constituted the conversion of the largest religious group in Magadha even if we do not take at face value the numbers in the text. It was therefore only natural that word of this singularly effective new religious teacher should be brought to Seniya Bimbisāra, the king of Magadha. The king, five years younger than the Buddha, is said thereupon to have called upon the teacher with "twelve myriad Brāhmans and householders of Magadha."

The question put to the Buddha in the presence of the retinue of the king and of his own disciples was whether Kaśyapa of Uruvilvā was the teacher and he the disciple or vice versa. The Buddha requested Kaśyapa to give his own testimony, which he did in the context of a description of the sharp contrast between the old and new religious ways. The Buddha then proceeded to instruct the king and his followers,

[57] Cf. *Thera-gāthā* 1082-1086; PEB, part II, pp. 366-367. *Anguttara-Nikāya,* I, 23; BGS, I, 16. *Anguttara-Nikāya,* I, 169-172; BGS, I, 153-156.

[58] *Vinaya-Piṭaka, Mahāvagga,* I, 22, 4-5; BD, part IV, p. 48. Cf. *Sutta-Nipāta* 1077-1083; WCEB, pp. 155-157.

whereupon the king and one myriad of the twelve of his retinue are said to have declared themselves to be lay followers of the Buddha.

This description should not be taken to mean that King Bimbisāra became a follower of the Buddha in any exclusive sense, for he apparently continued to serve as the patron of other religious teachers, notably Mahāvīra of the Jain tradition. Nevertheless, his support and encouragement of the Buddha was evidently both warm and unfailing throughout his lifetime. In addition to grants of food and probably of other necessities he donated a bamboo grove located in a place neither too far nor too near a village, quiet and yet accessible for people whenever they wanted to come. We may perhaps detect in this description something of the Buddha's own understanding of his mission, that is, meditation and the religious life as means for the welfare of the "manyfolk" as well as of the monastics. We may take as significant for the same purpose the frequent references to Buddhist monks as (properly) pleasing in appearance and possessed of pleasant behavior. In contrast to the harsh and evidently at times repulsive manners and appearance of certain of the ascetics of the time, the life style inculcated by the Buddha was refined and generally pleasing to high and low.[59] This aspect of the man and the movement was clearly an important addition to his insight into the truth, "the sorrowless path, unseen, neglected for many myriads of ages." We note the importance of this factor in the conversion of two of his chief disciples, Śāriputra and Maudgalyāyana, both Brāhmans who were already leading the homeless life under one Sañjaya and brought with them all the others of the latter's two hundred and fifty disciples.

Events of this kind obviously could not occur without social repercussions. Sañjaya himself is said to have been so vexed that hot blood issued from his mouth. The number of young men of promise from distinguished families of Magadha who had entered upon the homeless life under the tutelage of the Buddha was evidently large enough to generate nervous criti-

[59] *Vinaya-Piṭaka, Mahāvagga,* I, 23; BD, part IV, p. 52. Cf. *Dhammapada* 141-142 (but see also 395); SBE, X, 38-39, 92.

cism among their parents and wives, such as had occurred also at Benares. The relatives charged that he created his movement by breaking up families, by making parents childless and wives widows, and they wondered who would be next.

The reply of the Buddha was that truth-finders (*tathāgata*) lead men by the truth and who should be jealous of the wise who lead by this truth?[60] We may well doubt whether an answer of this sort was sufficient to satisfy the complaints of the families of his monastic disciples. Nevertheless, there are other reasons than the life style adduced above to account for the generally favorable reaction to the Buddha and his teaching from particularly the leading classes of the larger Ganges river basin of the period.

In the context of the expanding mercantile economy and concomitant increase of wealth in this area, there is considerable evidence to indicate that many persons of the time preferred to use their wealth in a hedonistic pursuit of pleasure. The Buddhist movement of course opposed this trend with its teaching of the infinity of natural human greed and the need to check such greed. This is not to say, however, that either the Buddha or the primitive monastic community despised property as such. To the contrary, property was highly valued. The monk who had entered the homeless state was expected to take good care of his modest belongings of bowl and clothing. And in keeping with the spirit of the Middle Way neither monk nor layman was to be guilty of slovenly or disorderly living. But the Buddhist view of property emerges with particular clarity in the teaching given laymen and goes far to explain much of the popularity of the movement. It also gives us a necessary framework of reference properly to understand the more "spiritual" teaching.[61]

We note that by fulfillment of the four conditions of dwelling in a proper place, association with worthy persons, due application of the self and merit of prior deeds there "rolls" upon such a man "wealth of crops, fame, good report and happiness."[62] This condition is not the equivalent of

[60] *Vinaya-Piṭaka, Mahāvagga,* I, 22-24; BD, part IV, pp. 46-57.
[61] Cf. Nakamura Hajime, *Shūkyō to Shakai Rinri,* pp. 70-91.
[62] *Anguttara-Nikāya,* II, 31; BGS, II, 35.

Nirvāṇa, but it is held to be highly praiseworthy in itself and spiritually meaningful as a provisional stage to the highest goal. Not only is the accumulation of wealth considered a proper goal for laymen in the world, but strenuous efforts to achieve this goal are among their religious duties.

We read of an account of the Buddha's teaching one of the clansmen, by name Longknee, of the Koḷiyans, who were members of the Vajrian Confederacy and of Śākyan origin. The Exalted One affirmed four conditions for a clansman's advantage and happiness on earth. They are "achievement in alertness . . . in wariness, good company and the even life." The first achievement refers to deft and tireless ways by which a man is able to carry on his economic activity. Wariness refers to the efforts a man must make to insure that his wealth be not taken from him by rājas, thieves, fire, water or ill-disposed heirs. Even as such a man will gain his wealth in a just and lawful manner, he will strive for it "by work and zeal," "by the strength of his arm," "by the sweat of his brow."

Good company means the company of householders of virtue, faith, charity and wisdom. The even life affirms serenity in the conduct of business, a calm confidence in the midst of the experience of economic loss and gain. A principal measure inculcated to achieve such serenity is a careful ordering of business and family life so that expenses will not exceed income. The four vices of "looseness with women, debauchery in drinking, knavery in dice-play and friendship, companionship and intimacy with evil doers" are cited as particularly contributing to the loss of wealth amassed.

This kind of zealous and careful householder who is "up and alert about his task and toil" must be, it is emphasized, "virtuous, believing, kind and bountiful." But his way of life is seen as the "onward way" of spiritual progress leading to "happiness both here and then, to bliss hereafter and to welfare now." Such a man makes and keeps happy also his parents, his wife and children, his slaves and workers. Indeed, the welfare of himself and these others constitutes the first reason for getting rich. Other reasons given are that the householder is enabled to make and keep happy his friends and companions, to make suitable offerings to gods and men, especially to worthy recluses. Such offerings ripen unto happiness and lead heavenward.

If such a man should lose his wealth even while pursuing his virtuous way, he is not disturbed. He is confident of the ripening of the fruit of his good conduct. But the emphasis of the text is clearly upon the blessings of wealth rightly gained and wisely and bountifully used. For such householders there is praise on earth and delight in heaven.[63]

As Professor Nakamura has pointed out, this regimen is clearly reminiscent of the later "Protestant ethic" denoted by Max Weber. We find the same praise of industry and reproof of idleness. The vices of immorality, drunkenness and gambling are cited, as we have seen, with reference to their deleterious economic effects. The virtues approved are "puritanical" but not severely ascetic. The way of life inculcated is the Middle Way of balanced proportions. The housefather should not covet nor wrongfully desire, but he will make both himself and others happy and cheerful with the wealth that he has lawfully acquired. He will avoid both excessive luxury and meanness of life.

A "capitalistic" pattern emerges in the strictures for the good layman to spend one quarter of his income for personal expenses, use two quarters in the conduct of his business (reinvestment?) and save the last quarter.[64] We note in one of the Chinese texts injunction to reinvest in the business three quarters of the income.[65]

Not only is the good and wise householder to pay his debts, but he may also, according to later texts, lend at interest. Positive advice is offered in another Chinese Agama to loan out at interest a quarter of one's income. It is doubtful, however, that this advice on lending goes back to the Buddha, although we note that later the Buddhist order itself in some cases loaned out money at interest. In the *Jātakas* we find the forgiving of debts cited as a virtue even as a wise investor is praised.[66]

[63] *Anguttara-Nikāya,* IV, 279-287; BGS, IV, 187-191. Cf. *Anguttara-Nikāya,* II, 63-67; BGS, II, 73-77; also *Anguttara-Nikāya,* III, 44-47; BGS, III, 37-38.

[64] *Dīgha-Nikāya,* III, 188; DB, part III, p. 180.

[65] Nakamura, *Shūkyō to Shakai Rinri,* p. 81.

[66] *Ibid.*, pp. 83-85.

In short, we find in the early texts a remarkably consistent socio-economic ethical teaching. Merchants and craftsmen are warned against covetousness or attachment to material things. In the context of belief in the workings of the principle of *Karma* they may, however, indeed should, strive zealously to increase their wealth. They may also enjoy it in moderation. Their methods of gaining wealth must be honest and hurt no one. Within this framework of understanding the newly emerging world of mercantile activity is positively affirmed and assigned high religious value. Unjust economic methods are severely reproved, with the specific warning that they bring the perpetrator to punishment (limited) in hell, even as laymen are enjoined to follow the examples of love and mercy. Yet economic activity as such is praised, a high value is assigned to property. In fact there is apparently no instance of the praise of poverty among householders, no concept of the nobility of poverty in itself apart from those who have left the world. This positive understanding and appreciation of the life of laymen in the world goes far to explain the wide and continuing acceptance of Buddhism both in India and in the lands beyond its borders. In this context we may also understand the frequent references in the early texts to the many "youths of good family" who had left home and kin to follow the Buddha into the homeless life.

It is equally necessary to affirm, however, the Buddha's acceptance of men—and women—of other classes than the wealthy and powerful. We have noted that even slaves could enter the order provided their masters freed them.[67] One account cites an instance of a debtor who ran away from his creditors and sought refuge by entrance into the order of monks. By this time full protection of the order had been granted by King Bimbisāra of Magadha and the creditors had no further recourse. But in the context of public criticism of this situation the Buddha is recorded as forbidding reception into the order of anyone who had debts outstanding. Similarly a runaway slave should not be received.[68] These qualifications

[67] Iwamoto Yutaka questions this assertion on the basis of his study of the lists of disciples given in the early texts (*op. cit.*, pp. 134-137).

[68] *Vinaya-Piṭaka, Mahāvagga*, I, 46-47; BD, part IV, pp. 95-96.

orm an integral part of the larger picture, but the otherwise ıniversal concern and openness of the Buddha and the order onstitute the predominating motif. There is reason to believe hat among other religious groups of the time, especially those of the ascetics (*śramaṇa*), comparable transcendence of caste was to be found.

A moving instance of this openness is seen in the account of he conversion of the streetsweeper Sunīta. One of the poems of the *Thera-gāthā* records the scene wherein the scavenger, oor and of humble birth, "one for whom no man cared, lespised, abused," accustomed to bend the head before the nost of men, saw the Buddha accompanied by a number of nonks enter into Rājagriha near his place of work.

> I laid aside my baskets and my yoke,
> And came where I might due obeisance make,
> And of his loving kindness just for me,
> The Chief of men halted upon his way.
> Low at his feet I bent, then standing by,
> I begged the Master's leave to join the Rule
> and follow him, of every creature Chief.
> Then he whose tender mercy watcheth all
> The world, the Master pitiful and kind,
> Gave me my answer: Come, Bhikku! he said.
> Thereby to me was ordination given.

The poem goes on to describe Sunīta's experience of enightenment as a result of faithful observance of the Master's eaching. The concluding verses relate the Buddha's smiling in pproval as he states that supreme holiness is gained (not by irth or aught external but) "by discipline of holy life, retraint and mastery of self."[69]

One consequence of this transcendence of the distinctions of caste and status was that a former Brāhman who entered nto the order might be in the position of receiving instruction n the doctrine and rules from a dark-skinned member of a ower caste who had preceded him in ordination. He would of

[69] *Thera-gāthā* 620-631; PEB, part II, pp. 273-274. Cf. the account of the rdination of the cowherd Nanda (*Sanyutta-Nikāya*, IV, 181; BKS, IV, 115). Cf. lso *Sutta-Nipāta* 136; WCEB, p. 22.

course necessarily have to respect him and call him friend or brother. In the poem of Sunīta the gods Indra and Brahmā are described as coming to him after his enlightenment to offer homage with clasped hands. They hailed him as "nobly born" and "highest among men."

We must note, however, that certain gradations of rank existed in the order from the beginning as a consequence primarily of differing abilities and degrees of zeal among the monks. Some were closer to the Buddha than others, for these and perhaps other reasons, such as consanguinity in the case of Ānanda. We read in the account of the death of the Buddha that he advised Ānanda to have the order change the prevailing practice of addressing each other as "Friend" (*Āvuso*). A younger brother might be addressed by an elder with his personal or family name or by "Friend." But an elder was to be addressed as "Sir" or "Venerable Sir."[70] It is highly doubtful that this injunction goes back to the Buddha himself. It does, however, reflect later practice, when monasteries, like their counterparts in Europe, tended to reflect at least in part the class distinctions of secular society.

There is also evidence that the monastic disciples of the Buddha continued to be aware of the significance of the social distinctions of those in secular life. In the context of contemporary understanding of *Karma* the gradations of caste may be presumed to have had spiritual as well as social value in their eyes. Ānanda is once cited as mentioning to the Buddha the importance to the movement of faith in his *Dharma* and discipline by well-known and distinguished laymen.[71] In one account the young Brāhman Ambattha is received by the monks with the thought that because he is of distinguished family and Brahmanic education, the Blessed One would "not find it difficult to hold conversation with such." Whereupon they, fellow Brāhmans, courteously directed him to the Buddha's door. It is significant, however, that when Ambattha is reproved a bit later by the Buddha for his specific rudeness he replies with a taunt about the "shavelings, sham friars

[70] *Dīgha-Nikāya,* XVI, 6, 2; DB, part II, p. 171.
[71] *Vinaya-Piṭaka, Mahāvagga,* VI, 36, 3; BD, part IV, p. 341.

menial black fellows, the offscourings of our kinsman's heels" who also made up the Buddha's monastic entourage.[72]

The names of a number of the Buddha's monastic disciples are given in the Scriptures and considerable detail is recounted of a few. The outstanding figures, as we have noted, are Śāriputra and Maudgalyāyana, both Brāhmans. Ānanda was a younger cousin of the Buddha and like him of Kṣatriya caste. With his quiet manner, humility and devotion to the person of the Buddha, Ānanda was the "beloved disciple" of the fellowship. Sharply different in style of life was the Brāhman Mahākaśyapa, who was noted for his moral strictness as well as his psychic gifts. After the death of the Buddha he became the head of the order.

The Buddha's son Rāhula also became a member of the order. He is occasionally mentioned together with the other disciples of note, but there is no evidence of his exercising a leading role. A disciple who became the first teacher or authority regarding the monastic rules was the Śākyan barber Upāli. He had long served as the barber attendant upon a group of Śākyan youth who entered into the order together with him. The kind of understanding engendered by the Buddha's teaching and practice is suggested by the request of the young men. Though proud Śākyans, as they affirmed, they asked that the Buddha allow Upāli to be ordained before them. "We will greet him, rise up before him, salute him with joined palms, and do the proper duties. Thus will the Śākyan pride be humbled in us Sākyans."[73]

Another cousin of the Buddha who became a monastic disciple was Devadatta, whom the texts describe as a kind of Judas Iscariot. The oldest account of Devadatta describes him as having acquired ordinary psychic power, a later commentary as having won the eight attainments of spiritual life. But he presumably had sufficient psychic gifts to impress Prince Ajātaśatru, the son and later murderer of King Bimbisāra of Magadha. The accounts relate how the prince had Devadatta waited on with chariots and served with "five

[72] *Dīgha-Nikāya,* III, 1, 7-11; DB, part I, pp. 111-112.
[73] *Vinaya-Piṭaka, Cullavagga,* VII, 1, 4; BD, part V, p. 257.

hundred offerings of rice cooked in milk" both morning and evening. In this context Devadatta is said to be so "overcome by gains, honours and fame, his mind obsessed by them," that the longing arose in him to lead the order of monks himself. When the Buddha heard of the prince's generous patronage of his cousin and, we may presume from the numbers cited, of not a few followers, he is recorded as saying that his "gains, honours and fame" may be expected to lead to decline rather than growth in his spiritual condition.

The account also relates that toward the end of the Buddha's life Devadatta personally requested of him permission to lead the order and was refused. The hostility of Devadatta was evidently confined to this latter period of the Buddha's life, and we read of the high respect both for psychic gifts and personal dignity that he had evidently enjoyed among the chief disciples and lay followers in earlier years. After the refusal he is said to have resorted to various attempts to murder the Buddha: the use of assassins, hurling a great stone down the mountainside, loosing a fierce elephant upon the Blessed One. The latter was able to thwart these attempts by his psychic powers, but he was evidently saddened by Devadatta's hostility and above all by the schism that he was able to effect, the first in the order. Devadatta's religious position was evidently in the direction of more severe austerity in mode of life.[74] As a result of this schism a sect arose that was to last for many centuries. The Chinese Buddhist pilgrim Fah-Hian, who traveled from China to India (A.D. 400-415), reported that a body of Devadatta's disciples was still in existence in Kośala (north of the Ganges River) in his time.[75]

The extent of the Buddha's concern for the wider dissemination of his teaching among the "manyfolk" and the authentic significance in terms even of ultimate salvation that he saw in the religious life of his lay followers should not be understood in the sense of detracting from what he clearly held to be the central role of the monastic order. This was the "better way," that most conducive to insight and rapture

[74] *Vinaya-Piṭaka, Cullavagga,* VII, 1-5; BD, part V, pp. 257-290. Cf. *Sanyutta-Nikāya,* II, 242; BKS, II, 163-164.

[75] Samuel Beal, *Travels of Fah-Hian and Sung-Yun,* p. 82.

eading to *Nirvāṇa.* With the monks he shared the deeper levels of his understanding. Above all they were expected to be the primary agents of missionary activity. And, we should add, the monastic orders have been over the centuries the dominant, usually the only, organized form of Buddhist life until the development of the Pure Land schools in Japan in the twelfth and thirteenth centuries and Buddhist lay societies within the past century.

The Buddhist monks were received and ordained perhaps with a fixed formula and ceremony from an early period. In the texts, however, we find instances, as in the case of Sunīta, of the Buddha's calling—and receiving—men into the order with the simple phrase, "Come, O monk." A probationary period of at least four months between acceptance into the order and ordination became customary, but there were exceptions to this practice during the lifetime of the Buddha. Later, youngsters seven years of age or older came to be accepted as novices, but they could not be ordained until they reached the age of twenty. The monks clearly understood their commitment to the homeless life as properly involving lifelong mendicant poverty and chastity. Although not a few came from other ascetic groups, some had lived as husbands and fathers of children like the Buddha himself.[76] The saffron—variations of this color are recorded—robe and tonsured head were symbolic both of their order and of the "decency" of their way of life. They became known as the ascetics who follow the son of the Śākyans. Their way of life may be characterized as meditative, mendicant and missionary.

The monks were under one head, the Buddha, who was, however, more their teacher and spiritual master than their commander. In fact, as we shall see, he disavowed the role of leader in a formal sense. There existed certain rules probably from the beginning that over several generations developed into the elaborate system formulated in the several volumes of the *Vinaya-Piṭaka,* or *Book of the Discipline.* The more primitive formulation is the *Pātimokkha* or list of 227 rules, many—probably not all—of which may have their origin within the lifetime of the Buddha.

[76] Cf. *Therī-gāthā* 291-303; PEB, part I, pp. 131-133.

The rules evidently developed much like the English Com mon Law, from the succession of cases handled. Over the year there were, according to the accounts, not a few problems o discipline. Indeed, it is recorded that the monks quarreled s often as to create a public scandal. Wherever possible it wa the custom to bring each case to the Buddha for his prope disposition. There are one or two instances, apart from Deva datta, where his authority was resisted, but otherwise through out his long ministry his decision was apparently accepted a the law for the case submitted and formed the basis for th rules created.

We should note, however, that the rules and courses c training prescribed by earlier forms of the *Vinaya,* especially i the *Suttavibhaṅga*, are primarily concerned with extern morality. The rules are not designed to teach the methodolog of salvation but are guidelines for the ordering of life that "fitting," "suitable" and "worthy of a recluse." The concern for the avoidance of conduct that does not serve "for th benefit of non-believers." We sense, in other words, procedur developed on an *ad hoc* basis for the purpose of ordering community structured to serve a primarily missionary purpos

The Buddha, as far as is known, exacted no vow of obed ence to himself, and except for the ultimate possibility c expulsion from the order, imposed no punishment. We do nc find him legislating for laymen—as distinguished from th enunciation of moral principles—in the manner of his co temporary, the Jain Mahāvīra. Yet the texts are clear that h was regarded as having unique authority, and there are man indications that he did not hesitate to use that authorit within the context of the monastic community, especial when his decision was asked for. He made use of his mo eminent disciples, such as Śāriputra and Maudgalyāyana, in th work of both teaching and discipline, but he himself w clearly the court of final appeal. After his death the *saṅgha* di not claim in itself to possess either legislative or hermeneutic authority. The authority for both legislation and doctrin even in the case of material obviously of later provenance, w always ascribed to the Buddha.[77] This development occurr

[77] Cf. BD, part I, pp. vi-xix.

in spite of the fact, which we shall discuss later, of the Buddha's specific directions to his disciples before his death not to depend in any ultimate way on his person. He directed them rather to depend upon the eternal *Dharma* and their higher selves as their source of truth and moral power. The monastic community in fact exercised no little religious creativity in the first centuries after the Buddha's death but was evidently unable to assert the right and authority of the community to act in its own name. This fact led on the one hand to the notable conservatism or tendency to immobilization of both doctrine and life of southern expressions of Buddhism in the Theravāda. We shall also find, however, extremes in quite another direction in the Mahāyāna of the North, extraordinary creativity in the context of what may at times seem rejection of meaningful continuity with the past.

The Buddha also founded an order of nuns (*bhikṣunī*) at the request of his widowed aunt and stepmother, Mahāprajāpatī Gautamī, who wished to enter the homeless life under his discipline. Three times he refused her, advising against the going forth of women into homelessness. He later consented only with grave misgivings and the assignment of stricter rules than for men after Ānanda supported the aunt's request. He prophesied that the duration of the true *Dharma* (teaching) and life in conformity thereto would be reduced from one thousand to five hundred years if women were allowed to go forth into homelessness.[78]

The question has been raised whether the Buddha shared the fairly common Indian view of woman as an inferior being.[79] The texts give clear evidence that woman was regarded as one of the monks' chief obstacles to progress in the spiritual life. Among the sayings recorded on the eve of the Buddha's death are his instructions on this point to Ānanda:

> "How are we to conduct ourselves, lord, with regard to womankind?"

[78] *Vinaya-Piṭaka, Cullavagga,* X, 1; BD, part V, pp. 352-356.

[79] Cf. the story of Viśākhā in Buddhaghosa's commentary on *Dhammapada* 53, where the statement is made that Indian maidens are considered but "goods for sale" (Warren, *op. cit.*, pp. 456-457).

"As not seeing them, Ānanda."
"But if we should see them, what are we to do?"
"No talking, Ānanda."
"But if they should speak to us, lord, what are we to do?"
"Keep wide awake, Ānanda."[80]

The Buddha, however, always treated women with grave respect and boldly proclaimed his message to both men and women with apparently full confidence that both, within the context of family life, could attain to the highest, to *Nirvāṇa.* His apparently ambivalent attitude toward women may derive primarily from his concern to develop an order of itinerant missionary monks for whom women could be only spiritual temptation and physical hindrance. It is likely that he feared women were not suited to the homeless life. It was perhaps unseemly for them to beg, although the texts indicate that they did beg. It was more difficult to provide for their physical needs; their menstrual period created additional problems. Furthermore, in the very earliest period the monks did not live in buildings but in forests, caves or in groves of trees. For these reasons, we may presume, the Buddha initially opposed the creation of an order of nuns and insisted that their discipline, if such an order had to be, be of a stricter kind. For instance, we note that the probationary period of nuns was to be two years in place of four months for men. Admonition of monks by nuns was forbidden, although the reverse was allowed. A nun, even though a hundred years had passed since her ordination, was required to pay "proper homage to a monk ordained but that day."

This deference to the male monks—the nun was expected to be ordained in both orders—may properly be understood in the context of the contemporary structure of families, in which the householder was always male. But with reference to women as such there is reason to believe that the Buddha entertained both respect and the highest expectations of their spiritual potential. The Buddha is recorded as saying to King

[80] *Dīgha-Nikāya,* II, 141; DB, part II, p. 154. Cf. *Anguttara-Nikāya,* I, 1; BGS, I, 1-2. *Anguttara-Nikāya,* I, 27; BGS, I, 26. *Anguttara-Nikāya,* I, 77; BGS, I, 72. *Anguttara-Nikāya,* II, 80; BGS, II, 92-93.

Prasenajit of Kośala in response to his unhappiness over the birth of a daughter that there are some women who are superior to men. Some are notable for their knowledge, morality, respect of their mothers-in-law and faithfulness to their husbands.[81]

In this context we may properly mention the incident recorded of the Buddha's meeting with the courtesan Ambapāli of Vaiśālī, the capital city of Videha, north of the Ganges River. The position of certain courtesans of Indian society of the time was apparently similar to that of the *hetairai* of the classical period in Greece. Ambapāli had learned that the Buddha was staying at her mango grove and went out to meet him there with her retinue in carriages of state that she evidently either owned or could afford to order. The Buddha "instructed, aroused, incited and gladdened her with religious discourse." She thereupon invited him with the brethren to dine at her house the following day. The Buddha accepted with the customary silence denotive of assent.

Later the same day a number of Licchavis of Vaiśālī, men of social position and wealth, hearing of the Buddha's arrival, also rode out to the mango grove to meet him. They were received and instructed in the same manner as Ambapāli. When they likewise invited the Exalted One and the brethren to dine with them the following day, he refused because of his prior promise to dine with the courtesan.

When on the next day the preparations had been completed, Ambapāli sent word that the meal was ready. The Buddha, "who had dressed himself early in the morning, took his bowl and his robe, and went with the brethren" to the residence of Ambapāli. Here she served them sweet rice and cakes "and waited upon them till they refused any more."

After the meal, when the Buddha had washed his bowl and hands, Ambapāli sat at his side on a low stool. She addressed him by offering to the order of mendicants of which he was head the property where they were. The Buddha accepted the gift and after further religious discourse rose from his seat and departed.[82]

[81] Cf. Iwamoto, *op. cit.*, pp. 104-113.
[82] *Dīgha-Nikāya*, II, 95-98; DB, part II, pp. 102-105.

The implication of this incident is clearly that Ambapāli was converted to the Buddha's teaching and way of life. The passage, however, nowhere states specifically that she changed her profession. In the *Psalms of the Sisters* there is a poem ascribed to one Ambapāli that is the product of reflection on the transitoriness of physical beauty by an aged woman. The introduction, of later origin than the poem, states that she strove for enlightenment in her old age.[83] We sense a certain ambiguity in the incident as recorded, but there is, on the other hand, no word from the Buddha in any of the texts in approval of the profession. If there is no clearly spoken "go, and do not sin again," there is as warm and unambiguous acceptance of the person as we find in Jesus' treatment of the woman taken in adultery.[84]

We may note in concluding this theme that in spite of the Buddha's reluctance and the physical difficulties mentioned above, a relatively large number of women sought entrance into the order of nuns, many of them from the highest levels of society. An analysis of the names of the nuns in the *Psalms of the Sisters* shows that out of seventy-three twenty-three are of "royal" origin, thirteen from merchant families, eighteen Brāhman, other castes four, courtesans four and eleven uncertain.[85] One of the most famous of early nuns was the consort of King Bimbisāra of Magadha, who entered the order after her husband's murder. The *Psalms of the Sisters* reveal clearly the new spiritual quality of life of these women. The testimony to joy and a higher alertness of mind is as frequent as to peace and calm. One of the sisters is bold enough to compare herself in spiritual attainment with the great Kaśyapa, the leader of the order after the Buddha's death.[86] We do not find, however, any instance among the poems of a relationship to the Buddha such as has occurred in Christian tradition, where, to use the words of Mrs. Rhys Davids, "He, the Central Figure, intervenes, and gratitude is blent with adoration." These poems reveal "no word of quasi-amorous self-surrender

83 *Therī-gāthā* 252-270; PEB, part I, pp. 120-125.
84 John 8:1-11.
85 Iwamoto, *op. cit.*, p. 104.
86 *Therī-gāthā* 63-66; PEB, part I, p. 49.

to the person or image of the Beloved." The highest expression to which a Buddhist sister presumed was to attribute spiritual fatherhood to the Master "whom she perhaps first saw late in his long life."[87]

6

THE DAILY LIFE OF THE BUDDHA

We should note again that we have no chronological ordering of the Buddha's life in the older texts after the conversion of Śāriputra and Maudgalyāyana and his dealing with the complaints of the families of Magadha. We have also no ordered itinerary, but the variety of locations cited for his various sermons or teachings strongly suggests an essentially missionary program. As we have seen, almost immediately after the formation of the order of monks the Buddha sent them forth to share with him the work of spreading the teaching. The monks often went out one by one. A phrase in what is perhaps the oldest of texts describes the life style of the missionary monk in the repeated injunction, "Fare lonely as a rhinoceros."[88] There was, however, no objection in principle to companionship in the life task. The monk is urged to walk alone, "like an elephant in the forest," if he can find no prudent companion to walk with him.[89]

The Buddha did not only send, he went himself. For the remainder of his long life he wandered, usually accompanied by a considerable band of his disciples, throughout the entire Ganges river basin, proclaiming the teaching to whoever would hear. The formal number of his monastic disciples is given as 1250, but we find other passages listing the number simply as in the hundreds.[90] It is likely, however, that he often traveled

[87] PEB, part I, p. xxxii.
[88] *Sutta-Nipāta* 35-75; WCEB, pp. 6-11.
[89] *Dhammapada* 329-330; SBE, X, 79-80.
[90] *Dīgha-Nikāya,* II, 52; DB, part II, p. 40. Also *Dīgha-Nikāya,* III, 77; DB, part III, p. 74.

with smaller numbers, as we read of groups of monks or individuals being in widely scattered places at the same time.

We note that at first the monks walked on their missionary tours regardless of the season or weather. They were criticized for this action on the basis of popular sympathies akin to Jain thinking, namely that in the rainy season they injured or destroyed the small life then afoot. In consequence the Buddha directed—the word used was "allow"—the monks to follow what was already the common practice of other sects, to spend three months of the rainy season in rest at one spot.[91] As time passed, the Buddha and his monks were able increasingly to reside, especially during the rainy season, in houses and halls provided for them by wealthy laymen. We read most frequently of stays at residential parks granted them in the two capital cities of Magadha and Kośala, Rājagriha and Śrāvastī, which appeared to constitute the southeastern and northwestern borders of their common range of itineration. Jeta Grove in Śrāvastī, given the order by a rich merchant named Anāthapiṇḍika, was particularly beloved.[92] The Buddhist monks, however, did not all spend the rainy season in any one location. In fact, we note the emergence of the custom of monks who had passed the season elsewhere to make a special effort to visit the Buddha afterwards. Such visitors were regularly greeted with expressions of concern for their physical as well as spiritual well-being.

During the rest of the year the Buddha and the monks went from village to village, city to city begging their nourishment and taking their rest often in the shade of trees. When traveling the Buddha apparently walked no more than approximately ten miles a day, regulating his course so as to reach a suitable place to beg food for the noon meal.

Buddhaghosa of Ceylon, writing in the fourth century A.D., has given an account of the daily life of the Buddha that may

[91] *Vinaya-Piṭaka, Mahāvagga,* III, 1-4; BD, part IV, pp. 183-185.

[92] *Vinaya-Piṭaka, Cullavagga,* VI, 4; BD, part V, pp. 216-223. Cf. *Sanyutta-Nikāya,* I, 33; BKS, part I, pp. 46, 79. Notable is the affection for the Magadhan park recorded in *Sutta-Nipāta* 1013-1014; WCEB, p. 146. Some of the places where the Buddha and his disciples stayed were apparently rest houses built for members of any monastic sect to use (*Majjhima-Nikāya,* I, 353; MLS, II, 18).

be faithful in its main lines. The Master's custom was to rise early in the morning, and after taking care of his personal needs alone, he would sit in meditation until it was time to go begging for his food. He usually took only one meal a day, at noon. Sometimes he went out to beg alone, on other occasions accompanied by a number of monks. We read also of requests by laymen to feed a certain number of the monks, each according to his means. There were also frequent invitations in advance to dine at the home of a devout and generally prosperous layman who invited all the attendant monks and whose women made the correspondingly strenuous preparations. The Buddha always accepted with the silence of consent.

After the meal the Buddha would teach his disciples, the monks if he were alone with them, or also the lay people if he were at a home of invitation. Crowds often came out to meet him from a nearby town or village, and he taught them always "with due consideration for the different dispositions of their minds." After this he spent a time in rest and meditation. We read that during the last month of the hot season, in conformity with the principle of the Middle Way and in spite of the criticism of extreme ascetics, he lay down to sleep during the early afternoon.[93]

The Buddha generally devoted the late afternoons and evenings to instructing his disciples again or larger groups of laymen. In the case of monks some would ask for exercises in meditation and be assigned such as "suited to their several characters." Others asked questions or requested a discourse. He always taught the laymen "as suited the time and occasion." He often carried on discussions with Brāhmans and members of various religious sects, usually impressing his hearers with his wise and apt answers to questions and Socratic leading of their train of thought.[94]

In the story of the conversion of the householder Anāthapiṇḍika we find what may be an authentic account of the

[93] *Majjhima-Nikāya,* I, 249; MLS, I, 303-304. Paul Younger sees the Buddhist monastic life as illustrative of the Indian tendency to "develop patterns of experience that are close to the rhythms of nature" (*Introduction to Indian Religious Thought,* pp. 28-30).

[94] Buddhaghosa, *Sumañgala-Vilāsinī,* I, 45-47; Warren, *op. cit.,* pp. 91-95.

Buddha's methodology of teaching. He gave what the text calls a "progressive" talk. He first gave "talk on giving, talk on moral habit, talk on heaven, he explained the peril, the vanity, the depravity of pleasures of the senses, the advantage in renouncing (them)." After the mind of the householder was "ready, malleable, devoid of the hindrances, uplifted, pleased, then he explained to him that teaching on *dhamma* which the awakened ones have themselves discovered." This is the Four Noble Truths of suffering, the origin, the stopping of suffering, the way thereto.[95]

The Buddha without doubt taught his monastic followers in greater fullness and depth, but he apparently had no secret doctrine and modified his teaching only according as he sensed the extent of receptivity and needs of his hearers.[96] He offered his teaching freely to all but recognized that not all were equally able to perceive and apply the truth as he understood it. A layman once questioned him on this matter, asking first whether he dwelt "in compassion for every living thing." The Buddha answered that he did. Then the layman, headman of his village, asked whether the Exalted One taught the *Dharma* in full to some and not in full to others. In place of a direct answer, the Buddha told a parable of three fields, "one excellent, one moderate, and one poor, hard, saltish, of bad soil," asking whether the farmer would not sow them in that order. So the Buddha preaches first to monastics, both men and women, then to lay believers, and lastly to "his" wandering recluses and Brāhmans that hold other views than his own. A similar lesson is given with a parable of three waterpots of varying quality. We note that in each case the content of the teaching given is the same. Also the Buddha is determined not to neglect teaching the third group "because if so be they understand but a single sentence of it, that would be to their profit and happiness for many a long day."[97]

[95] *Vinaya-Piṭaka, Cullavagga,* VI, 4, 5; BD, V, 219-220. Similar is the account o the conversion of Sīha, a general of the Licchavis (*Anguttara-Nikāya,* IV, 179-185 BGS, IV, 124-130).

[96] In the chief account of the utterances made shortly prior to his death, th Buddha specifically denied his ever having made any distinction between exoteri and esoteric doctrine (*Dīgha-Nikāya,* II, 100; DB, part II, p. 107).

[97] *Sanyutta-Nikāya,* IV, 314-316; BKS, II, 220-223. We may recall that Jesus similar parable (Mark 4:2-20 and parallels) should properly be named a parable o the soils. Cf. George A. Buttrick, *The Parables of Jesus,* p. 41.

It is clear from the above that the Buddha had numerous critics and religious opponents. Yet apart from the opposition of Devadatta, his long career seems to have been characterized throughout by nonviolence on both sides of disagreement. With but a few exceptions he was received with respect and friendliness. The general openness and religious tolerance of Indian society of his time and place were of course important factors behind this friendly reception. It has been observed, we should add, that the Buddha himself apparently made no attempt to travel to northwestern India, the heartland of Vedic-Brahmanism.[98] But the man himself and his teaching were also important reasons for his reception.

While the Buddha boldly asserted certain priestly ceremonies to be religiously useless, he apparently never urged his disciples to take steps to secure their abolition. Similarly, while allowing no distinction of class or caste in the order of monks, he did not oppose the caste system as a social institution. While residing at Vaiśālī, north of the Ganges, the Buddha is recorded as teaching a number of Licchavis, who were one of the constituent groups of the Vajrian Confederacy, the seven things that make for national prosperity. The import of the teaching is for responsible political, economic and personal morality. Significantly—the context implies recognition of the political implications of the act—the Licchavis are told to "honour, respect, venerate, revere the Vajjian shrines within and without (their borders)."[99]

Similarly the Buddha told Sīha, general of the Licchavis, who had long been a disciple of the Jain movement but asked for acceptance among the Buddha's lay followers, that he should "deem it right" to continue to give alms to monks of his former allegiance. The text cites Sīha as commenting with pleased surprise on this rare generosity. He was also pleased that when he announced his intent of discipleship to the Buddha, the latter urged him to "make a thorough examination of the matter. . . . Investigation is profitable to well-known men like yourself." Sīha observed that if he had been won over by some other sect, "they would have paraded

[98] Cf. Hermann Oldenberg, *Buddha*, p. 137.
[99] *Anguttara-Nikāya*, IV, 15; BGS, IV, 10-11.

through the whole of Veśālī with banners, shouting: 'Sīha, the general, has joined our discipleship.' "[100]

The Buddha's gentleness in "taking the offensive against error" is further expressed by the words delivered to the last convert before his death, Subhadra. Subhadra had asked whether the teachers of other sects and traditions had thoroughly understood things, had in fact fulfilled the claims they made. The Buddha's answer was that Subhadra should leave the question aside and simply listen to him, for he would speak the truth. He proceeded to assert that any system of doctrine or discipline that lacks the Noble (Aryan) Eightfold Path, that is, the way of interior and exterior morality, does not produce men of true saintliness. Such systems are void of true saints.[101] In this evaluation of other teachers the Buddha significantly does not refer to the area of more abstruse doctrine but bases his recognition of religious authenticity on the criterion of quality of ethical content and its fruit in life.

In one of the oldest Scriptures we find reference to the Buddha's dislike of verbal disputation with opponents, of "wordy issue" or "argument with folk." He preferred not to speak of things in the world that he could not accept and would fain keep aloof from.[102] In another passage we note the Buddha's affirmation that he does not quarrel with the world but that the world quarrels with him. His contention was that a preacher of the true *Dharma* does not quarrel with others. This latter passage also affirms the essential identity of the main elements of the Buddha's world view with the views of the "world of sages," a phrase that may mean the best thought of his own time as of the past.[103] In the *Sutta-Nipāta* the Buddha is recorded as stating that truth is one and that differences of men's opinions emerge from their own minds and private surmises.[104] The clear inference, however, of these and related passages is that the Buddha had a low opinion of the verbal wrangling and passionately partisan dis-

[100] *Aṅguttara-Nikāya,* IV, 179-188; BGS, IV, 124-130.
[101] *Dīgha-Nikāya,* II, 148-153; DB, part II, pp. 164-170.
[102] *Sutta-Nipāta* 841-847; WCEB, pp. 125-126.
[103] *Sanyutta-Nikāya,* III, 138; BKS, III, 117.
[104] *Sutta-Nipāta* 883; WCEB, p. 130.

cussion characteristic of many of the religious teachers of his day. He felt that they saw but one part of the whole, a truth illustrated with singular aptness by his famous parable of the blind men and the elephant. A certain rāja brought together a number of blind men and told them each to feel a single different part of an elephant's body. The resultant description of the elephant was that in the case of one blind man it looked like a pot, of another like a winnowing basket, or a plowshare, the pole of a plow or a broom, each according to the part the several blind men had felt over.[105] The Buddha's position was that men arrive at the truth only as they are freed from the vagaries of both metaphysical speculation and traditional views.

The Buddha is recorded as having once addressed a group of Kālāmas from Kesaputra, a district of Kośala, who questioned him as to how to distinguish between true and false religious teachers. Their experience was that generally both ascetics and Brāhmans proclaimed in full their own view but reviled that of others. The Buddha replied that the Kālāmas should not be misled by report or tradition, nor by men's knowledge of sacred Scriptures. They should not be misled by mere logic or rational reflection, nor by the apparent fitness of the view or by respect for the recluse who held it. Rather, they should judge for themselves, and their criterion of judgment should be whether teachings, "when performed and undertaken," lead to moral loss and sorrow or the reverse, to the ethical disintegration of a man or to "his profit and happiness for a long time," that is, to his moral and spiritual development. The Buddha's thought at this point would seem to be particularly close to Jesus' teaching that prophets are properly evaluated according to their ethical fruit.[106]

The Buddha is recorded as giving considerable personal instruction to kings and rulers, although he apparently took no part in politics or other secular activity in a direct way. An exception may be the somewhat uncertain account of his successful moderating of a dispute between the Śākyans and

[105] *Udāna*, VI, 4; MA, part II, pp. 81-83.

[106] *Anguttara-Nikāya*, I, 187-192; BGS, I, 170-175. Cf. Matt. 7:15-20; 11:19; 12:33; Luke 6:43-45; James 3:11-12; Rom. 12:2.

the Koḷiyas over water rights for irrigation.[107] We may say that the Buddha's disengagement from phenomenal existence through nonattachment took the form of aloofness or detachment from social institutions and public events that was yet combined with benevolence toward men.

The Buddha's concern was not only for the peace and harmony of the order as a whole but also for its members as individuals. He frequently gave individual instruction as he sensed the need. He taught the monks to care for their sick brethren, insisting that one sick brother is the responsibility of all. One account tells how the Buddha once found a monk suffering from dysentery who lay in his own filth. With the aid of Ānanda he washed him with his own hands and laid him on a couch. On this occasion he gave the teaching, "Monks, you have not a mother, you have not a father who might tend you. If you, monks, do not tend one another, then who is there who will tend you? Whoever, monks, would tend me, he should tend the sick."[108]

This incident, which brings to mind the saying of Jesus, "as you did it to one of the least of these my brethren, you did it to me" (Matt 25:40), is reinforced by another account. A certain monk whose progress in the spiritual life was admittedly "sluggish and halt" was dismissed from the order by his (mentor) brother. As he stood in inward misery at the gateway of the brethren's park still longing to remain,

> there he came to me, the Exalted One,
> And laid his hand upon my head; and took
> My arm, and to the garden led me back.
> To me the Master in his kindness gave
> A napkin for the feet. . . . [109]

The accounts are in agreement that the Buddha not only taught but was himself characterized by a remarkable resoluteness and strenuousness of mind. The monks are also addressed as strenuous-minded even as they are urged to be such; the achievement and practice of this mode of mental life was a

[107] Christmas Humphreys cites what may be a reconstruction of this event from a Burmese life of the Buddha (*Buddhism*, p. 38).

[108] *Vinaya-Piṭaka, Mahāvagga*, VIII, 20, 1-3; BD, part IV, pp. 431-432.

[109] *Thera-gāthā* 557-566; PEB, part II, p. 258.

central element of their vocation.[110] In keeping with his vigor of thought the Buddha had great skill in reasoned discourse so as to make him veritably unconquerable in disputation. His determination to refrain from discussion of certain metaphysical questions did not keep him from holding and expounding a remarkably consistent world view. But this mental vigor appeared always in the context of calm self-control and serenity. He was the "Tamed One," who had tamed self well.[111] This quality could be coupled with the references, which may be authentic, to his calm and bright expression. The overall effect of his personality was evidently that of a bright and positive spirit manifesting a serene dignity that had been achieved as a result of profound spiritual victory.[112]

The accounts agree also on the Buddha's "unruffled courtesy" in discussion, in spite of the fact that by no means all of his questioners were of good intent. He is recorded as directing his disciples to avoid anger or ill will if others spoke against him or the teaching or the order. Rather, with the calmness of men who have conquered themselves, they should perceive what is well or ill said in the speech of others. In pointing out what is false they should say, "For this or that reason this is not the fact, that is not so, such a thing is not found among us, is not in us."[113] We note instances that point to his fine tact. On one occasion a number of monks were gathered in discussion at the hermitage of the Brāhman Rammaka. The Buddha acceded to the request of Ānanda to go there, but on arrival he perceived that the monks were engaged in discussion of the *Dharma* and he stood outside the porch awaiting its end. "Then the Lord, knowing that the talk had finished, coughed and knocked on the bar of the door." Whereupon the monks opened the door for him.[114]

Regarding the Buddha's manner of teaching, there is general scholarly agreement that the extant Pāli and Sanskrit texts preserve the main elements of his teaching, as well as much

[110] *Sutta-Nipāta* 964-975; WCEB, pp. 140-142. Cf. *Sutta-Nipāta* 63-75; WCEB, pp. 10-11.

[111] Cf. *Dhammapada* 321-323; SBE, X, 78.

[112] We may note in this context the moving words of Romano Guardini regarding the Buddha (*The Lord*, p. 305).

[113] *Dīgha-Nikāya,* I, 3; DB, part I, p. 3.

[114] *Majjhima-Nikāya,* I, 161; MLS, I, 204.

later material. Moreover, some of his very words may be preserved, although it is impossible to be certain in particular cases. The texts as they stand show him as capable of terse and homey language that went straight to the point. Humor is also on occasion discernible in his teaching. On the other hand, much of the material accords with the Indian scholastic predilection for detailed classification of material, repetition in an attempt to catalogue almost every conceivable aspect of a subject.[115] This fact of course must be understood in light of the present format of the texts, which is clearly the result of the arrangement of materials so as to facilitate memorization and oral transmission by recitation, the sole method of transmission during the four hundred years prior to their reduction to writing in the first century B.C. The Buddha was evidently committed to a variety of modes of teaching, a scholastic disputant with the Brāhmans, an exhaustive expositor to his monks, likewise a teacher of understandable and winsome truth to the populace. The texts relate that he used the current speech of Magadha in his teaching and allowed the monks "of various names, various clans, various social strata" to learn and therefore to teach the doctrine each in his own dialect.[116]

There is evidence, however, that the Buddha was not regarded by his disciples as completely without fault. In the account of his last utterances an incident is recorded wherein Ānanda reproved the Master for what he thought was the latter's harshness to the venerable monk Upavāna for standing in front of him as he fanned him. The Buddha explained in answer to Ānanda's remonstrance and request for a reason that Upavāna by standing in front of him at this critical time was impeding the view of "the gods of the ten world-systems" who had come together in great numbers to watch the Tathāgata die. This notion of invisible spirits having their vision thus impeded seems quaint, to say the least, but the episode, with its clearly implied reproval of the Buddha, seems hardly of such a kind to be created by a later generation. The fact that

[115] Cf. Nakamura Hajime, *The Ways of Thinking of Eastern Peoples*, pp. 117-118.

[116] *Vinaya-Piṭaka, Cullavagga*, V, 33; BD, part V, p. 194.

Ānanda so boldly addressed the Blessed One on this occasion suggests that he may have done so before.[117]

The weight of the Buddha's personal authority, moreover, was felt by some of the monks, probably only a small minority, to lie upon them with undue heaviness. One account, which could hardly have been invented later, tells of an old monk who said immediately after the Master's death, "Weep not, neither lament! We are well rid of the great Samaṇa. We used to be annoyed by being told: 'This beseems you, this beseems you not.' But now we shall be able to do whatever we like; and what we do not like, that we shall not have to do!"[118] The tradition as a whole, however, strongly suggests that this kind of resentment was felt by only a very few of the first generation of disciples. It is significant that even this critical account witnesses to the nonauthoritarian mode of the Buddha's ethical teaching.

7

THE END OF THE BUDDHA'S LIFE

The end came during one of the Buddha's missionary journeys; all the evidence points to his continuing this mode of life to the very last year. The account of his last days in the *Mahā-Parinibbāna Sutta* begins at Rājagriha, the capital of Magadha, perhaps a half year before his death. We read of the incident of King Ajātaśatru's (son of Bimbisāra) prime minister asking advice as to the wisdom of a plan to attack the Vajrian Confederacy. The Buddha advised against the plan and taught the conditions of right conduct, concord and religious worship that make for national prosperity, even as he had formerly taught the Licchavis of the Vajrian Confederacy. He then taught similar conditions for the welfare of the monastic order. We note in the "comprehensive religious talk with the

[117] *Dīgha-Nikāya,* II, 139; DB, part II, pp. 151-152. Rhys Davids calls the whole episode "absurd."

[118] *Dīgha-Nikāya,* II, 162; DB, part II, p. 184.

brethren" during these last days repeated emphasis upon the great fruit of upright conduct combined with earnest contemplation and understanding.[119] In the context of what we shall consider later as the Buddha's analysis of phenomenal existence it is significant to observe that the text records him at this time as recollecting how he had formerly remarked that many of the places where he and other monks had stayed for periods of time were so "pleasant," "delightful" and "charming."[120]

The last journey was made with Ānanda and a group of disciples. He traveled in a north and northwesterly direction, possibly with intent to reach his birthplace. He held "comprehensive religious talk" in perhaps a half dozen different towns enroute. He spent the rainy season in the region of Vaiśālī, north of the Ganges River, which he is alleged to have crossed without use of boat or raft. During this stay he experienced a "dire sickness" with severe pains, which he bore without complaint.

Here at Vaiśālī, after he had quite recovered from his sickness, the Buddha was delicately asked by Ānanda for some definitive instructions regarding the order of monks. Ānanda confessed to his body becoming weak and his sight dim when he beheld the sickness of the Exalted One. His only comfort was that the Master would not pass away before he left instructions concerning the order. The answer of the Buddha reveals clearly at least his own intentions regarding his relationship to the order and the refuge and source of truth of both himself and his disciples.

He specifically denied that he was the leader of the brotherhood or that the order was dependent upon him. Only one who harbors such a thought was qualified to leave such instructions. Rather he directed Ānanda and the other disciples to themselves and the Truth (*Dharma*).

> Be ye lamps unto yourselves. Be ye a refuge to yourselves. Betake yourselves to no external refuge. Hold fast to the Truth as a lamp.

[119] *Dīgha-Nikāya,* II, 81, 84, 94; DB, part II, pp. 85-86, 89, 100. We should note that according to another account the minister was the prime figure in a sustained plot that three years later resulted in the attack and destruction of *Vaiśālī* by Ajātaśatru.

[120] *Dīgha-Nikāya,* II, 102, 117-118; DB, part II, pp. 110, 124-125.

> Hold fast as a refuge to the Truth. Look not for refuge to anyone besides yourselves.[121]

We shall see later that the Buddha's understanding of Truth (*Dharma*) went considerably beyond that of mere propositional statement to affirm cosmic Reality with an inner dynamism of its own. The incident, however, shows with succinct clarity the paradox of the Buddha's disavowal of a unique or indispensable religious role in his own person and the touching dependence of perhaps the closest of his disciples.

We may mention in this context an incident that is also recorded as having occurred in the last period of the Buddha's life. Śāriputra, whom we have noted as among the chiefest disciples, expressed to the Buddha singularly high faith in his person, "Lord! such faith have I in the Exalted One, that methinks there never has been, nor will there be, nor is there now any other, whether wanderer or brahmin, who is greater and wiser than the Exalted One, that is to say, as regards the higher wisdom."

The Buddha answered ironically, "Grand and bold are the words of thy mouth, Sāraputta: verily, thou hast burst forth into a song of ecstasy." He then proceeded with further irony to say that in order to make such a statement Śāriputra must have known all the enlightened sages (Buddhas) of the past, perceived those to come in the future, and come to know the Buddha himself, all to the extent of comprehending in full their conduct, wisdom, mode of life and manner of spiritual liberation. Upon Śāriputra's disavowal of this knowledge, the Buddha asked again why he resorted to such extravagant words. Śāriputra then confessed that he knew only the outline of things, "the lineage of the faith."[122]

The *Sutta-Nipāta,* however, records a dialogue in which one Sela, a Brāhman, addressed the Buddha with comparably exalted language, calling him worthy to be rāja of rājas, king of men, too glorious to waste his talent in the life of a recluse.

[121] *Dīgha-Nikāya,* II, 99-101; DB, part II, pp. 106-109. Cf. *Sanyutta-Nikāya,* V, 162; BKS, V, 143.

[122] *Dīgha-Nikāya,* II, 82; DB, part II, pp. 87-89.

The Buddha answered that he was indeed a rāja but rāja of *Dharma* and that without a peer. He rolled by *Dharma* the wheel of authority and cosmic power, "which none can backward roll!" He was the physician without equal, wholly enlightened, all his foes conquered, rejoicing without fear. The evidence taken together seems to point to the Buddha's having in fact a sublime self-consciousness of his knowledge of the truth, of his own moral victory, even as he was generally hesitant to thrust his person into the foreground. The oldest materials show his consistently pointing beyond himself to *Dharma* as the way and *Nirvāṇa* as the goal. The Buddha's role was evidently to set the wheel of *Dharma* rolling in the world, that is, to manifest its reality and power in a way rare but not totally unknown in the history of men, a process to be carried on by his disciples.[123]

The text affirms that the Buddha had a clear premonition of death, or rather that he had consciously chosen this as his time to die. We read his recollection that he had prophesied immediately after having attained enlightened that he would not die until his monastic and lay disciples, both men and women, "shall have become true hearers, wise and well trained . . . correct in life, walking according to the precepts—until they, having thus themselves learned the doctrine, shall be able to tell others of it, preach it, make it known, establish it, open it, minutely explain it and make it clear." The testimony of Māra, the Evil One, now that the time of death approached, was that this had all happened and indeed that "this pure religion" had already become "successful, prosperous, widespread, and popular in all its full extent . . . well proclaimed among men." The Buddha did not contest this witness but announced that he would die three months hence.[124] Some such consciousness of the fitness of the time seems to have been the context of the final journey.

From Vaiśālī the party went on to Bhaṇdagāma and thence to Pāvā. Here the Buddha and his disciples were invited to eat

[123] *Sutta-Nipāta* 548-561; WCEB, pp. 87-88. Cf. *Sanyutta-Nikāya,* I, 33, 55; BKS, I, 46, 79.

[124] *Dīgha-Nikāya,* II, 104-106, 113-114; DB, part II, pp. 112-113, 120-121.

at the home of an earnest lay disciple, one Cunda, a worker in metals. There is some difference of scholarly interpretation as to whether the food (*sūkara-maddava*) eaten by the Buddha at this time was boar's flesh or something like truffles. It may have been the former as the Buddha expressly refused to require abstinence from the eating of meat as a monastic rule. The consequence of the meal, however, which included rice, was that he became severely ill of dysentery. In spite of the pain he continued his journey with Ānanda, and possibly other disciples, though slowly and with many stops. At one stop the text records the miracle of a small muddy streamlet coming to flow clear and fresh in order that the Buddha might drink of its water.[125] At another place he urged Ānanda to tell the smith Cunda that he should not feel remorse about the effect of his well-intended food. When he reached the city of Kuśinagara, he was exhausted and lay down to rest between two Sāla trees.

Here, though weak in body, yet with full consciousness, the Buddha gave final instructions to his sorrowing disciples. Addressing Ānanda, he affirmed that the worthiest homage was paid to himself by "the brother or the sister, the devout man or the devout woman" who is "correct in life, walking according to the precepts."[126] He urged the monks not to be concerned over the honoring of his remains but to leave that to devout laymen; they should rather be zealous for their own spiritual good. He spoke words of comfort to Ānanda when he learned that the latter was weeping apart at the thought of the passing away of his Master, "he who is so kind." With fulsome repetition he praised Ānanda for his acts, words and thoughts of "love, kind and good," over a long time. He reminded his close and faithful disciples that he had always taught that whatever is born or made within this world must be dissolved. Ānanda should be zealous in his spiritual effort and he too would soon be delivered from the intoxications of mind that bind men to rebirth.[127]

[125] *Dīgha-Nikāya,* II, 129; DB, part II, pp. 139-141.
[126] *Dīgha-Nikāya,* II, 138; DB, part II, p. 150.
[127] The text clearly implies that Ānanda had not yet experienced enlightenment unto *Nirvāṇa.*

The Buddha then told Ānanda to inform the people of Kuśinagara, Mallas by tribe, that he would pass away during the coming night. The text records that the Mallas were overcome with grief and requested the privilege of visiting the Buddha in his last hours. Ānanda made this possible by presenting the people by family groups. It was on this day also that the conversion of the ascetic Subhadra occurred and his immediate reception into the order without the usual four months probation. Shortly afterwards Subhadra "attained to that supreme goal of the higher life," which "did he by himself, and while yet in this visible world, bring himself to the knowledge of, and continue to realize, and to see face to face."[128]

Then Buddha inquired three times of the assembled brethren whether there was some "doubt or misgiving" in their minds regarding "the Buddha, or the doctrine, or the path or the method" that they wished to ask him of while they were still face to face with him. Each time silence was the answer. The Buddha's last words were "Decay is inherent in all component things! Work out your salvation with diligence."[129]

The text describes in some detail the ensuing events of a series of stages of rapture or transitions from one stage of consciousness to another. Twenty-one different stages in all are listed. The Buddha expired after passing out of the fourth stage of rapture for the last time. Little more can be said than that he died while in deep meditation. The date was close to the year 480 B.C. According to the Sanskrit texts the month was that of Kārttika (November) at the time of the full moon; according to the Pāli the month was Vaiśakha (April-May) as were the traditional dates of the birth and the enlightenment.

The text of the *Mahā-Parinibbāna Sutta* describes those of the brethren "who were not yet free from the passions" as prostrate with grief. Those who were free "bore their grief collected and composed" with the thought that all component things are impermanent and subject to dissolution. The elder Anuruddha exhorted the brethren to refrain from sorrow and

[128] *Dīgha-Nikāya,* II, 153; DB, part II, p. 169. We may note the "quasi-personal" element perhaps to be inferred from the phrase "face to face."

[129] *Dīgha-Nikāya,* II, 156; DB, part II, p. 173.

tears for this same reason.[130] The Mallas also were deeply grieved, and they were the ones who took "perfumes and garlands and all the musical instruments, and five hundred suits of apparel" to pay homage to the remains of the Exalted One. For six days they did honor "with dancing, and hymns, and music, and with garlands and perfumes, and in making canopies of their garments and preparing decoration wreaths to hang thereon." On the seventh day the body was cremated in a manner befitting a "king of kings." The remains were then shared with the eight greatest political units of northeastern India, whose kings built cairns (*stūpa*) to house the relics in dignity.[131]

[130] *Dīgha-Nikāya,* II, 157-158; DB, part II, pp. 177-178.
[131] *Dīgha-Nikāya,* II, 159-167; DB, part II, pp. 180-191.

III

THE TEACHING OF THE BUDDHA

1

The teaching of the Buddha, generally called the Law (*Dharma;* Pāli: *Dhamma*) in Buddhist tradition, is, as we have seen, not easily to be distinguished from the developments thereof made by disciples in the various schools in the first generations after the death of the Master. Heinrich Zimmer went so far as to say that there is not a single word that can be ascribed with unqualified certainty to the Buddha himself.[1] This statement cannot be specifically denied, but it does not give us the whole picture. By comparing the recensions of the Pāli and the Sanskrit versions of the Scriptures, we are able, in the case of essential agreement, to be relatively certain that the material dates back to a time antedating the separation of the two schools responsible for these versions, i.e., about 250 B.C. In other cases, where we can use the fewer surviving texts of

[1] Zimmer, *Philosophies of India,* pp. 466-467.

the Mahāsanghika school, we are able to achieve relative textual certainty a century earlier.[2] Furthermore, there is a wide scholarly consensus that certain main lines of the recorded teaching derive from the Buddha; it is with these that we shall primarily deal.

The Four Noble Truths (*Ārya Satya*) apparently constitute the core of the original teaching. Their discovery by the Buddha, according to the Scriptures, was the primary basis of his enlightenment. The fourfold structure has been compared to the four divisions of Hindu medicine: disease, the cause of disease, the absence of disease, medicine. A similar parallel can also be shown with Yoga philosophy, but as there is no evidence that either of these parallels existed before the time of the Buddha, we are not able to draw any conclusions as to possible influence.

The Scriptures record this teaching as having been given in fully developed form in the Buddha's first sermon to his former disciples, the five ascetics, in the Deer Park at Isipatana near Benares. In the account in the *Mahāvagga* of the *Vinaya-Piṭaka* the preaching of the sermon is described as the rolling of the *Dharma*-wheel, constituting a cosmic event that no man or spirit or god could reverse.[3] The two main accounts of the sermon are in essential agreement and are almost universally accepted by Buddhists as conveying the authentic teaching of the Buddha.

The gist of the sermon is simple and easy to follow. The Buddha began by saying that the homeless religious must reject the two extremes of ignoble and unprofitable sensual indulgence and of painful, ignoble and useless self-mortification. "By avoiding these two extremes the Tathāgata has gained knowledge" of the Middle Way that gives sight and knowledge and leads to calm, to insight, enlightenment, *Nirvāṇa.*[4]

[2] Cf. Conze, *Buddhist Thought in India,* p. 31; Bareau, *Die Religionen Indiens,* III, 32.

[3] *Mahāvagga,* I, 6, 30; BD, part IV, pp. 17-18.

[4] *Sanyutta-Nikāya,* V, 420; BKS, part V, pp. 356-357. Thomas J. J. Altizer observes that Westerners might well wonder at the use of the term "Middle Way" because the monk who followed it was obligated to deprive himself of everything that we would call pleasure or enjoyment (*Oriental Mysticism and Biblical Eschatol-*

In the form of the sermon as it is recorded, the Buddha significantly describes the Middle Way by listing first the Noble Eightfold Path (*Marga*), which constitutes the fourth of the Four Noble Truths as these are ordinarily cited. This order is to give priority to ethical conduct. The Noble Eightfold Path consists of "right view, right aim, right speech, right action, right living, right effort, right mindfulness, right concentration."

This path is an ethical way, both primarily and comprehensively. Primarily, the word for "right" (*samyak;* Pāli: *sammā*) is related to the Latin *summum*, the highest or best. It also has the meaning of "real" or "true." The statement of these "right" ways is one of the "noble" truths.

The path is also comprehensively ethical; it is concerned not only with external conduct but also with right thought and intent. The teaching insists that the ethical quality of men's motives, attitudes and thoughts is as important as their formal words and deeds. Throughout the religious history of India from the Vedic period onward there has been strong emphasis upon ethical conduct.[5] The Buddha did not differ appreciably from his contemporaries in his understanding of what constituted right ethical behavior. He emphasized, however, as few others, the importance of the inner aspects of human behavior. Going beyond the Upanishadic concept of thought control as a technique for spiritual breakthrough into Ultimate Reality, the Buddha taught the inherent goodness as well as the cosmic importance or effectiveness of right thinking.

The proper control of thought and feeling is frequently stressed in the Scriptures. In an account of his early struggle with Māra, the evil one, the Buddha described himself as "with

---

ogy, p. 120). We may recall, however, that in the context of contemporary ascetic practices for the Buddha categorically to reject all self-mortification was unquestionably a move toward the "middle." In the *Dhammapada* we find two suggestive aspects of this position. On the one hand the ideal monk is described as "pure, serene, undisturbed, and in whom all gaiety is extinct" (*Dhammapada* 413; SBE, X, 94). But on the other, the homeless monk should "look for enjoyment where enjoyment seemed difficult" (*Dhammapada* 88, 99; SBE, X, 25, 30). The ordinary pleasures of life are to be rejected, but the text affirms that there is a joy and satisfaction in the homeless religious life beyond what men expect. As we shall see, *Nirvāna* is often described as a state of unalloyed bliss. Cf. Buddhadāsa Indapaññо, *Buddha Dhamma for Students*, pp. 31-32.

[5] Cf. Brown, *Man in the Universe*, p. 10.

purpose bent (to order), with mindfulness well set." Strong mental watchfulness and concentration are more effective in the human dilemma than the old ideal of a pious life characterized by the faithful observance of sacrifices that Māra (or Namuci) urged.[6] In the *Dhammapada* we read: "This mind of mine went formerly wandering about as it liked, as it listed, as it pleased; but I shall now hold it in thoroughly as the rider who holds the hook holds in the furious elephant." "Be not thoughtless, watch your thoughts." "A wise man makes straight his trembling and unsteady thought." "It is good to tame the mind, . . . a tamed mind brings happiness." "Let the wise man guard his thoughts, . . . thoughts well guarded bring happiness." "Whatever a hater may do to a hater, or an enemy to an enemy, a wrongly directed mind will do him greater mischief. Not a mother, not a father, will do so much, nor any relatives; a well-directed mind will do us greater service."[7]

A classic Buddhist expression of the primary importance of human thought in the working of the karmic process is that of the opening verses of the *Dhammapada*: "All that we are is the result of what we have thought: it is founded on our thoughts, it is made up of our thoughts. If a man speaks or acts with an evil thought, pain follows him, as the wheel follows the foot of the ox that draws the carriage. . . . If a man speaks or acts with a pure thought, happiness follows him, like a shadow that never leaves him."[8] In a discussion with a disciple of Nātaputra (Mahāvīra), leader of the Jains, the Buddha learned that Nātaputra had affirmed wrong of body to be more blamable in the doing of an evil deed. In response to this disciple's inquiry as to the Buddha's own view, the latter affirmed unequivocally that deed of mind is more blamable, of another order of importance.[9]

For the Buddha the proper control of thought consisted negatively in overcoming the mental defilements of craving, ill will and delusion. When these cease, the *Karma* of a man

[6] *Sutta-Nipāta* 425-449; WCEB, pp. 63-65. Cf. *Dhammapada* 106-108; SBE, X, 32.

[7] *Dhammapada* 326-327, 33-43; SBE, X, 79, 12-15. Cf. *Dhammapada* 79, 91, 94, 103-105, 185, 234; *Anguttara-Nikāya*, I, 4; BGS, I, 4-5.

[8] *Dhammapada* 1-2; SBE, X, 3-4.

[9] *Majjhima-Nikāya*, I, 372-373; MLS, II, 36-38.

ceases, that is, the karmic results of his past, in this or previous lives, even though certain consequences may remain, no longer have spiritually harmful or constraining effects upon him. Positively, proper thought meant the consistent practice of benevolence (*mettā*) toward all beings, active concern for their welfare, and a tranquillity of mind that is at the same time characterized by alertness and energy of mind, the opposite of sloth and torpor. Such thought is also characterized by friendship with (or aspiration for) that which is lovely, which in one passage is equated with the whole of the Noble Eightfold Path, and, as we shall see, with *Dharma* and probably with *Nirvāṇa.*[10] The mind of such a thinker is thus free and empty, free of clinging to aught in this world as though it had immortal substantiality or ultimate value in itself, free to aspire to that which is truly valuable and eternal, *Nirvāṇa*.

The discovery of this teaching was a significant element in effecting a veritable revolution in the spiritual climate of many Americans in the early nineteenth century. It was of fundamental importance to Ralph Waldo Emerson and others of the New England Transcendentalists. It was a major factor in the emergence of what has been variously termed New Thought or the Metaphysical Movement in American history.[11] Admittedly these movements have developed theological positions and world views that at some points have seemed opposed to the mainstream of the Christian tradition. Yet it is difficult to understand the long hesitancy of Protestant orthodoxy in particular vigorously to endorse this Buddhist insight. For the notion of the central importance of the ethical quality of men's thoughts is clearly an integral element of the Christian gospel as given in the New Testament. We are reminded in particular of Jesus' "morality of intention," whereby to think adultery is the same as doing it.[12]

[10] *Anguttara-Nikāya,* I, 2-16; BGS, I, 2-12. *Sanyutta-Nikāya,* V, 32-39; BKS, V, 30-31. Cf. Buddhadāsa, *op. cit.*, pp. 21-22.

[11] Cf. Stillson Judah, "Indian Philosophy and the Meta-physical Movement in the United States," *Religion in Life,* XXVIII, 3 (Summer, 1959), 353-364; Arthur Christy, *The Orient in American Transcendentalism,* passim.

[12] Cf. Matt. 5:21-22, 27-28, 44; 6:14-15, 22-23; 12:34; 15:8, 18-20; 18:35; 22:37-40; 25:13 (and parallel passages in the other Gospels). See also I Cor. 13; 14:20; 16:13-14; II Cor. 11:3; Gal. 5:19-24; 6:7-9; Phil. 2:5; 4:8; Col. 3:14-15; James 3:17; 4:8; I Pet. 1:13, 22; 2:1; 3:4; 5:8; I John 2:9-10; 4:7-12; II John 5-6; Rev. 2:4, 23; 16:15.

The Eightfold Path begins with "right view," for right understanding was basic to attainment of the goal in the Buddha's teaching. Such understanding did not mean merely intellectual apperception of propositional truth. From the Scriptures it appears that the Buddha had no hesitancy to express truth in propositional terms, but he was evidently even more concerned to teach an existential insight that leads to commitment and changed modes of living. "Right view," however, included knowledge of the Four Noble Truths, which, as we shall see, constituted the basic elements of both his world view and soteriological method. It included the evaluative understanding that there is nothing in this world worthy to be grasped at or clung to in any ultimate sense and the faith-vision that the truly Real exists and also the way to it. Right view was presumed, as was each of the eight elements of the path, to end in the restraint of craving, of ill will and delusion.[13]

"Right aim" meant the resolve to renounce the selfish self and sensual pleasures (for the unalloyed bliss of *Nirvāṇa*), to have malice toward none, to harm no living creature. Positively it meant aspiration toward benevolence and kindness to others as also toward *Nirvāṇa*. "Right speech" was to abstain from falsehood, from slander, from harsh words and frivolous talk. "Right action" meant to abstain from "taking life, taking what is not given," from sexual immorality. It also included the entire range of human ethical conduct. As we have noted, the Buddha seemed to differ little in his basic ethical judgments from what was commonly accepted as good or evil in his society. We perceive, however, an essentially nonlegalistic orientation from his use of expressions like: "This beseems you," or "This does not beseem you." He evidently considered spiritual discernment indispensable to ethical decisions.

"Right living" meant to quit a wrong occupation and to earn one's living by a right one. From this item we clearly perceive that householders as well as monastics were included among the objects of this teaching. "Right living" was understood to mean that one should refrain from work that brought harm to any living being. Specifically, later Buddhism taught

[13] *Dīgha-Nikāya,* II, 313-314; DB, part II, pp. 343-345. *Sanyutta-Nikāya,* V, 32-39; BKS, V, 30-31.

that any profession that involved killing was proscribed, such as that of soldier, butcher or fisherman. Selling weapons, harmful drugs or intoxicating liquor was forbidden, as was the profession of slave dealer or even caravan merchant.

We may classify the eight items of the Path under three headings: the first two under the category of wisdom or understanding, the next three under ethical conduct, the last three under mental discipline.[14] Later Buddhist literature summarized the category of ethical conduct in the Five Precepts, which have come to play a central role in popular teaching and are considered as binding on all Buddhists, both lay and monastic:

> To abstain from taking life.
> To abstain from taking what is not given.
> To abstain from sexual immorality.
> To abstain from false speech.
> To abstain from intoxicating liquors.[15]

These precepts, like the Ten Commandments of Hebraic tradition, are negatively phrased, but the Eightfold Path itself is expressed in positive terms and reveals thereby the primarily positive thrust of the Buddha's teaching. More typical therefore is the brief summation of the Buddha's ethical teaching as: "Avoid evil, do good, purify the mind."

The third heading of mental discipline, the category frequently emphasized by the Buddha, began with "right effort." This refers to effort of will that evil or unwholesome states of mind not arise, that those already arisen may be abandoned. The effort is also to be made that good and wholesome states of mind arise and be preserved, developed and perfected. The particular ethos of this way is properly realized only if we note the emphasis in the texts that in "right effort" the disciple "puts forth will, he makes effort, he stirs up energy, he grips and forces his mind."[16] This is one of the many instances

[14] George Appleton, *On the Eightfold Path*, p. 95.

[15] Cf. Edward Conze, *Buddhist Scriptures*, p. 70. There is another list of ten prohibitions that adds an additional five to the first group. The added items apply only to monks and forbid their eating after noon, participating in theatrical arts, adorning their persons, sleeping on a high couch or accepting money.

[16] *Dīgha-Nikāya*, II, 313; DB, part II, p. 344.

cited in which the Buddha summoned his followers to the most vigorous exertion of will, especially with reference to states and habits of mind. Strenuousness of mind is a primary characteristic of the Buddhist disciple.

"Right mindfulness" refers to a program of disciplined mental attentiveness. In one passage the setting up of mindfulness is denoted as the "one and only path" to the realization of the final goal of Buddhist aspiration.[17] It is, as it were, a summation of the total methodology. Right mindfulness involves an alert observation of the body, "ardent, self-possessed and mindful," to the end of overcoming both the craving and despair "common in the world." The same attentiveness is to be directed to one's feelings, thoughts and ideas. The end in each case is to achieve the victory of nonattachment, of freedom from both craving and dejection. The process of right mindfulness, in short, involves a comprehensive control of body, mind and feeling.

We find this teaching of self-control repeatedly emphasized in the *Dhammapada:* "If one man conquer in battle a thousand times a thousand men, and if another conquer himself, he is the greatest of conquerors." "The gods envy him whose senses, like horses well broken in by the driver, have been subdued." "By rousing himself, by earnestness, by restraint and control, the wise man may make for himself an island which no flood can overwhelm." "Good people fashion themselves." "If a man hold himself dear, let him watch himself carefully."[18]

The last item of the Eightfold Path is "right concentration," sometimes translated as right rapture. The term specifically denotes the progressive process of mental states by which the final goal of *Nirvāṇa* is to be attained. It is essentially a process of meditation, the discipline to which the Buddha devoted a substantial part of his daily life, and which has remained ever afterward a primary element of the Buddhist way of life. This discipline is properly and necessarily, however, in Buddhist context, practiced as the crown of the other parts of the Eightfold Path.

[17] *Dīgha-Nikāya,* II, 290; DB, part II, p. 327.
[18] *Dhammapada* 103, 94, 25, 145, 157; SBE, X, 31, 28, 10, 40, 45.

Right concentration is described in a major text as a process of four progressive states of mind, which are designed to bring not only the conceptions of the mind but also the feelings of the heart into ever deeper and purer levels of integration and peace. The first stage of meditation (*dhyāna*) is "born of solitude and is full of joy and ease." It is characterized by cogitation and deliberation. This is to say that the practicer abandons sensual pleasures and all unwholesome qualities of mind, even as the exercise of reason is still a part of the mental process. In the second state "the mind grows calm and sure." This state is produced by concentration of the mental faculties but with subsidence of the reasoning process and reflection. Joy and ease are still sensed. We note that the description of each state is almost identical to that of the Buddha's Enlightenment.

The third stage involves the paling of joy but with mental alertness unimpaired. One is aware, self-possessed, calm and contemplative, still feeling a deep ease in himself. The fourth stage knows neither happiness nor sadness, neither ease nor dis-ease; the practicer experiences what is called "rapture of utter purity of mindfulness and equanimity, wherein neither ease is felt nor any ill."[19] This stage represents the culmination of the Eightfold Path and the goal of Buddhist life. The rapture clearly indicates not the loss but the refinement of consciousness, awareness purified of all defilement or emotional involvement that is possessive. This is to know *Nirvāṇa,* to have achieved detachment and thereby liberation. Herein is "Nothingness" experienced, awareness that true Reality is empty of grasping, separative selfhood. The religious life has been lived, the way out of the human dilemma has been found and followed, from this point onward human life on earth is presumed to be lived in a new dimension of Reality.

The central importance of the Eightfold Path as *the* way for early Buddhism, and at least in its essence for the Buddha himself, is suggested by Buddhaghosa's description of the Path as "unconditioned."[20] This mode of expression assumes the unconditioned as an aspect of *Nirvāṇa* and ascribes to the

[19] *Dīgha-Nikāya,* II, 313-314; DB, part II, pp. 343-345.
[20] *Visuddhi-Magga* 21; Warren, *Buddhism in Translations,* p. 379.

Eightfold Path the dignity of being the solely pure manifestation in phenomenal existence of unconditioned, Ultimate Reality. As we noted among the last utterances of the Buddha, the presence of this Path in any religious teaching or practice was the determining element in its power to produce the fruit of right living and the attainment of *Nirvāṇa.*

The last item of the Eightfold Path clearly involves a progressive development, but otherwise the eight parts are to be practiced simultaneously, constituting the Buddhist way of daily life designed to lead to the goal of right concentration (*samādhi*), which may be understood as the human experience of *Nirvāṇa.* The Eightfold Path, however, is not the only description of the Way recorded in the Scriptures. A fourfold formula is also found and repeated eight times in the *Mahā-Parinibbāna Sutta.* According to this formulation, the Way begins with observance of the rules of morality (*śīla*), proceeds to concentration or the rapture of enlightenment (*samādhi*), whereby saving knowledge (*paññā*) is acquired, a state of mind or understanding that is liberation (*vimutti*). The ethical content, however, and mental-spiritual development envisaged in this formula are essentially no different from those of the eightfold version.

2

Following this brief consideration of the central role of ethics in the teaching of the Buddha, it is in order that we inquire into the provisions made for what we may call recovery from ethical failure. Aside from a very few instances of criticism of the Buddha within the order, as we have noted, we find perhaps no case in the Scriptures where he acknowledges or is charged with formal wrong. There are, however, many instances given in the *Vinaya-Piṭaka* of wrongs done by individual monks, and the problem of restoration of the man and of his relationship to the order existed apparently from a very early period.

We read that it was the custom for the "wanderers" of other sects to meet together four times a month, "on the fourteenth, fifteenth and eighth days of the half-month," to discuss among themselves and also to proclaim to the people their own particular tenets. King Seniya Bimbisāra of Magadha thereupon suggested to the Buddha that his own disciples do the same. The fact that the suggestion came from the king rather than originated with the Buddha himself points to the looseness of the early organizational structure of the order. The Buddha consented, however, but, according to the text, the monks first met only to sit, as popular criticism gave it out, "in silence like dumb pigs." Following this criticism the Buddha "allowed" them to proclaim *Dharma,* their word of truth, to the people on such occasions.

The text relates that subsequent to this event the Buddha "allowed," that is, prescribed, a form of confessional service for the monks to use when they thus met together. "An experienced, competent monk" recited the *Pātimokkha,* or list of rules, developed as a result of the Buddha's teaching. Most scholars hold that the present form of 227 rules was drawn up in part during his lifetime and in part later, but it is possible that all or nearly all are drawn from elements of his teaching. The list was apparently read three times, and if a monk were innocent of the offense stated in the rule, he indicated his purity by silence. If he were guilty, he was duty bound to reveal his fault before the assembled brethren. If he failed to do so, he was guilty of conscious lying, and this had been called a stumbling block by the Lord. The confession of his offense was therefore the moral obligation of a monk who desired purity, and it furthermore brought him comfort.[21]

After the avowal of offense the penalty, which is stated in conjunction with each rule in the present form of the *Pātimokkha,* was assigned. The extreme penalty was expulsion from the order. The intent of the process, however, was evidently to constitute, as Miss I. B. Horner has put it, courses of training with the upbuilding of the ethical and spiritual life of the monk as the goal. Furthermore, in particular instances in the texts a monk who had committed an offense is usually cited as making his avowal either to the Buddha or to one or more monks soon after the offense. In this way he became "pure"

[21] *Vinaya-Piṭaka, Mahāvagga,* II, 1-3; BD, part IV, pp. 130-135.

prior to the time of formal assembly and needed not to make confession before the whole congregation.[22]

A custom evidently developed early for groups of the monks to hold a meeting at the end of their joint residence during the rainy season for the purpose of inviting mutual criticism. This period of enforced proximity apparently furnished more temptations to disharmony and unfriendly relationships than other times. The criticism invited was with respect to what had been seen or heard or suspected of the speaker. A formula of invitation developed wherein each monk, beginning with the senior, invited criticism from his brethren "out of compassion" and ended with the words: "I will make amends."[23] The monk was of course obligated to make amends in terms of the formal penalty assigned by the community for his offense. This action, however, was clearly not viewed as a substitute for the strenuous inner work that the disciple was obligated to initiate and carry out himself.

We read in the *Dhammapada* that the worthy monk cleanses himself from evil. "By oneself one is purified. The pure and the impure (stand and fall) by themselves, no one can purify another."[24] The Scriptures reveal a sense of the solidarity of mankind and indeed of all sentient beings; love for all is taught even as a part of charms for self-protection from poisonous snakes and insects.[25] But while the significance of the effect of one's good and evil deeds upon others is not lost sight of, the emphasis of the teaching is that good or evil done by a man works its good and evil effects primarily upon himself. Evil is done by the self and crushes the foolish self. He whose evil is very great brings himself down to that state where his enemy wishes him to be. The working of the law of *Karma* is unfailing. However slowly, both good and evil deeds ripen and bear appropriate fruit, which comes home to the doer.[26]

[22] Cf. BD, part I, pp. viii-xxvi.

[23] *Vinaya-Piṭaka, Mahāvagga,* IV, 1; BD, part IV, pp. 208-212.

[24] *Dhammapada* 9, 165; SBE, X, 5-6, 46.

[25] *Vinaya-Piṭaka, Cullavagga,* V, 6; BD, part V, pp. 148-149. All living beings share also with inanimate things the characteristic of being composed and therefore conditioned, as a part of the causal process that is by definition other than *Nirvāṇa.*

[26] *Dhammapada* 161-162, 116-128; SBE, X, 45, 34-35.

A central element of the Buddha's teaching was that a man himself should change, turn from doing evil to doing good, orient his whole self toward *Nirvāṇa.* "Hatred ceases by love." He evidently thought that it was within the range of human power to effect such change and to initiate a sustained course of doing good. "Good people fashion themselves."[27] The astonishing aspect of this conviction-claim, however, is that by this change the process of *Karma,* with all of its cosmic implications, is essentially nullified in its effect upon the one who changes. The liberation of the *arhat* (one who has attained the last stage of enlightenment-rapture) is as much liberation from this process as from the mental defilements. Within this life certain karmic effects from the past, whether good or evil, may be experienced by the liberated man, but they have no real power over his mind or cosmic destiny. The *arhat* may enjoy—without attachment—the effects of good *Karma;* evil *Karma,* which he cannot formally escape, cannot harm him, that is, cause his moral or spiritual disintegration.[28] He is liberated, free.

The Buddha did not explain in "theological" terms how such a momentous change could be effected within a cosmos where the law of *Karma* was seen to work as rigorously as he held it. He believed, however, not only that the change was possible but that he himself had achieved it. We read in the *Dhammapada* that "He whose evil deeds are covered by good deeds, brightens up this world, like the moon when freed from clouds."[29] In the context of the India of the day this affirmation of the possibility of radical release was a veritable "gospel." We shall consider later the nature of *Dharma,* as the "Power" or "Force" that, according to the early teaching, was available to help men make the change and carry it through.

[27] *Dhammapada* 5, 145; SBE, X, 5, 40. The Japanese Zen Buddhist Hakuin wrote that meditation has the power to wipe clean all evil *Karma* (Bernard Phillips, ed., *The Essentials of Zen Buddhism,* p. 270).

[28] *Dhammapada* 221; SBE, X, 59.

[29] *Dhammapada* 173; SBE, X, 47.

3

We come now to a consideration of the first three of the Four Noble Truths. From our study thus far we may well agree with the observation of Sir Charles Eliot that "the Buddha regarded practice as the foundation of his system." He was concerned to show a way and quality of life with the primary goal of liberation from the human dilemma as he perceived it. But he clearly regarded certain knowledge or understanding as essential to the practice of the way and attainment of the goal. In particular, he evidently regarded knowledge of the nature of the human dilemma in its cosmic context as essential to liberation. Although, as we have noted, the Buddha regarded metaphysical speculation of little moment in the way to liberation, he and his early disciples clearly had a coherent view of the world as of human psychology.[30] But the knowledge that he considered essential was not primarily intellectual in the modern, Western sense of the word; it involved rather a proper perception of values, knowing what is truly good, real, dependable and therefore worthy of aspiration.

The First Noble Truth is that of suffering or ill (*duḥkha;* Pāli: *dukkha*). This term is frequently translated as pain, but it meant pain of mind and heart as well as of body, including grief, anxiety, despair and frustration. While there was clearly consciousness of wrongdoing in the Buddhist tradition, we may note here that what we call guilt apparently did not play a role comparable to that in the Western world. A main element of the first Truth, however, is the all-pervasiveness of the condition described. We read that "birth is painful, old age is painful, death is painful, grief, lamentation, suffering, misery and despair are painful, painful is it not to get what is wished for, in a word, the Five Groups (of material and mental qualities) that arise from Grasping are connected with pain."[31]

[30] Cf. *Dīgha-Nikāya,* I, 18-22; DB, part I, pp. 30-35; Bareau, *Bouddha,* pp. 21-34.

[31] *Dīgha-Nikāya,* II, 305; DB, II, 337-338.

This teaching is not to be understood as meaning that the whole of phenomenal existence is one totally unrelieved mass of suffering. Certain forms of provisional or temporary happiness are allowed to human life. According to the world view of primitive Buddhism, dwellers in the northern continent (Uttarakuru) were believed to live in perfect felicity, as were the gods, although for a limited period of time. The Buddha, moreover, viewed the present human situation as the one potentially most productive of good. To be born a human being means that one has the opportunity to hear the Truth and to attain *Nirvāṇa.* It is good to help others. "The accumulation of good is delightful." Friends are held to be pleasant; indeed, any enjoyable experience is pleasant. Virtue is pleasant, as is "faith firmly rooted," "attainment of intelligence" or the "avoiding of sins."[32]

The First Noble Truth therefore would seem to be more affirmative of religious values than descriptive of physical conditions, although the latter remain a part of the whole. The Buddha was concerned in the affirmation of religious values to turn the attention of men away from that which neither satisfies nor has ultimate value or reality to that which does satisfy and is Ultimate Reality. He saw the life of all sentient beings in their natural state as being characterized by impermanence, inadequacy, purposelessness, as lacking true reality or ultimate value. He taught that sense-pleasures are of little satisfaction, of much pain, tribulation, peril; that which is impermanent, liable to change, is painful.[33] The sense of the transitoriness of all things in this world looms large in this understanding; they lack permanent or dependable reality. The Buddha's search for the Good led him to find it not in the changing but in that which changes not and is "Other" than phenomenal existence in flux, that is, *Nirvāṇa,* and its manifestation in *Dharma.*

[32] *Dhammapada* 118, 331-333; SBE, X, 34, 80.

[33] *Majjhima-Nikāya,* I, 132-138; MLS, I, 168-178. On one occasion the Buddha is recorded as saying that the basic characteristic of the world and all of its elements is that "it crumbles away" (*Sanyutta-Nikāya,* IV, 52; BKS, IV, 28). We may note in this context the similar understanding of Rudolf Bultmann, who writes "Das Sichtbare, Verfügbare ist vergänglich, und deshalb ist, wer von ihm her lebt, der Vergänglichkeit, dem Tode verfallen" (*Kerygma und Mythos,* I, 28).

In this awareness of the fundamental inadequacy of the situation of empirical man and in pointing to a way out therefrom based on such recognition, the Buddha seems akin to most other great religious teachers of mankind.[34] In a suggestive passage in the *Dhammapada* the Buddha is recorded as likening the situation of empirical man, who is under the dominion of Māra, the Tempter, to "a fish taken from his watery home and thrown on the dry ground."[35] The role of understanding is to realize that the existential situation of empirical man and his natural environment does not have (is "empty" of) ultimate or real value. Religiously and ethically, it is not worthy, not any part of it, to be grasped at or clung to. True religious and ethical aspiration lies in committal to the truly and ultimately desirable, *Nirvāṇa* and its dynamic principle of operation in this world, *Dharma.* We may say therefore that rather than affirming phenomenal existence in itself to be entirely painful or evil—although we find statements regarding its evil nature in later materials—the Buddha evidently intended to affirm that the source of suffering lies in man's grasping or clinging to that which cannot give true or ultimate satisfaction.[36]

The Buddha is recorded as ascribing the quality of suffering to what is impermanent, and in that sense the empirical human body-mind with its feelings and consciousness may be reckoned as an ill. The full ethos of this understanding, however, at least as our texts stand, is seen only as we note the spiritual direction that is regularly added as the proper consequence to the awareness that the body and its feelings, perceptions and consciousnesses constitute an ill. That is, "the well-taught Aryan disciple" is repelled and feels disgust at the empirical body-mind and its activities. He learns not to lust.after these things by creating attitudes of revulsion and disgust toward

[34] William James declared the "common nucleus" of the intellectual content of all authentic religion to consist in two parts, an uneasiness and its solution. The first he described as "a sense that there is something wrong about us as we naturally stand" (*The Varieties of Religious Experience*, p. 383).

[35] *Dhammapada* 34; SBE, X, 12.

[36] *Sanyutta-Nikāya*, III, 68-69; BKS, III, 60-62. Cf. Buddhadāsa, *op. cit.*, pp. 2, 42, 51, 60-61, 66; Helmut von Glasenapp, "Nachträge und Ergänzungen," in Oldenberg, *Buddha*, p. 416.

them.[37] Whether this spiritual direction represents faithfully the teaching of the Buddha or is an interpretive addition made by the later monastic community we are perhaps unable to determine.

The weight of the texts, however, is clearly on the side of a relatively negative evaluation of human life as empirically known. We have noted the record of the Buddha's early experience of the impermanence and vanity of the common forms and values of life as constituting a basic element in his decision to seek the Good by entering the homeless way. In a later discourse he is recorded as counting the tears shed on the long road of rebirth, "crying and weeping as ye fare on, run on this long while, united as ye have been with the undesirable, sundered as ye have been from the desirable," as more than the waters in the four seas.[38] In this evaluation of phenomenal existence, moreover, he was clearly not far removed from many of his contemporaries in India. Sir Charles Eliot has pointed out that while the Scriptures record many incidents where the Buddha's assertions called forth discussion and contradiction, there is no evidence that anyone disputed his principle that all empirical existence involves suffering.[39]

On the other hand, the Buddha, as we have noted, was reproved by some of his contemporaries as "living in abundance" because of his abandonment of extreme asceticism for the Middle Way.[40] He taught his monks to enjoy what they got (in food) from laymen "without greed or longing."[41] The wrong or un-Aryan quest seeks that which is liable to birth, which participates in the cyclical process of rebirth and is always liable to aging, decay and stain even as to birth and hence has no abiding reality or value. The right or Aryan quest

[37] *Sanyutta-Nikāya,* III, 20-21; BKS, III, 20-21.

[38] *Sanyutta-Nikāya,* II, 180; BKS, II, 120. Cf. *Therī-gāthā* 51, 495-497; PEB, I, 38-39, 172-173.

[39] Eliot, *Hinduism and Buddhism,* I, 202. It is in order to cite Paul's summation of the "natural" man in Rom. 7:24, "Wretched man that I am! Who will deliver me from this body of death?" and Rom. 8:22, "We know that the whole creation has been groaning in travail together until now." Similarly to developments in later monastic Buddhism, we find extreme and morbid views of the world also in the later Christian ascetic tradition, as in the *De Contemptu Mundi* of Pope Innocent III (J. P. Migne, *Patrologia Latina,* vol. CCXVII, col. 701-746).

[40] *Majjhima-Nikāya,* I, 171; MLS, I, 215.

[41] *Sanyutta-Nikāya,* II, 269-270; BKS, II, 181.

seeks "the undecaying, the undying, the stainless, the uttermost security from the bonds," *Nirvāṇa.* The origin of mischief lay in attachments, being "enslaved, infatuated, addicted" to that which is not worthy of such quest or commitment.[42]

4

The Second Noble Truth is the cause or origin of suffering. The cause is craving leading to rebirth, joining itself to pleasure and passion, seeking satisfaction here and there (or in every existence), craving, namely for sensual pleasures, craving for a particular existence, craving for permanent existence.[43] The key word is craving or thirst (*triṣṇā*; Pāli: *taṇhā*). The Buddha used the word to denote a fundamentally self-centered desire not only for sensual pleasures but also for separate self-identity in phenomenal existence or in any other form of existence.[44] The understanding of craving was in the widest sense of what men yearn and strive for: health, wealth, power, fame or pleasure, but the Buddha apparently saw the primarily evil aspect of this craving to be in its self-centeredness. He saw it as both evil and foolish.[45] The Buddha's concept of the all-pervasiveness as well as perniciousness of selfish desire is revealed in the famous Fire Sermon.

The Buddha was staying at Gayā Head on one occasion and addressed the thousand monks who are said to have come there with him. "Monks, everything is burning," he declared. All organs of the body, all feelings, consciousness, the mind are burning with the fire of passion, of hatred and stupidity, burning because of the experience of frustration from all the ills of sentient existence. He then proceeded to state how the

[42] *Majjhima-Nikāya,* I, 161-163; MLS, I, 205-207.

[43] *Dīgha-Nikāya,* II, 308; DB, part II, pp. 339-340.

[44] Cf. Winston L. King, *Buddhism and Christianity,* p. 112.

[45] We may note that the word ἐπιθυμία, which is sometimes translated in the Bible (as in Rom. 6:12, RSV) as passion, is perhaps better rendered as desire and suggests a wider emotive range than the merely sensual. Cf. W. F. Arndt and F. W. Gingrich, *A Greek-English Lexicon of the New Testament and Other Early Christian Literature,* p. 293.

instructed Aryan disciple will "disregard" the whole range of forms and sensory impressions, including mental states and consciousness. By disregard he becomes dispassionate, by his freedom from attachment he is delivered from the canker-sores of phenomenal existence.[46]

In other passages the primary evil of man's natural condition is traced from desire back to ignorance (*avidyā*). The principle of derivation is called dependent origination (*pratītyasamutpāda*). The term occurs frequently in the Scriptures and represents an important principle in primitive Buddhism. It is a way of explaining not only the phenomenon of suffering but all phenomena in existence.[47] The Buddha is recorded as having thought through the principle during the first night after his enlightenment; it was, moreover, a basic element of his world view and subsequent teaching. Simply stated, it is that all the elements of being depend upon preceding causes; in particular the dilemma of man suffering in the futility of phenomenal existence is the consequence of specific causes, which are knowable.

These causes are seen to work in progression as a chain of causation, and thus the present condition of "natural" man in his aggregation of misery is derived by causal progression from ignorance. On ignorance depend the habitual tendencies (*saṃskāra*) or elemental aspects of being in phenomenal existence. On these depends consciousness, on consciousness depend name and form, and so on through twelve stages to empirical man who experiences "old age and dying, grief, sorrow and lamentation, suffering, dejection and despair."[48]

We may note that there are shorter versions of the chain recorded with only nine or five links to make the whole.[49] Also, in the form of twelve links, the form accepted by all schools of Buddhism and represented in Buddhist art by the Wheel of Life motif, the progression apparently involves a

[46] *Vinaya-Piṭaka, Mahāvagga,* I, 21; BD, part IV, pp. 45-46.

[47] The fullest exposition is found in *Dīgha-Nikāya,* II, 55-71; DB, part II, pp. 50-70.

[48] *Vinaya-Piṭaka, Mahāvagga,* I, 1; BD, part IV, pp. 1-3. Cf. *Sanyutta-Nikāya,* II, 1; BKS, II, 1-2.

[49] Cf. *Dīgha-Nikāya,* II, 56; DB, part II, pp. 51-52; *Milindapañha* 51-52; MQ, I 70-73.

repetition whereby a human being is brought into existence twice, once through consciousness by means of ignorance, secondly through birth by means of desire.

The great Ceylonese scholastic Buddhaghosa recognized the difficulty and endeavored to dispose of it by saying that while from one point of view ignorance may be said to be a primary cause, it is in itself not causeless and is merely chief of the elements of being. He emphasized that the process is a "Wheel of Existence without known beginning, continuing to exist by virtue of a concatenation of cause and effect." He concluded that the factors of both ignorance and desire are the root cause but that the first beginnings of either cannot be discerned.[50]

We cannot be certain that the Buddha thought of the matter in this way. But there is reason to believe that ignorance and desire are two sides of the same coin. As we have noted, ignorance is not primarily want of facts but a misplaced sense or system of values. It is not to know that all the elements of phenomenal existence lack true reality and value; desire is craving for any of these elements based on the misapprehension that they are worthy of such grasping. Conversely, as we shall see, liberation emerges from aspiration—and practice—toward that which is worthy of it.

We read that ignorance is not to know the Four Noble Truths or not to know that everything must have an origin and cessation.[51] In either case the insight played a role in the larger world view of the Buddha and of early Buddhism. The Master's primary concern, however, for the fact and progression of causal relationships was to the end of isolating the elemental factors of existence and by eliminating them to reverse the progression and end the whole process of causes leading to phenomenal existence with its suffering. Basic to his teaching was the conviction, evidently substantiated in his experience, that the causal chain may be stopped by the right method.

Thus the doctrine of dependent causation also works backward. The Buddha is recorded as having thought it through on

[50] *Visuddhi-Magga* 17; Warren, *op. cit.*, pp. 171, 174-175.

[51] *Majjhima-Nikāya,* I, 54; MLS, I, 68-69. *Sanyutta-Nikāya,* III, 170; BKS, III, 146-147.

that first night in both direct and reverse order. As the whole mass of ill arises, so may it cease.[52] The principle has been termed a statement of the interdependence of the different stages of the human spiritual condition. But of primary significance in the history of religions is the fact that it represents a sublime faith in the possibility of a solution to the human dilemma. It constitutes a restatement of the Second and Third Noble Truths. In its forward progression leading from ignorance through craving to empirical man in his suffering, it is equivalent to the Second Truth. In its reverse order leading from the cessation of ignorance to the cessation of the entire aggregation of ill, it is equivalent to the Third Truth.

5

The Third Noble Truth is of the cessation (*nirodha*) of suffering. It is the complete cessation of and disengagement from craving, "giving it up, renouncing it, emancipation from it, detachment from it." These terms are regarded by Buddhist commentators to be synonyms for *Nirvāṇa,* which we shall consider in detail later. The point of reference, however, for the cessation of craving is craving for all the things—material, sensory, mental—in this world "that are dear, that are pleasant." The text repeats the phrase with reference to the main elements of existential experience and in each instance affirms that "Here may this Craving be put away, here does it cease."[53]

At first glance this approach appears exceedingly negative, as if it were to take the heart out of life. The essence of the message, however, is that nothing among the elements of this world should be grasped at or clung to as if it were ultimately real or valuable. There is nothing in these elements worthy of such religious aspiration. But the obverse of the negative aspect of the Third Noble Truth, the cessation of craving, is the positive reorientation of self away from separate self-

[52] *Vinaya-Piṭaka, Mahāvagga,* I, 1; BD, part IV, p. 2.
[53] *Dīgha-Nikāya,* II, 310-311; DB, part II, pp. 341-343.

centeredness, from infatuation with all that has "form and name," to find a mode of being in that which is radically "Other," *Nirvāṇa.* Moreover, the cessation of craving for the things or elements (or persons) of this world does not mean the cessation of relationships or use. The goal is such relationships that we are not "hooked," infatuated or carried away by them. Only then are we free to be unselfishly benevolent and kindly toward others.[54]

The Third Truth of the cessation of suffering is thus intended to strike a positive note. It is the heart of his message and points to the ultimate solution of the human dilemma as the Buddha understood it. It is the prescription for the cure. In the passage cited above the term used is "cessation," but the concept is elsewhere expressed by the word "liberation," which gives the dominant flavor of the teaching. A statement that may go back to the Buddha himself is this: "As the great ocean has one taste, the taste of salt, even so, monks, does this *dhamma* and discipline have one taste, the taste of freedom."[55] Buddhaghosa denoted the achievement of the reverse process of dependent causation from the cessation of ignorance through craving, etc. as in effect the gaining of deliverance.[56]

E. Steinilber-Oberlin described the "essence" of Buddhism as teaching escape from suffering and the winning of the pure and calm refuge.[57] This is to say that deliverance is unto an end and that end is a refuge, a mode of being utterly good and subject to none of the failings of impermanence, inadequacy, purposelessness, lack of true reality or value that characterize the names and forms of phenomenal existence. The term "refuge" (*ratna*) literally meant jewel, that which is of surpassing value, and came to have the force of a *terminus technicus* in later Buddhist tradition. The Buddha, the teaching (*Dharma*) and the community (*Saṅgha*) became the three jewels or refuges to which man in his existential dilemma may turn. But the ultimate and utterly dependable refuge, the only

[54] Cf. Buddhadāsa, *op. cit.*, pp. 5-6, 19-20, 25, 50, 55, 63, 67.

[55] *Vinaya-Piṭaka, Cullavagga,* IX, 238; BD, part V, p. 335.

[56] *Visuddhi-Magga* 17; Warren, *op. cit.*, p. 174.

[57] E. Steinilber-Oberlin, *Les Sectes bouddhiques japonaises*, p. ix.

true Reality, for primitive Buddhism was *Nirvāṇa,* and *Dharma* more in the sense of eternal Right than a system of teaching.

Since liberation from phenomenal existence is seen as integral to attainment of the goal, we may properly ask at this point if physical death is necessary to a true realization of such liberation. In one sense this is true. Evidently one of the most distasteful aspects of phenomenal existence to the Buddha was involvement in its apparently endless round of rebirths, and liberation was understood as freedom from this process. Again and again we note the Buddha's affirmation of victory in that he was done with the whole process of becoming. No more would he be reborn into this world.

The final aspect of release through physical death with no return to phenomenal existence was called, perhaps as a later term, *Parinirvāṇa.* But this aspect of the goal appears to have been of only secondary significance in the early teaching. The primary goal was *Nirvāṇa,* seen as a state or mode of being attainable in this life. Indeed, we note that we have to do with "a visible process, not a matter of time, but one that invites to come and see."[58] The Buddha was apparently utterly convinced that he had attained this goal and that it was attainable by all others who would fulfil the necessary conditions.

The summation of the Buddha's ethical way as radical disengagement from phenomenal existence by nonattachment involves therefore not primarily a physical but a spiritual event. What is sought is not death or annihilation but a new relationship to phenomenal existence that is nonpossessive and non-self-assertive. Nonattachment means that one does not crave, does not cling to the ever changing forms of phenomenal existence, not even, as we shall see, to the fact or concept of an abiding individual self.[59] An expression frequently repeated is that the liberated brother "abides independent, grasping after nothing in the world whatever." The end result of this posture, however, is properly not negative or weak but an attitude "ardent, self-possessed, and mindful." The victorious brother looks upon all things, his body, feelings, thoughts and ideas as "having overcome both the hankering and the

[58] *Anguttara-Nikāya,* I, 141, 147, 158, 221, 236; BGS, I, 125, 130, 141, 201, 216.

[59] *Sanyutta-Nikāya,* III, 35; BKS, III, 33.

dejection common in the world."[60] "Sitting loose in the saddle," to use a modern American expression, the liberated practicer is free to love, to exercise benevolence, without being possessive or otherwise harmful. We note in the texts the association of passion, or possessive emotion, with malice.[61] Conversely, the practice of goodwill becomes possible only by freedom from possessive emotions.

We need to be reminded at this point that the understanding of nonattachment in the context of primitive Buddhism was not intended to lead to extreme asceticism. The Buddha's was the Middle Way. He taught a radical rejection of phenomenal existence not for the purpose of abandoning it, for even the homeless life of a monk is but another, although presumably better, more efficient mode of living in relation to phenomenal existence.[62] The crux of the matter is the kind of relationship, whether attached or not. If attached, one is caught and at the mercy of the ebb and flow of that which is impermanent and not ultimately real or valuable. If not attached, one is free to be moved by that which is unchanging and truly Real. The event of liberation is one with cosmic as well as psychological implications.

Perhaps we can clarify this understanding by a brief comparison with the teaching of Jesus. Jesus likewise taught a radical rejection of self and all the relationships of life—for the sake of the kingdom—and a reorientation to all that has been rejected. "Seek first his kingdom and his righteousness, and all these things shall be yours as well" (Matt. 6:33). In Mark 8:34-35 we note the affirmation "for my sake and the gospel's": "If any man would come after me, let him deny himself. . . . whoever loses his life for my sake and the gospel's will save it." In Luke 14:26 we find even stronger language: "If any one comes to me and does not hate his own father and mother and wife and children and brothers and sisters, yes, even his own life, he

[60] *Dīgha-Nikāya,* II, 290-304; DB, part II, pp. 327-337.

[61] *Anguttara-Nikāya,* I, 156-158; BGS, I, 140-141.

[62] A distinct tradition existed that the Buddha had forbidden suicide (*Milindapañha* 195-196; MQ, I, 280-282). An exception, however, was apparently made in the case of the permission granted the elderly monk Godhika (or Vakkali), who had already attained release into mental calm but was afflicted with an apparently incurable disease (*Sanyutta-Nikāya,* III, 118-123; BKS, III, 101-106; Warren, *op. cit.*, pp. 381-383).

cannot be my disciple"; in 14:23: "whoever of you does not renounce all that he has cannot be my disciple."[63] In Luke 18:29 the renunciation of house or wife or brothers or parents or children is "for the sake of the kingdom of God," of which Jesus claimed to be the authorized representative.

The act of renunciation called for in these cases is termed renunciation for discipleship, but it is insufficiently noted how radical was the renunciation asked for. Jesus demanded the total renunciation of all that is closest and dearest, the most intimate of human ties, one's own life, his very self. Admittedly renunciation is not destruction. It is the offering of all to receive all, or almost all, back again, but all is received back under the aegis of the kingdom of God, under the ultimate control of his Spirit. In any case an integral element of the religious understanding involved in such renunciation is that no part or all of that renounced, even the "whole world," is worthy in itself to receive ultimate value or loyalty.[64]

Jesus was in the mainstream of Hebraic tradition in affirming the creation of the entire phenomenal universe by God and in seeing the world as an arena where not only evil, but also God, who is good, is present and at work.[65] According to the record of the New Testament, Jesus had an historical-eschatological perspective wherein the events of human life and history, however they may in themselves be contrary to the divine will, are subsumed within the divine control so as ultimately to minister to the final purposes of God.[66] One element of the divine control is the operation of the principle of compensation.[67] But affirmation of the presence and working of God and his good in the world was not to ascribe to the world itself or any of its parts ultimate value or meaning.

For Jesus the distinction between Creator and creation was apparently absolute, and he did not deviate from the Hebraic tradition that to render ultimate value or loyalty to aught of

[63] Cf. Matt. 10:37-39; Luke 18:29-30 (Mark 10:29-30).
[64] Cf. Mark 8:36; Matt. 6:19-21.
[65] Mark 10:6, 13:19; 10:18 (Matt. 19:7); Luke 11:20.
[66] Cf. Mark 12:1-11; Luke 12:42-48.
[67] Matt. 7:2; 5:21-22, 26, 29-30; 7:19. Cf. Gal. 6:7; Col. 3:25; Rom. 7:5.

the creation is idolatry. He preceived, however, the divine origin of and presence within the created universe and was able therefore to assign authentic though secondary and derivative meaning and value to phenomenal existence and its events. This is to affirm "history." The Buddha differed from the Christ in that he saw no comparable cosmic meaning or purposeful progression in the events of existence; he was aware, so far as we can discern from the texts, of no goal therein.[68] As we have seen, he affirmed certain positive aspects, but he had no hope, as did Paul, of the creation itself being set free from its bondage to decay.[69] Only the Self, as we shall see, is the proper ruler of the self. But with unvarying consistency he refrained from assigning ultimate value to the phenomenal universe in order to give it solely, with complete personal commitment, to the ontologically "Other." At this point of religious orientation he was remarkably akin to Jesus–and Muḥammad.[70]

Like the Buddha, the Christ saw the renunciation of all in commitment to the "Other," in his case God and his kingdom, as being not only the cosmically true destiny of man, but as also bringing its own present reward. This is the way for a man to save or find his own life. A reorientation with return to the relationships of phenomenal existence is also clearly implied in Jesus' teaching that there is no one who has renounced all for his sake and the gospel's who "will not receive a hundredfold now in this time, houses and brothers and sisters and mothers and children and lands, with persecutions, and in the age to

[68] We find in certain modern interpreters of the Buddhist tradition an affirmation of purpose in life, because, for instance, of the opportunities it offers to come to know *Nirvāṇa.* The Buddha himself affirmed this kind of value, but the question remains whether it constitutes "purpose." Cf. Buddhadāsa, *op. cit.*, p. 42.

[69] Cf. Rom. 8:21.

[70] The New Testament reveals somewhat differing nuances in its views of the "world." A typical view is that of Heb. 13:14: "For here we have no lasting city, but we seek the city which is to come." The Johannine literature reveals a more negative view with the Tempter as the "ruler of this world" (John 12:31; 14:30; 16:11). The concept of "principalities and powers" in Col. 2:15 or Eph. 6:12 suggests a somewhat less radical view of the subjection of the world to demonic forces. Paul's understanding that "the creation was subjected to futility" (Rom. 8:20) implies that in the context of the distinction between the realms of flesh (sin) and spirit, the former represents essentially purposeless activity even as it comprises a substantial part of phenomenal existence.

come eternal life."[71] Perhaps the reward is primarily future, but we read that "blessed *are* you *when* (ἐστε ὅταν) men revile you and persecute you and utter all kinds of evil against you falsely on my account" (Matt. 5:11).

There are, however, differing nuances in the evaluation of phenomenal existence to be found in the Buddhist Scriptures as in the Christian. We note, for instance, a more negative view of married life in Paul than in Jesus, although both, according to the New Testament records, held the single life to be most appropriate for their own apostolate.[72] In the Buddhist texts the superior religious advantage of the homeless life as contrasted with the life of men in families is frequently affirmed.[73] As we have noted, there are also passages where loathing and disgust for the physical are stressed as elements in spiritual development. With regard to family ties, one account tells how, when the monk Sangāmaji was sitting beneath a tree in meditation, his wife, whom he had left for the homeless life, laid their child before him and asked him to nourish her and the child. He was silent, and the woman finally took the child and went away. The Buddha is recorded to have observed the incident and said, "He feels no pleasure when she comes, no sorrow when she goes: him I call a true Brāhman released from passion."[74]

The narrative is distasteful to most modern sentiment, both East and West, although happenings like it must have occurred in the early period when many men left their wives and children to enter the homeless life. It is necessary to note, however, that there are other accounts of a different tenor. Buddhaghosa relates the story of a young monk who in response to his mother's concern for his welfare returned to his home community to spend three months, begging his food at his mother's home alone.[75] We must also recall the "definite

[71] Mark 10:29-30. Cf. Matt. 19:29; Luke 18:29-30. There are numerous problems connected with the exegesis of these texts, but Werner Kümmel overstates the case for future orientation when he affirms the "Anschauung Iesu . . . die Gottes Vergebung nicht irdisch festlegt" (*Verheissung und Erfüllung*, p. 43 n.).

[72] I Cor. 7:25-40; Matt. 19:10-12.

[73] Cf. *Jātakamala* XXVIII; Conze, *Buddhist Scriptures*, p. 27.

[74] *Udāna*, I, 8; MA, part II, p. 7. The quotation is from Eliot, *op. cit.*, I, 160, who also cites language of comparable spirit from Angela of Foligno (1248-1309). Cf. also the case of Cāpā and Upaka (*Therī-gāthā* 300-303; PEB, part I, p. 133).

[75] *Visuddhi-Magga* III; Warren, *op. cit.*, pp. 434-436.

and honorable position" accorded laymen who attempted to follow the Buddha's teaching without abandoning their life in the world. The view of primitive Buddhism in general was evidently that a good and zealous layman might attain *Nirvāṇa* on his deathbed.[76]

Laymen were consistently urged to fulfil their family responsibilities, to "cultivate friendliness, cultivate compassion, joy and indifference; wait on your mothers; wait on your fathers; and honor your elders among your kinsfolk."[77] In the *Dhammapada* we read: "Pleasant in the world is the state of a mother, pleasant the state of a father, pleasant the state of a samaṇa (*śramaṇa*—ascetic), pleasant the state of a brāhmana." This apparent equation of the spiritual state of family people with that of a representative of the homeless life as of the historic spiritual leadership of India obviously emerged from no low view of the life of men in the world. We note further that the above quotation is made in the context of affirmation of other "pleasant" aspects of human life: "Friends are pleasant; enjoyment is pleasant, whatever be the cause. . . . Pleasant is virtue lasting to old age, pleasant is a faith firmly rooted; pleasant is attainment of intelligence, pleasant is avoiding of sins."[78]

André Bareau has reminded us that the documents of primitive Buddhism form no consistent system but rather constitute elements that are at points distinctly heterogeneous and that later scholasticism sought vainly to harmonize.[79] Perhaps, however, a valid balancing of the themes we have been discussing may be seen in the words recorded of the woman known as Punabbasu's mother. She quoted with approval the Exalted One's words that *Nirvāṇa* is the deliverance from every tie and affirmed her love for that truth as "passing great." Dear to her was her child and dear her husband, but dearer to her than these was to seek out the path of the Buddha's teaching.

[76] Cf. the references to the possibility of deliverance at the moment of or shortly after death in W. Y. Evans-Wentz, *The Tibetan Book of the Dead,* pp. 102-104.

[77] Introduction to the *Jātaka,* I, 47, 27; Warren, *op. cit.*, p. 39.

[78] *Dhammapada* 331-333; SBE, X, 80. We note another passage, however, that regards pleasant feelings as an ill (*Sanyutta-Nikāya,* IV, 207; BKS, IV, 139).

[79] Bareau, *Die Religionen Indiens,* III, 32-34.

For neither child nor husband, though they be
So dear to us, can save us from all ill,
As can the hearing of the blessed Norm (*Dharma*)
From pain and sorrow set a creature free.

The mother stilled her children that both mother and children might hear the liberating words of Truth. Happy was she at her own deliverance, happy for the understanding and love for the Truth shown by her son and hopeful for the awakening of the younger child.[80]

[80] *Sanyutta-Nikāya*, I, 210; BKS, I, 270-271.

IV

NIRVANA

1

We noted that the cessation of suffering, the Third Noble Truth, is in effect to attain *Nirvāṇa* (Pāli: *Nibbāna*). It will be helpful if we now consider in some depth this central term and concept of early Buddhist teaching. *Nirvāṇa* is the goal of Buddhist vision and effort, the Ultimate. The Buddha, however, consistently refused to define the word in intellectual terms. We need to consider once again therefore the problem of his reserve with reference to metaphysical speculation.

The Buddha was by no means what we call anti-intellectual. He employed close reasoning and, as we have seen, considered certain knowledge essential. But knowledge for him was unto practice and achievement, and knowledge or speculation that did not conduce to these ends he believed of little use. The lesser discourse to the monk Māluṅkyāputta expresses this position with particular clarity.

The monk was concerned because the Lord had left unexplained the traditional problems of Indian metaphysics: whether the world is eternal or not, finite or infinite, whether the soul or life-principle and the body are identical or not, whether the Tathāgata exists after death or not, both is and is not, or neither is nor is not. The monk forthrightly asked the Buddha to explain these matters or honestly say that he did not know.

The Buddha answered by first asking whether he had invited Māluṅkyāputta to lead the religious life under his guidance with the promise that he would explain such matters. The monk acknowledged that he had not. The Buddha then pointed out that anyone who insisted on learning the answers to such questions as a prior condition to entering the religious life might die before the explanation could be made.

> It is as if a man were pierced by an arrow that was thickly smeared with poison and his friends and relations were to procure a physician and surgeon. He might speak thus: "I will not draw out this arrow until I know of the man who pierced me whether he is a noble or brāhman or merchant or worker."

The Buddha went on to recount the various items of information regarding the assailant, his background, details of the materials and manufacture of the bow, string and arrow that the man insisted on knowing before he would allow the physician to proceed with the treatment. This man, too, the Buddha affirmed, might die before he had learned all this.

Because the living of the religious life does not depend on knowing whether the world is eternal or not, etc., the Buddha had not explained these matters. Such teaching "is not connected with the goal," is not fundamental to the true religious life and "does not conduce to turning away from (form and name), nor to dispassion, stopping, calming, super-knowledge, awakening nor to nibbāna."

And what has the Buddha explained? Suffering, its origin, cessation and the path to its cessation. And this "is connected with the goal, is fundamental" to the true religious life and "conduces to turning away from, to dispassion, stopping, calming, super-knowledge, awakening and nibbāna."[1]

[1] *Majjhima-Nikāya,* I, 426-432; MLS, II, 97-101. Cf. *Sanyutta-Nikāya,* V, 418; BKS, V, 354, 378.

Another Sūtra gives an account of a somewhat similar questioning of the Lord by the wandering ascetic Vaccha. The Buddha's answer is that the theory that the world is eternal—various other current theories are also cited, each receiving the same following ascription—"is going to a (speculative) view, holding a view, the wilds of views, the wriggling of views, the scuffling of views, the fetter of views; it is accompanied by anguish, distress, misery, fever; it does not conduce to turning away from, nor to dispassion, etc."

In answer to the question whether the Buddha (Vaccha addressed him as Gautama) had any theory of his own, he replied that the Tathāgata is rid of all speculative views, but what he knows (has seen) is the nature of form, how it arises and goes down. He listed the elements (in this case five) in the chain of causation from form to consciousness. By the destruction, stopping of "all imaginings, all supposings, all latent pride" of self, he had achieved liberation without attachment.[2]

The Buddha was thus primarily concerned with the attainment or realization of *Nirvāṇa,* not its definition. The manner of its usage, however, and its connotations in the texts give us a fairly clear idea of what the term was intended to mean. The word does not originate with or belong exclusively to the Buddhist tradition. It was used in Jainism of Mahāvīra's death and in the *Bhagavad Gītā* to denote the attainment of spiritual peace in this world as well as the realm of peace beyond.[3] It also appears in the later Tantric literature of Hinduism.[4] But the term *Nirvāṇa* acquired a distinctive significance and degree of usage in the teaching of the Buddha, to the extent of revealing important elements of his originality as a religious teacher.

2

Nirvāṇa has the etymological meanings of a condition of being "blown out" or "extinguished," "become cool," "extinct."

[2] *Majjhima-Nikāya,* I, 484-489; MLS, II, 162-167.
[3] Franklin Edgerton, *The Bhagavad Gītā,* 2.72; 5.25; 6.15, pp. 17, 30, 33.
[4] Zimmer, *Philosophies of India,* p. 596.

The image is of the unfed flame, no longer given the materials by which its formal continuity may be sustained.[5] These meanings refer, with reference to the human psycho-physical condition, primarily to liberation from the mental defilements of craving, ill will and delusion. *Nirvāṇa* is where there is no-thing, where naught is grasped.[6] A reverse form of the image may be seen in the contemporary Thai word for "anxiety," which has the literal meaning of "hot-heart."[7] The concept is of the cooling of the otherwise uncontrolled fires of feeling, of anger, fear and grief as much as of sensual passion. Coolness of mind, however is not dullness of mind; rather its clarity, alertness and creativity are enhanced.[8] We find *Nirvāṇa* repeatedly at the end of the stock series of ethico-spiritual qualities that constituted the goal of the way. Such and such "redounds to the beginnings of right conduct, to detachment, to purification from lusts, to quietude, to tranquillisation of heart, to real knowledge, to the insight of the higher stages of the Path, and to *Nirvāṇa*."[9] This is to say that detachment from phenomenal existence, liberation from passions and uncontrolled desires unto calming of the heart lead to both knowledge and insight, without which *Nirvāṇa* in this world cannot be conceived. And, it must be emphasized, *Nirvāṇa* is, in the recorded teaching of the Buddha, attainable in this world.[10]

The coolness of *Nirvāṇa* is also not coldness. We note frequent references in the texts to the happiness, bliss and boundless peace of *Nirvāṇa*. Not only griefless, it is that in which men delight.[11] *Nirvāṇa* is deliverance from every tie, as

[5] *Sutta-Nipāta* 235; WCEB, p. 37. *Therī-gāthā* 116; PEB, part I, p. 73. Cf. *Sanyutta-Nikāya,* I, 159; BKS, I, 198.

[6] *Sutta-Nipāta* 1109, 1131, 1094; WCEB, pp. 161, 165, 159. *Anguttara-Nikāya,* V, 65, 111; BGS, V, 46, 76.

[7] Buddhadāsa, *Buddha Dhamma for Students,* p. 59.

[8] *Sutta-Nipāta* 19, 739; WCEB, pp. 3, 111. There is also, however, an expression "mind-at-work" (*viññaṇassa*), which is used in the pejorative sense of busy but pointless intellection (*Sutta-Nipāta* 734-735, 1037; WCEB, pp. 110, 149).

[9] *Dīgha-Nikāya,* I, 189; DB, part I, p. 255. *Anguttara-Nikāya,* III, 82; BGS, III, 68, etc.

[10] *Sutta-Nipāta* 514, 186, 228; WCEB, pp. 77, 30, 37. *Anguttara-Nikāya,* IV, 352, 358, 453; BGS, IV, 233, 237, 298.

[11] *Sutta-Nipāta* 593, 86; WCEB, pp. 92, 15. *Anguttara-Nikāya,* III, 213, 297; IV, 14; BGS, III, 157, 211; IV, 9.

we have seen, not the abandonment of concern.[12] Indifference to phenomenal existence is one side of a coin whose obverse is the spirit not only of joy but of friendliness and compassion. Control of mind is not merely the repression of ill will but its transformation into these positive qualities. We find this ideal expressed in a later Scripture: "Even as a mother watches over and protects her child, her only child, so with a boundless mind should one cherish all living beings, radiating friendliness over the entire world, uncramped, free from ill-will or enmity."[13] Furthermore, the Buddha did not think of the bliss and happiness of *Nirvāṇa* in self-centered terms. In a discussion with the Jain ascetic Udāyin, for whom the attainment of a "world that is exclusively happy" was the proper goal of the religious life, he affirmed that there are things superior and more excellent, the understanding and freedom of *Nirvāṇa*. His intent was evidently to say that perfect happiness is attainable only by abandoning the conscious pursuit of happiness as a goal.[14]

As one aspect of a larger whole, *Nirvāṇa* appears in the early Scriptures as another and more exalted or deeper mode of human consciousness. Many of the passages, including those cited above, lend themselves naturally to this interpretation. The role of meditation in the path to the goal, particularly in the eighth item of the Eightfold Noble Path, concentration or rapture, indicates that the mindful disciple was expected to penetrate the upper layers of "ordinary sense-imposed consciousness" in order to enter into what Miss I. B. Horner has termed the "transcendent and abounding plenitude of the extra-sensory Wisdom beyond."[15] The Scriptures do not specify as to whether this mode of consciousness was understood to be in itself, or in contact with, what we may term a more universal consciousness.

From the image of the extinguished flame, however, as from other figures, we perceive that a mode of consciousness tran-

[12] *Sanyutta-Nikāya,* I, 210; BKS, I, 270-271.

[13] Conze, *Buddhist Scriptures,* p. 186.

[14] *Majjhima-Nikāya,* II, 30-39; MLS, II, 228-236.

[15] MLS, I, xix. Miss Horner's phrase is her rendering of *Dīgha-Nikāya,* III, 57; DB, part III, p. 52. T. W. Rhys Davids translates the phrase more noncommittally as "full and abounding insight."

scending the ordinary was clearly envisaged. In considering the problem of the self, we shall see that considerable evidence in the early Scriptures points to the Buddha's having a concept of a higher Self that seems similar to C. G. Jung's understanding of the *self.* Jung termed the *self* a new totality figure in which the ego is properly subordinated to but not dissolved in identification with the *self.*[16] The Buddhist Scriptures do not give us specific information as to the nature of the relationship between the ordinary self and the higher, nor do they tell us precisely how the latter relates to *Nirvāṇa*. Such concerns evidently went "too far" and were beyond the compass of an answer for the Buddha. What is clear, however, is that in entering *Nirvāṇa* a radically integrative and unitive experience or event has occurred. The old separate and self-centered self has been transcended and found itself in a new unity, *Nirvāṇa,* which is One.[17] We may say, indeed, that the primary thrust of the teaching of the Buddha was orientation from the many to the One.

Nirvāṇa, however, is not merely a state of human consciousness. We note that it is perfection's state, completely freed from ill. But in the context of primitive Buddhism such liberation included freedom from specific cosmic processes. It meant the "end of becoming," the cessation of the process of rebirth.[18]

One of the Sūtras records the conversion of the robber Aṅgulimāla, a "bloody-handed" merciless scourge of the realm of Kośala, whom King Prasenajit himself feared and was unable to control. Him whom the king "was unable to tame with stick and sword, the Lord has tamed without stick and sword." The king marvelled at the Buddha's power to tame the

[16] *The Basic Writings of C. G. Jung,* Violet Staub de Laszlo, ed., pp. 94-95. We note elsewhere that Jung felt that the Buddha had seen and grasped the "cosmogonic dignity of human consciousness" as having power to overcome the world (*Memories, Dreams, Reflections,* Aniela Jaffé, ed., p. 309).

[17] We find reference to *Nirvāṇa* as "one" in the commentary to *Dīgha-Nikāya,* II, 310; Warren, *op. cit.*, p. 372.

[18] *Anguttara-Nikāya,* IV, 238; BGS, IV, 163. *Anguttara-Nikāya,* V, 9; BGS, V, 7. Cf. Günter Lanczkowski, "Das Heilsziel des Nirvāṇa in der Lehre des Buddhas," *Asien Missioniert im Abendland,* Kurt Hutten and Siegfried von Kortzfleisch, eds., p. 148.

untamed and calm the uncalmed. But the account in describing Aṅgulimāla's subsequent experience as a monk of abuse and physical mistreatment from his former victims records the Buddha's urging the bloodied monk to endure his pains with patience. The Lord affirmed that his disciple was experiencing the immediate ripening of *Karma,* which he would otherwise have had to endure as punishment for untold years in Niraya Hell. Aṅgulimāla's consequent understanding of the event was that his evilly done *Karma* was closed, the account concluded, "debtless I enjoy an owner's state." Not only had the harmful man become harmless, the cord that bound him to the process of becoming, of rebirth, had been severed.[19] This is to say that the process of *Karma* characteristic of phenomenal existence, the causal law of rebirth dependent upon prior deeds, had been essentially overcome and stopped.

Furthermore, *Nirvāṇa* was frequently spoken of in the early texts as if it were an independent Reality with its own dynamic. We note the use of the expression "come and see" (*ehipassikam*), of *Nirvāṇa* as something to be seen for oneself, presumably as manifested in persons, particularly in the Buddha himself, not involving time and yet leading men onward.[20] In one Sūtra the Buddha is recorded as flatly affirming his conviction, a conviction shared by his Brāhman interlocutor, that *Nirvāṇa* is, even as the way to it, the unchanging goal, is. The context of the affirmation was the Buddha's intent to explain why some of his disciples attain the goal and some do not. He himself was only the shower of the way, but of the fact of the existence of *Nirvāṇa,* even though specifically other than phenomenal existence, there could be no doubt.[21]

Cosmologically, the question may be put whether the Buddha conceived of the cosmos in monistic or dualistic terms. He clearly saw the world of phenomenal existence as a unitary whole with *Karma* as its integrative principle. But the whole thrust of his religious teaching was to see *Nirvāṇa* as

[19] *Majjhima-Nikāya,* II, 98-105; MLS, II, 284-292.

[20] *Anguttara-Nikāya,* I, 158; BGS, I, 141. *Anguttara-Nikāya,* IV, 453; BGS, IV, 298.

[21] *Majjhima-Nikāya,* III, 4-6; MLS, III, 55-56. Cf. *Milindapañha* 270-271; MQ, II, 88-89.

other than this process-realm, and his religious thought therefore can in one sense be termed consistently dualistic. Later Buddhist thinkers, especially in the Mahāyāna tradition, endeavored to develop a higher unity, an ultimately monistic world view, out of this mode of analysis. Earlier Buddhism was content to affirm two realms, this world (*loka*) and the "world outside the world" (*lokuttara*), "this side" and "that side," and at the same time to refrain from ascribing to *Nirvāṇa* the kind of differentiation known in phenomenal experience.[22]

Nirvāṇa is the deathless calm, the eternal realm, the utter destruction of aging and dying. The goal to which men may attain is the deathless.[23] *Nirvāṇa* is the unborn, the undecaying, the unaging, the undying, even as it is the uttermost security from the bonds of existence, the unsorrowing, the stainless. The ethical conquests of the attainment of *Nirvāṇa* continue to be stressed—indeed, the incomparable bliss of *Nirvāṇa* is said to be steeped in the holy life—but something more is clearly involved than personal moral victory.[24] The overcoming is unto understanding, higher consciousness and participation in a greater Reality. In the *Dhammapada* we read, "Drive away the desires, O brāhmana! When you have understood the destruction of all that was made (compounded or put together), you will understand that which was not made."[25]

In the *Udāna Sūtra* we find the clearest affirmation of the ontological otherness as well as the soteriological necessity of *Nirvāṇa*: "Monks, there is a not-born, a not-become, a not-made, a not-compounded. Monks, if that unborn, not-become, not-made, not-compounded were not, there would be apparent no escape from this here that is born, become, made, compounded. But since, monks, there is an unborn, not-become, not-made, not-compounded, therefore the escape from this here that is born, become, made, compounded is apparent."[26]

[22] *Sutta-Nipāta* 1, 765, 915; WCEB, pp. 1, 114, 134. Cf. Masutani Fumio, *A Comparative Study of Buddhism and Christianity*, pp. 148, 157.

[23] *Sutta-Nipāta* 204, 1094; WCEB, pp. 32, 159. *Vinaya-Piṭaka, Mahāvagga*, I, 23; BD, part IV, p. 54.

[24] *Majjhima-Nikāya*, I, 163; MLS, I, 206-207, 211. *Anguttara-Nikāya*, I, 168; BGS, I, 151-152.

[25] *Dhammapada* 383; SBE, X, 90. For the thought of participation cf. *Sutta-Nipāta* 228; WCEB, p. 36.

[26] *Udāna*, VIII, 3; MA, part II, p. 98.

This passage would seem to indicate that for the Buddha *Nirvāṇa* is not only a new mode of consciousness attainable by human beings but also and primarily an independent Reality of its own. As Buddhaghosa later phrased it, *Nirvāṇa* is causeless whereas the whole of phenomenal existence is characterized by subjection to the chain of causation. It is unconditional whereas existence is conditioned.[27] It is of another or further world (*lokuttara*).

The Scriptures also use the figure of a stream to suggest the independent dynamism of *Nirvāṇa.* The *Sutta-Nipāta* speaks of *Nirvāṇa* as the "place" to which one goes, or has gone, and uses the term stream (*sota*) pejoratively as life's stream of becoming, of "dark propensities." The victor is the stream-crosser or cutter.[28] Elsewhere, however, we note references to the stream of *Nirvāṇa* into which one plunges, and the religious life taught by the Buddha goes toward that plunge. The Aryan disciple is a stream-winner, he plunges into the Deathless. He descends or enters into *Nirvāṇa.* In the *Dhammapada* we read that "he in whom a desire for the Ineffable (*Nirvāṇa*) has sprung up, . . . he is called *ūrdhvamsrotas* (carried upwards by the stream).[29]

Although we find the expression "one who goes upstream" used of the victorious disciple freed of the five fetters binding him to rebirth,[30] the figure perhaps more generally implies a large course of water flowing downhill in a particular direction toward a specific goal.[31] It is not always clear whether the stream itself is *Nirvāṇa* or the spiritual force (*Dharma*) that carries men there. A later distinction affirms that a stream-enterer has not yet attained the real *Nirvāṇa* but once in the stream will never be drawn back to attachments.[32] This distinction does not emerge in many of the earlier passages, but there is reference to a spiritual state wherein a man is said to be near to *Nirvāṇa* and incapable of falling away.[33] In many

[27] *Visuddhi-Magga* 21; Warren, *op. cit.*, p. 379.
[28] *Sutta-Nipāta* 233, 514, 355; WCEB, pp. 37, 77, 53, etc.
[29] *Anguttara-Nikāya,* II, 25; BGS, II, 28. *Sanyutta-Nikāya,* V, 340-410; BKS, V, 296-351. *Anguttara-Nikāya,* IV, 111; BGS, IV, 74. *Dhammapada* 218; SBE, X, 58.
[30] *Anguttara-Nikāya,* I, 233; BGS, I, 213.
[31] *Sanyutta-Nikāya,* V, 40; BKS, V, 32.
[32] Cf. Buddhadāsa, *op. cit.*, pp. 56-57, 62-63.
[33] *Anguttara-Nikāya,* II, 37; BGS, II, 45-47.

more instances, however, particularly in the Buddha's own reported consciousness, we note the strongest kind of affirmation of spiritual victory with reference to having attained *Nirvāṇa,* consistently a liberation whereby a man will never again come to birth. There is reason to believe, however, that such consciousness of spiritual, indeed cosmic, victory was not understood as meaning freedom from temptation. The evidence is also clear, even apart from the *Vinaya-Piṭaka,* that on the way to the goal the monks experienced temptations and in numerous cases moral failings of various kinds.[34]

3

Nirvāṇa is the Ultimate and the ideal.[35] Primitive Buddhism and evidently the Buddha himself accepted much of the world view of earlier Hinduism with its gods, heavens and hells. But for the Buddha these all belonged to the universe of changing phenomena. Even the gods and their abode of celestial bliss he considered to be part of the world of impermanence and subject to its causal chain, to the karmic process of rebirth. Insight into even the details of this process at work was ascribed to the Buddha as part of his psychic powers. The *arhat* therefore passes beyond even the leader of the *devas* into *Nirvāṇa;* heaven or the heavens are not the highest good and must end. Hell or the hells are a part of the same process and are accordingly of limited duration.[36]

There is no precise evidence, however, within primitive Buddhism that *Nirvāṇa* was ever conceived in personal terms, although its "come and see" aspect has been termed quasi-personal. It was a state and realm of Reality. But the Scriptures record no intelligible communication or revelation as issuing from this realm. It took no specific action toward the phenomenal world. It manifested no affection or compassion for men in this world wandering about as the captives of craving, ill will and delusion. But those who experienced this

[34] Cf. the Vangīsa Suttas, *Sanyutta-Nikāya,* I, 185-196; BKS, I, 185-249.

[35] *Anguttara-Nikāya,* III, 363; BGS, III, 258-259.

[36] *Visuddhi-Magga* 23; Warren, *op. cit.,* p. 391. *Anguttara-Nikāya,* III, 18; BGS, III, 13. *Anguttara-Nikāya,* I, 144; BGS, I, 127-128.

state were presumed to manifest such qualities of heart and action. Furthermore, the realm was "at hand" and, as we shall see, singularly expressed through *Dharma,* which was also perceived as moving like a stream in which men may plunge. And Buddhas are born into this world to teach *Dharma* to men (cf. *Dhammapada* 276).

We have frequently noted the emphasis in the teaching upon the abandonment of desire or craving for any or all of the elements of phenomenal existence. There is, however, an acceptable and noble desire. This is the Aryan quest for "the unborn, the uttermost security from the bonds," *Nirvāṇa,* the undecaying, the undying, the unsorrowing, the stainless."[37] This is what we noted in the *Dhammapada* as "desire for the Ineffable" or what the *Sutta-Nipāta* terms "joy in what is lovely."[38] Herein we see a summation of early Buddhism and a view of the primary orientation of the Buddhist disciple. He is to disengage himself from attachment to the "many" in the flux of phenomenal existence to cleave to the "One," which is good, pure and unchanging.[39]

We find recorded among early fragments of the teaching the aspiration of a disciple; this may give us authentic insight into the daily spiritual orientation of the Buddha as well. This disciple aspired not only to the rooting out of all evil tendencies within himself but also to the doing of what ought to be done and to "minister to the Teacher with loving service." But the foundation of this activity was to be the thought of *Nirvāṇa* always with him in the midst of all phenomena, "as a slayer with drawn sword." This thought was the weapon by which he could rise above every world and become a "seer at peace in Nibbāna."[40]

A primary element of the inner life of the Buddha would seem to be revealed in the recorded teaching on friendship or

[37] *Majjhima-Nikāya,* I, 161-163; MLS, I, 204-207. Translators differ as to the acceptability of the term "desire" (*rāga*) in this context. Some prefer "quest" or "aspiration." Thus Henri de Lubac writes: "Le nirvana ne peut être désiré, sous peine d'être manqué. Mais l'aspiration authentique au nirvana n'est plus un 'désir' " (*Amida,* p. 14, n. 13).

[38] *Sutta-Nipāta* 969; WCEB, p. 141. Cf. Matt. 5:6; 6:33.

[39] Cf. Luke 10:42; Mark 10:18; Matt. 6:24. We find reference to *Nirvāṇa* as "one" in the commentary to *Dīgha-Nikāya,* II, 310; Warren, *op. cit.,* p. 372.

[40] *Anguttara-Nikāya,* III, 442; BGS, III, 309.

intimacy with the "lovely" (*kalyāṇa*). "Monks, I know not of any other single thing of such power to cause the arising of good states if not yet arisen, or the waning of evil states already arisen, as friendship with the lovely. In one who is a friend of what is lovely good states not arisen do arise and evil states already arisen wane." "Indeed, friendship with the lovely conduces to great profit."[41] We learn elsewhere that friendship with the lovely is the forerunner or prior condition for both the beginning and the sustained practice of the Noble Eightfold Path. A monk who is a friend of the lovely is expected to practice this path with full earnestness. Indeed, on one occasion the Buddha is recorded to have said to Ānanda that the whole of the holy life he taught "consists in friendship, in association, in intimacy with what is lovely." The primary event of liberation is possible "because of my friendship with what is lovely."[42] These passages constitute the focus of a clear tradition that for the Buddha the religious life consisted not merely in strenuous moral effort or "self-help" but also and more primarily in orientation to the "Other" and spiritual "participation" therein.

We find elsewhere references to *Dharma* as lovely, and the association of the lovely with the Noble Eightfold Path further emphasizes the loveliness of the Noble (Aryan) moral qualities and practices of life taught by the Buddha. In the next section we shall consider in more detail the integral relationship that evidently obtained in the thought of the Buddha between *Nirvāṇa* and *Dharma,* the former as the goal, the latter as the way. In the passages we have just noted, however, "friendship with the lovely" seems to imply a basic orientation of life toward that which is seen primarily as goal or "Other." This orientation is held to be singularly effective in man's moral strivings on the way, but the lovely is evidently more than a description of the quality of the way. Aspiration as well as a sustained relationship of intimacy would seem to be envisaged. We seem therefore to be able to affirm that *Nirvāṇa* is also that which is lovely. Furthermore, the kind of orientation to the

[41] *Anguttara-Nikāya,* I, 14-16; BGS, I, 10-12.

[42] *Sanyutta-Nikāya,* V, 29-35; BKS, V, 27-31. *Sanyutta-Nikāya,* V, 2; BKS, V, 2-3. Cf. Winston L. King, *Buddhism and Christianity,* p. 227.

lovely that this teaching implies the Buddha himself had tells us more than perhaps anything else of the nature of his own interior life. He seems to have practiced with remarkable effectiveness the essence of the injunction of Paul: "Finally, brethren, whatever is true, whatever is honorable, whatever is just, whatever is pure, whatever is lovely, whatever is gracious, if there is any excellence, if there is anything worthy of praise, think about these things" (Phil. 4:8).

Apart from references to the bliss and loveliness of *Nirvāṇa*, the early Scriptures tend to denote the sublimity of the state with the use of negative terms. This usage may be understood as pointing to the limitlessness of all the connotations of the term, even as in the Upanishadic literature negative language was preferred to denote the indefinability of Brahman. Later writings, however, do not hesitate to use more positive language. We find *Nirvāṇa* described as a lake that "exists to wash away corruption's stain" and is bliss itself, the giver of joy.[43]

In the later Scripture *Milindapañha* (first century A.D.), which purports to give conversations between the Graeco-Bactrian king Milinda (Menander) and the monk Nāgasena, we find even more positive language. To the king's questions regarding the nature of *Nirvāṇa*, Nāgasena answers first that it is not possible by simile or other method to indicate the "shape or configuration or age or size" of *Nirvāṇa*. But in response to the king's prodding, he affirms that there are special qualities that mark it. It is like the lotus plant in that it is unstained by any defilement. Like water it cools and allays the fever of all the mental defilements. It quenches the thirst of craving. Like medicine it protects from the poison of passions and puts an end to the sickness of suffering; it is the very nectar of immortality. Like the great ocean it is empty of evil, great and unbounded; it is the abode of *arhats.* In number like the waves of the ocean, it is filled with "unnumbered, various, abundant and quite pure flowers of knowledge and freedom." Like space (*ākāśa*) it is neither born, nor grows old, dies, passes away or is reborn, both are unconquerable, cannot be stolen, are unsupported, the realm of Aryans, unobstructed, infinite. *Nirvāṇa* is like the wishing jewel in being the granter

[43] Introduction to the *Jātaka,* I, 4, 22; Warren, *op. cit.*, p. 7.

of desires, brings delight and sheds luster. Like red sandalwood it has a lovely scent; like the cream of ghee it has the scent of moral habit. Like a mountain peak it is lofty and hard to scale, immovable, unaccessible to all the passions and evils of desire.[44]

To my knowledge there is no discussion in the Scriptures of the cosmological problem as to how *Nirvāṇa*, seen always as specifically "Other," is able to be effectually known, attained and, in an authentic way, manifested within phenomenal existence. We shall consider this problem later with reference to *Dharma.* But we may note again at this point the primary witness of the Scriptures that the Buddha himself not only remained in this world but continued after his enlightenment to maintain for forty-five years an astonishing consistency not only of nonattachment to phenomenal existence but concomitantly more positive qualities of compassion and loving concern that may be called "consonant" with *Nirvāṇa.* Such conduct was taught not only as the way to the goal but the proper life style of the *arhat* who had attained *Nirvāṇa.* And yet he is free from this world. The *arhat's* continued life on earth was likened to the rolling of a wheel from which the initial impelling force has been removed. The wheel continues to roll for a while, but the impetus to its movement has ceased to be applied and it will stop in due time. The relationship is that of being in the world but not of it.

4

Nirvāṇa in the thought-experience of Gautama the Buddha, both cosmologically and spiritually considered, is not unlike the kingdom of God for Jesus the Christ. We have noted the apparent absence of the personal element in the early accounts of *Nirvāṇa,* while this aspect must be acknowledged as integral to Jesus' view of the kingdom. But, like the Buddha's focus of aspiration upon *Nirvāṇa* as the "One" other than the "many," Jesus taught men to seek first the kingdom of God and his

[44] *Milindapañha* 313-323; MQ, II, 148-160.

righteousness and only secondarily to relate to all other things or persons in this world (Matt. 6:33; 5:6). At no point in the New Testament record does he equate the kingdom with any person, institution or event in the world. Yet with paradox akin to the Buddha's, he proclaimed that the kingdom of God is at hand (Mark 1:15), in the very midst of men or within them (Luke 17:21). The future tense used by Old Testament prophets had become a present reality.[45] The kingdom is a realm within but not of the world, present even though ontologically "other," a reality realized always in the context of specific ethico-spiritual qualities. Paul phrased the point thus: "the kingdom of God does not mean food and drink but righteousness and peace and joy in the Holy Spirit" (Rom. 14:17).

Similarly to the Buddha's understanding of *Nirvāṇa,* Jesus proclaimed the kingdom of God as having both present and future aspects. The future will bring the consummation, the perfection of the reality, with judgment and with dimensions revealed that were previously unknown. But like the Buddha, he emphasized in his teaching present opportunities and responsibilities and the present reality of the kingdom. Much of Jesus' teaching is unintelligible unless his proclamation of the kingdom is understood to mean that the new order has already in some authentic sense broken in upon the old. The whole of the Sermon on the Mount, for instance, presupposes the present circumstances of human life, including all of its adversities, in the face of which the kingdom-life is to be entered into and lived out.

These points of similarity, however, are not merely matters of historical or antiquarian interest. The respective teachings represent religious perception and presumably experience. Considering therefore from the perspectives of Christian faith the range of the Buddha's teaching on *Nirvāṇa* I feel compelled to affirm that in some authentic way he was in contact with aspects or dimensions of the Reality that Jesus termed the kingdom of God. We shall consider some of the theological problems involved in this statement in the last chapter.

[45] Cf. John Bright, *The Kingdom of God,* p. 216.

V

DHARMA

1

Dharma (Pāli: *Dhamma*) is one of the basic terms of the Buddhist Scriptures, knowledge of whose meaning is necessary for understanding both the world view and the soteriological method of the Buddha. Something of its importance may be seen from its role as one of the three jewels (*ratna*) central to Buddhist devotion, the refuges every Buddhist is presumed to repeat before he begins to meditate:

> I go for refuge to the Buddha.
> I go for refuge to the *Dharma*.
> I go for refuge to the *Saṅgha*.

Dharma was a term of evidently long usage in Sanskrit-speaking India from before the time of the Buddha. Its primary meaning, from the root *dhṛ*, was to hold or support. In the extant Buddhist literature it apparently always bore religious or cosmic connotation in its variety of meanings. *Dharma* meant, for one thing, the natural or proper condition of both sentient beings and nonsentient things; it was "what supports them, the law of their being."[1] We note that the Buddha used the term "*Dharma*-men" to denote the faithful followers of his way; they were men as men were meant to be, truly human.

Probably from before the time of the Buddha *Dharma* came to be used in India to express the concept already present in the earliest Vedic literature, in the term *rita,* of a principle of order in the universe, with distinct moral as well as cosmogonic implications. It clearly had something akin to the meaning of universal principle of righteousness; it was that which ought to be done. But it also was used to mean any established, as if with cosmic sanctions, law, condition or fact, either of nature or of human institution.

In the context of thought of the last meaning *Dharma* was transformed so as to denote the duties and obligations of social life as they came to be formulated by the spiritual leadership of Indian society and expressed in the great law books written in the period from 550 B.C. to A.D. 300. Thus *Dharma* came to be applied to caste and the four stages of life and in turn to give ultimate religious sanction to the specific structures and customs of Indian society. According to the *Mahābhārata,* there are nine eternal duties that belong to all castes; otherwise each caste is to live by its own *Dharma,* the norm of behavior appropriate to its own station and function in life.[2]

We find, however, no such association of *Dharma* with particular societal structures in the teaching of the Buddha. For him, *Dharma* was apparently related in its cosmic aspect to *Nirvāṇa,* which is ontologically "other," and in its human, social aspect to the teaching and the ethical life of his followers. In this sense of the term there was only one *Dharma* and participation in the fellowship, whether as monk or layman, of *Dharma*-men was entirely independent of either caste

[1] MLS, I, xix.

[2] *Mahābhārata,* XII, 60; Ainslie T. Embree, *The Hindu Tradition,* pp. 80-83.

or stage of life. We may note that this position constituted in part a rejection of the emerging metaphysical basis of Indian society, of the Brahmanic concept of religion as the cement and sanction of established social practice.[3]

For the Buddha *Dharma* meant truth, primarily truth in the cosmic and inner sense, not propositional nor denotive of societal structure. We find this sense clearly emerging in a discussion recorded as between the Buddha and a certain Brāhman. Over against the Brahmanic practice of sacrificial offerings, the Buddha affirmed the better way of inner purification, the altar fire of an ardent mind, a well-tamed self. *Dharma* is truth that is also the norm, the standard of ethical choice, a lake, clear, undefiled, "praised by the good to good men," characterized by virtue, the water wherein the wise come to bathe and, "clean of limb," cross over to the goal beyond.[4] Through *Dharma* there is help in the world for men to do right.

The Buddha frequently used *Dharma* to denote his own teaching, and it later became the *terminus technicus* for Buddhist doctrine. But it is clear from the above quotation that in the early period the term was employed in a more dynamic sense. That is, the teaching was vital in that it communicated Ultimate Truth, and Ultimate Truth was in turn a manifestation or expression of Ultimate Reality and bore its own inner dynamic.[5]

Like certain other terms in the early community, *Dharma* had to carry the burden of several meanings. It was used to denote not only the proper but also the actual condition of beings and things. In one passage the Buddha is recorded to have identified the process of dependent origination or causation, also termed conditioned genesis, with *Dharma.*[6] This process, in effect the working of *Karma,* was for the Buddha

[3] Joseph M. Kitagawa, *Religions of the East,* p. 169.

[4] *Sanyutta-Nikāya,* I, 169; BKS, I, 212-213. Cf. *Sanyutta-Nikāya,* I, 32; BKS, I, 45. We note here the use of fire as an image to denote the well-tamed, ardent, alert mind of the disciple as contrasted with the more common figure of coolness.

[5] Richard A. Gard has suggested that the term Truth (*Satya*) as used in the Four Noble Truths has the twofold meaning of principle and essential constituent of Reality (*Buddhism,* p. 95).

[6] *Majjhima-Nikāya,* I, 190-191; MLS, I, 236-237.

the basic integrative principle of phenomenal existence and at the same time constituted the primary cosmic aspect of the dilemma of man. The Buddhist disciple was taught to be carefully observant of the elements of being (*Dharma* in plural form), that is, of the dependent process of their causation and cessation, to the end that he might grasp after naught of them and thereby become independent, self-possessed.[7]

Differently from classical Sāṅkhya, which ascribed eternal Reality to separate life-monads and elemental matter, the Buddha considered the *dharmas* to be void of ultimate or eternal reality in themselves.[8] All the elements of phenomenal existence, including ideas or perceptions, were termed *dharmas* and all living beings and crafted products were combinations of *dharmas;* neither any one nor all together constituted Ultimate Reality (*Nirvāṇa*), and the liberation of man consisted in nonattachment to any or all. But the fact that the Buddha–it seems probable that the usage goes back to the Master himself–thus used in plural number the term *Dharma,* with its consistently noble ethical connotations, suggests that he had no basic hostility to the phenomenal universe itself. The primary problem for him was human craving, not the physical universe. Not until much later do we read of "evil dharmas."[9]

There may be some similarity between this, the primitive Buddhist apprehension of *Dharma,* and the concept of the Logos in the pre-Socratic Greek philosophers, especially in Heraclitus. Like all others in this tradition, Heraclitus was impressed by the dominant aspect of change in the world of human experience. But even more central to his thought was his perception of a certain measure of stability inhering in change. He found an underlying coherence of things, an arrangement common to them all, which he termed Logos.[10] The Buddha's use of the term *Dharma* in the plural for the elements of being suggests some such apprehension of princi-

[7] *Digha-Nikāya,* II, 315; DB, part II, pp. 345-346. Warren translated *dharmas* in this passage as "elements of being," Rhys Davids as "ideas."

[8] Cf. von Glasenapp, "Nachträge und Ergänzungen," in Oldenberg, *Buddha,* pp. 420-424.

[9] *Saddharmapundarika* II; Conze, *Buddhist Scriptures,* p. 201.

[10] Cf. G. S. Kirk and J. E. Raven, *The Presocratic Philosophers,* pp. 186-187.

ple at work in phenomenal existence. But for him the religious goal of man lay beyond this.

We thus find the term *Dharma* in plural number associated with phenomenal existence in a way different from *Nirvāṇa*. But in singular number *Dharma* was properly Truth-Reality manifested within but not deriving from phenomenal existence. The Truth won to and understood by the Buddha through his enlightenment was *Dharma*. *Dharma* was the teaching by which men could grow, but a reality more than verbal. By his first teaching of the five ascetics at the deer park of Isipatana in Benares he had "rolled the *Dharma*-wheel," evidently a cosmic event that could not be reversed by any man, god or supernal spirit in all phenomenal existence.

The understanding-committal of Koṇḍañña and the other ascetics on this occasion is said to have given them *Dharma*-vision. They saw *Dharma*, attained it, plunged into it as they "crossed over doubt . . . put away uncertainty."[11] The language suggests that *Dharma* is the Truth taught by the Buddha and at the same time possessive of independent reality and dynamism of its own. It is significant in this context that a contemporary Thai Buddhist scholar prefers, without reference to personal elements, to equate *Dharma* with the Christian concept of God.[12]

The Scriptures, however, suggest a sense in which the Buddha and *Dharma* are one. In one passage we read that a number of his disciples agreed that he had become *Dharma* (*Dhamma-bhūta*), or *Dharma*-lord; in another we find the ascription "sovereign of the Norm" (*Dharma*).[13] In the conversation with the elderly and grievously ill monk Vakkali the Buddha is recorded as saying: "He who seeth the Norm (*Dharma*), Vakkali, he seeth me: he who seeth me, Vakkali, he seeth the Norm. Verily, seeing the Norm, Vakkali, one sees me: seeing me, one sees the Norm"

The precise significance of this quotation, however, is revealed by its context. Vakkali had just expressed his previous longing to see the Exalted One but had been prevented by his

[11] *Vinaya-Piṭaka, Mahāvagga*, I, 5-6; BD, part IV, pp. 6-21.
[12] Buddhadāsa Indapañño, *Christianity and Buddhism*, pp. 70-76.
[13] *Majjhima-Nikāya*, I, 111; MLS, I, 144. *Sanyutta-Nikāya*, I, 33; BKS, I, 46.

physical weakness. The Buddha turned aside the implications of personal reverence in Vakkali's words and said to him, immediately preceding the above quotation, "Hush, Vakkali! What is there in seeing this vile body of mine?"[14] The point of the account is that the *Dharma* the Buddha proclaims and represents in his quality of life is the only aspect of his person that has true significance, but the *Dharma* is not confined in its manifestations to Siddhārtha Gautama. Thus to salute the body of his physical birth is not to render him the proper homage.[15]

A similar point is made in one of the Buddha's final sayings, as we have previously noted. In answer to the concern of Ānanda and other disciples that upon the death of the Master his word would be ended, that the disciples would have no more teacher, the Buddha is said to have replied that the *Dharma* and the discipline he had taught and laid down for them would be their teacher after he had gone.[16] This phraseology might suggest a static concept of *Dharma*, as identical with propositional statements. More dynamic, however, is the understanding implied in the Buddha's injunction that Ānanda and the other disciples be grounded in *Dharma,* making it their refuge and none other, even as they are to be grounded in the Self, making it their refuge and none other.[17] We shall consider the problem of the self in the next section, but the association, or perhaps equation, of *Dharma* with the higher Self of man suggests a transcendent aspect in the Buddha's understanding of *Dharma*.

When the Buddha sent his disciples out to preach, they were to teach *Dharma,* the Truth-Norm, "which is lovely at the beginning, lovely in the middle, lovely at the ending," to "explain with the spirit and the letter the Brahma-faring completely fulfilled, wholly pure."[18] The "loveliness" of *Dharma*, an expression occurring frequently in the Scriptures, suggests both the bliss of the goal, which is *Nirvāṇa,* and the ethical nobility of the way, which is *Dharma.*

14 *Sanyutta-Nikāya,* III, 121; BKS, III, 103.
15 Cf. de Lubac, *Amida,* p. 18.
16 *Dīgha-Nikāya,* II, 154; DB, part II, p. 171.
17 *Sanyutta-Nikāya,* V, 162; BKS, V, 143.
18 *Vinaya-Piṭaka, Mahāvagga,* I, 11; BD, part IV, p. 28.

The way is also termed *sama,* or even. Aryans walk the uneven path "with an even stride."[19] It is the Brahma way, which is always defined by the commentaries as "Best" and is used in the texts to denote the way of moral purity and harmlessness—"who abstains from onslaught on creatures, the stick laid aside, the knife laid aside, he lives kindly, scrupulous, friendly and compassionate towards all breathing things and creatures."[20] The farer of this way torments neither himself nor others, has become cool, experiences bliss, his self become Brahma.[21] Brahma is thus also a term descriptive of the goal as well as the way, the Brahma-world (*Brahmaloka*) attained by the man loosed from craving.[22] Similarly, *Dharma* is not only the Truth principle by which men may grow, it seems to be both the power and quality of *Nirvāṇa* manifested in phenomenal existence. Indeed, the two terms at times seem to merge into one meaning.

We note exalted language used of *Dharma* as of *Nirvāṇa*: "The gift of the law (*Dharma*) exceeds all gifts; the sweetness of the law exceeds all sweetness."[23] The connection of the way with the goal is suggested by the statement that the monk who behaves with kindness and is happy in the *Dharma* of the Buddha will reach *Nirvāṇa*.[24] In what may be the earliest of extant Buddhist literature, the *Sutta-Nipāta*, we find reference to *Dharma* as the "aloof state," as also the way by which men may cross the flood. *Dharma* "reigns" over the enlightened man. *Dharma* is his delight; he takes his praise in *Dharma* and knows its judgments. He orders his conduct lest *Dharma* reveal his guilt. *Dharma* has might that may be seen; it is the state reached as the goal, the reality awakened, set astir by the Stainless One; *Dharma* is the ancient, deathless word of Truth, the goal in which "calm men stand fast." It is nigh men and yet a lofty bourn, not easily wakening in those overcome with life's cravings, a Reality inwardly seen, not handed down as tradition, that in accord with which the alert monk guides his

19 *Sanyutta-Nikāya,* I, 48; BKS, I, 69.
20 *Majjhima-Nikāya,* I, 179; MLS, I, 224.
21 *Majjhima-Nikāya,* I, 342; MLS, II, 6.
22 *Sutta-Nipāta* 139; WCEB, p. 22.
23 *Dhammapada* 354; SBE, X, 84. Cf. Ps. 19:7; 119:72, 77, 92, 97.
24 *Dhammapada* 368; SBE, X, 87.

conduct. The (ideal) universal ruler will rule "by *Dharma* without rod or sword." *Dharma* is that which ends craving, that by which he "who finds and knows and fares alertly may cross over the world's foul mire."[25] It is not only self-realized, it is "timeless, a come-and-see thing," that which leads men onwards. *Dharma* is also the "stream" that carries forward to the goal men of open mind, "in whom listening has effect."[26] We have noted that there is nothing more effective in the achievement of liberation than intimate friendship with *Dharma*, the "lovely." It is perhaps not possible to weave these usages and intimations into a harmonious whole. We seem to learn, however, from the Parable of the Raft, which is equated in the text with *Dharma*, that *Dharma* with all its loveliness and excellence is primarily the way to the goal, that which is to be transcended, is taught "for crossing over, not for retaining."[27]

In later Buddhism, on the other hand, *Dharma* came to be specifically identified with *Nirvāṇa.* We read in the *Saundaranandakavya* of Aśvaghoṣa (first-second centuries A.D.): "the holy, calm and fortunate *Dharma*, . . . which is the supreme place of rest, wherein all Worldly Activity is stopped, a shelter which abides eternally and which nothing can ever take away; that secure place which is final and imperishable," etc.[28] In Mahāyāna philosophy the concept of "Three Bodies" (*Trikāya*) was developed to denote Reality in its various degrees of relatedness to the phenomenal universe. The highest or absolute "Body" was termed *Dharma-kāya,* seen as identical with Void (*Śūnya*) and Suchness (*Tathatā*) as with *Nirvāṇa.* In the Chinese Mahāyāna *Dharma* was generally understood as the equivalent of Tao, although the ideogram signifying "law" was assigned to it rather than "way" (Tao), that is, understood as the eternal principle of order in the (phenomenal) cosmos.

[25] *Sutta-Nipāta* 1054, 1064-1065, 81, 327, 344, 361, 374, 384, 385, 453, 764-765, 934, 963, 1002, 1085; WCEB, pp. 152, 153, 13, 48, 52, 54, 55, 57, 66, 114, 136, 140, 145, 157.

[26] *Majjhima-Nikāya,* I, 265; MLS, I, 321. *Anguttara-Nikāya,* III, 347-348; BGS, III, 247-248.

[27] *Majjhima-Nikāya,* I, 134-135; MLS, I, 173-174.

[28] Conze, *op. cit.*, p. 114.

But in this context of thought the term *Nirvāṇa* came to play a less conspicuous role than in the teaching of the Buddha.

2

Dharma is a word-concept particularly difficult to understand in terms of Christian thought. There is clearly no one or even combination of terms that precisely corresponds to it. As noted above, it would seem at some points to be similar to Heraclitus' understanding of Logos. Later Stoicism used the latter term to denote the all-pervasive "divine" Reason, which they saw as the intelligent, purposeful and good force, but also necessary law, governing the cosmos. The Stoics attributed both will and forethought to the Logos, although without full personalistic consistency. Again, as in the case of *Nirvāṇa,* we have no textual evidence of the Buddha's assigning personal qualities to *Dharma.* The weight of the Buddhist scriptural witness, however, points to the Buddha's primary concern with the religious rather than the cosmological role of *Dharma.* It is the dynamic ethical norm.

In this sense *Dharma* seems akin to the concept and usage of wisdom in the Hebraic Wisdom literature of the Old Testament and of the intertestamental period in both its consistently ethical connotations and occasional transcendent attributes.[29] Perhaps we can also say that *Dharma* in its relationship to *Nirvāṇa* shows a comparable subordination to a higher integrative principle as wisdom is subordinated to the Lord God. "For the Lord gives wisdom," and "no wisdom, no understanding, no counsel can avail against the Lord."[30]

In later literature, such as the Wisdom of Solomon (first century B.C.), we find wisdom described as a kindly spirit, the veritable equivalent of the spirit of the Lord, more precious than all things, the guidance of the Lord. "In kinship with wisdom there is immortality, and in her friendship there is

[29] Cf. Ps. 37:30; 111:10; Prov. 4:11; 5:1-23; 7:4-5; 8:1-4, 11-12; 10:31; 14:33-34; 16:16; 17:24; 18:4; 23:24.

[30] Prov. 2:6; 21:30.

pure delight." Wisdom is said to know the works of God, to have been present when he made the world.[31] There is a context of personalism here somewhat different from the primitive Buddhist tradition, but again the ethical connotations suggest a similar awareness of moral force at work in the world and in the destiny of men.

Dharma in the teaching of the Buddha thus clearly suggests awareness of the presence in the cosmos of a force that "makes for righteousness." Its occasional identification with the karmic or causal principle suggests participation in the role of what is termed divine judgment in Christian context. Its function as the dynamic ethical norm points to activity similar to that of the Holy Spirit, the Spirit of truth, of life, as he is portrayed in the New Testament.[32] Its identification with the Buddha, who "became" *Dharma,* suggests some kinship of meaning with the concept of the Logos, who "became flesh," or even more with the Christ, who became the Law.[33] The Buddha's understanding of this Reality evidently lacked perception of its inherent personal aspect, but his apprehension of its ethical quality as well as cosmic import leads me, thinking again from the perspectives of Christian faith, to conclude that his basic awareness was not essentially misplaced either religiously or ethically.

[31] Wis. Sol. 1:6-7; 7:7-15; 8:17-18; 9:9.
[32] Matt. 7:2; Rom. 2:2-3, 5-6; John 14:16-17, 26; Rom. 8:14; Gal. 5:22-23.
[33] John 1:14.

VI

NON-SELF

1

An element of the early teaching that evidently played an integral role in the thought of the Buddha and yet occasioned considerable misunderstanding is the concept of *anātman* (Pāli: *anatta*). The term may be translated literally as non-self, but obviously the problem of interpretation lies with the meaning assigned to "self." Some Buddhists of the Theravāda School understand the Buddha to have meant that there is literally no such thing as the human self, soul or personal entity with continuity.[1] Mahāyāna philosophy, especially in the tradition of Zen, has approached the problem primarily from a monistic ontological perspective and has seen the self in its essence to be identical with the universe as a whole, or, more particularly, with its essence.[2] There are reasons to

[1] E.g., Walpola Rahula, *What the Buddha Taught*, p. 51.

[2] Cf. Richard H. Robinson, "Buddhism: in China and Japan" in *The Concise Encyclopedia of Living Faiths*, R. C. Zaehner, ed., p. 332.

believe, however, that the Buddha taught something other than either of these positions.

The Buddha's understanding also represented a different position from the Upanishadic equation of the *ātman* of man in its essence with Absolute Reality (*Brahman*). This latter view, a development from the *Rig-Veda* concept of *ātman* as the wind or breath, then self or essential nature of a thing, posited a metaphysics of an eternal and unchanging "substance" that the true Self of man shares with *Brahman.* The Sāṅkhya-Yoga School of Hinduism held the Ultimate to consist in a multitude of separate life-monads (*puruṣa*) and the true Self of each man to be one of these distinct but eternal monads. The Vedānta School of philosophy has in general viewed the Ultimate as One and the eternal aspect of the self as identical with, an indistinguishable part of, that One.

In each of these cases the essence of the self of man is seen as eternal. We are not certain to what extent the Upanishadic literature had been composed by the time of the Buddha and was known to him; the other traditions are both largely of latter provenance. But in the primitive Buddhist teaching only *Nirvāṇa,* and (probably) in a derivative sense *Dharma,* is eternal and changeless, and only the eternal and changeless can be depended upon. The Buddha did not teach in terms of a doctrine of grace, such as is found in the Mahāyāna, in later Hinduism, as in Christianity. But he urged men to orient themselves to that which is eternal and changeless, the good, and truly dependable. For him this was not the self. He never identified the self in any aspect with *Nirvāṇa,* but the true Self, as we shall see, is a part of the larger goal of man.

We may note again in this context that the Buddha's radical distinction between phenomenal existence and *Nirvāṇa* is not one between matter and spirit. The dilemma of man includes the whole of phenomenal existence, material and spiritual, physical and mental. Indeed, in the evil aspects thereof, as we have seen, wrong mental practices are the most pernicious. The direction of spiritual reorientation is away from all these elements of existence toward the totally "Other" (*Nirvāṇa*), which is the deathless element, the unchanging, perfect bliss. The doctrine of *anātman* would seem specifically intended to deny the notion that the salvation of man lies in his own spirit, or self, as empirically known.

The Buddha's analysis of the empirical situation of man led him to the conclusion that a leaning lies latent within man to wrong views or misunderstanding of the true nature-value of things and thereby a leaning to attachment to things, as also to malice. And, as we have seen, true understanding of their nature-value is necessary to overcome attachment to them. Part of the true understanding is to regard not only all things of material form but also men's "feeling, perceptions, the habitual tendencies (*saṃskāra*), consciousness" as "impermanent, suffering, as a disease, an imposthume, a dart, a misfortune, an affliction, as other, as decay, empty, not-self."[3] The last term in this context would seem to mean "devoid of eternal substance or reality." This is to say that all the elements of empirical man, including his mental and spiritual qualities, consciousness itself, have in themselves no ultimate or abiding reality; they are characterized by impermanence (*anicca*), suffering (*duḥkha*) and lack of substantive reality (*anātman*).[4]

Sentient beings are said to consist of five aggregates or elements (*skandhas*) of existence. These are the material qualities (*rūpa*, material form or the physical body), and four nonmaterial aspects: feeling, perception, habitual tendencies (also translated as predisposition) and consciousness. Habitual tendencies (*saṃskāra*) refer to inherent grasping activity that through karmic-causal process brings together a particular sentient being. We have seen that one element of the Buddha's understanding of salvation was liberation from the domination or the "calming" of these tendencies or predispositions of character. The Buddhist affirmation is that all five aggregates are conditioned, impermanent, not the self. "An instructed disciple of the pure ones" does not regard any of these as the self. "He does not regard consciousness as self nor self as having consciousness nor consciousness as in self nor self as in consciousness."[5] Frequent are the references in the texts to

[3] *Majjhima-Nikāya,* I, 433-437, 500-501; MLS, II, 102-107, 179-180.
[4] Cf. Introduction to the *Jātaka,* I, 48; Warren, *Buddhism in Translations,* p. 40.
[5] *Majjhima-Nikāya,* I, 228, 300; MLS, I, 281, 362.

the disciple's responsibility to regard all things, including all intellection or aspects of consciousness, so as to say, "This is not mine, this am I not, this is not my self." This is to see by "perfect intuitive wisdom" all consciousness as it really is.[6]

There appear to be three distinct meanings assigned to the term *self* in the early Scriptures. These are the selfish or self-centered self, the self that is the responsible agent of action and the higher Self. The first two are part of the samsaric process and hence subject to birth, aging, decay, dying, sorrow and stain. An important element of freedom of mind is to be "void of self and what pertains to self," that is, primarily void of self in the first sense and perhaps ultimately void of self in the second; man must not cling to "substantial" things.[7] The third or higher Self refers to a reality that we shall consider more fully below; this is that which is specifically other than the elements of existence. It was evidently the object of the religious quest of many Indians of the time, as, indeed, one part of the Buddha's.[8]

In the first sense we find the self as lustful, the begetter of its own snares, characterized by evil desires (and "in the thrall of evil desires"), self-exaltation, wrath, fault-finding, temper, ill will, sulkiness. This self is envious, grudging, treacherous, deceitful, stubborn, proud, in short "seizing the temporal, grasping it tightly, not letting go of it easily."[9] Therefore man's sorrows, vain longings, his suffering are self-bred. Self-will is one of the major elements of evil. Hence it is the self that hurts the self, that keeps it subject to birth, aging, decay, etc. [10]

Clearly, however, from the last sentence another concept of the self emerges, the responsible agent of action. This is the self that takes the initiative to "look after self," that reflects on self, that measures self against self, the self that is to take action to be purified, freed, awakened. Many are the refer-

[6] *Majjhima-Nikāya,* I, 40, 136, 139; MLS, I, 52, 175, 178.

[7] *Majjhima-Nikāya,* I, 162, 297; MLS, I, 205-206, 358.

[8] *Majjhima-Nikāya,* I, 205; MLS, I, 257. *Vinaya-Piṭaka, Mahāvagga,* I, 14; BD, part IV, pp. 31-32.

[9] *Majjhima-Nikāya,* I, 97-100; MLS, I, 128-131.

[10] *Sutta-Nipāta* 272, 592, 436-439, 585, 659; WCEB, pp. 43, 92, 64, 91, 99. *Majjhima-Nikāya,* I, 167, 173; MLS, I, 211, 217.

ences in the Scriptures to the self-awakened ones.[11] Men are instructed to draw out from self the dart of indolence; who seeks self-happiness draws out the dart of all self-bred pains. The self is responsible for making the path to utter cool; the self-resolute monk purges the self. For his self ill is quenched.[12]

We note references to the self as the self-blaming agent. The awakened man, "poised amid the restless," is neither soiled by the world nor blamed by self.[13]

From this understanding emerges in turn a higher concept of the self. We find the goal, the "wisdom of the still," described as the "self-at-one" (*ekatta*), which is the self integrated, not attached to or distracted by the "many," finding itself in the "One." The Buddha saw the "calm of the self within." Self becomes an island, a refuge, for liberated men, men who grasp at naught. Such men have uprooted the false view of self and regard the world as void of substantive reality; thus they are victors over death. In the man-of-calm exists neither self (*attaṃ*) nor non-self (*nirattaṃ*).[14] The Self and what belongs to Self, "although actually existing, are incomprehensible."[15]

Admittedly this teaching is not always easy to follow. Part of the picture was the Buddha's concern to affirm that the consciousness of empirical experience, that "experiences now here, now there," is generated by conditions and has no permanent continuity in itself. He included within this category various planes of consciousness, even what is termed the "plane of infinite consciousness," from which the mindful monk is to turn in order to "focus his mind on the deathless element." This means that in the continuity of rebirth, exemplified in the being called *gandharva* (Pāli: *gandhabba*) who in conformity with the mechanism of *Karma* enters into the womb of a mother before or at birth, there is no continuity of

[11] *Majjhima-Nikāya,* I, 288, 97-98, 283, 6, 17; MLS, I, 347, 128-129, 337, 7, 22. There is a passage in the *Sutta-Nipāta* that suggests that the self is not properly perceived by the self. Yet the worthy man is "poised-of-self" (477; WCEB, p. 70).

[12] *Sutta-Nipāta* 334, 592, 514, 961-962, 626; WCEB, pp. 49, 92, 77, 140, 95.

[13] *Sutta-Nipāta* 778, 912-913; WCEB, pp. 117, 133-134.

[14] *Sutta-Nipāta* 718, 837, 501, 1119; WCEB, pp. 107, 124, 74, 163.

[15] *Majjhima-Nikāya,* I, 138; MLS, I, 177.

ordinary consciousness, although we note that seers can perceive the events of their previous births.[16]

The last qualification suggests, indeed affirms, that there is continuity in another sense. According to Buddhaghosa (fourth century A.D.), there are consciousnesses, sensations, perceptions that are not subject to depravity.[17] The Aryan disciple turns away from both body and mind, but a "monk rules over mind, is not under mind's rule."[18]

Paradox becomes almost inevitable in the expression of this teaching. Buddhaghosa, perhaps the greatest representative of Theravāda scholasticism, in considering the problem of continuity in the karmic process, wrote that "behind the action there is no actor, and, although actions bear their fruit, there is no one that experiences that fruit." To speak of an actor or one who experiences is but to employ a conventional mode of speech. "Not a single element of being will go from this existence into the next . . . just as the words of the teacher do not pass over into the mouth of the pupil who nevertheless repeats them."[19] This strong language, however, was not intended to denote annihilation of existence. In the conversation recorded between the monk Yamaka and the leading disciple Śāriputra the doctrine, imputed by Yamaka to the Buddha, that the *arhat* upon death is "broken up and perishes . . . becomes not" is termed by Śāriputra an "evil heresy." None of the elements of existence is permanent, the body is not the Self. But the Self is affirmed, although it has no body. The body of man is not in the Self, nor is the Self in (or a part of) the body. We find repeated statements in the Scriptures that terminology based upon transitory phenomena is not adequate to denote the nature of a Tathāgata's "life" after physical

[16] *Majjhima-Nikāya,* I, 256-271; MLS, I, 311-324. *Majjhima-Nikāya,* I, 436-437; MLS, II, 106-107. The analyses of human psychology in the *Sutta-Piṭaka* are much simpler than the elaborate system developed in the later *Abidhamma (Abidharma)* literature. As F. Stcherbatsky has pointed out, the primary concern of the earlier materials with regard to this matter was moral rather than scholastic (*Buddhist Logic,* I, 3-4). Cf. Lama Anagarika Govinda, *The Psychological Attitude of Early Buddhist Philosophy,* pp. 79-142.

[17] *Visuddhi-Magga* XIV; Warren, *op. cit.,* p. 156.

[18] *Majjhima-Nikāya,* I, 215; MLS, I, 267.

[19] *Visuddhi-Magga* XIX; Warren, *op. cit.,* pp. 247-249.

death.[20] Buddhaghosa, however, attempted to affirm a continuity with the figure of a fruit that "is not the same nor something else. The fabricating power in seeds will show the meaning of the word." As sour cream arises from milk, neither an absolute sameness is obtained nor an absolute diversity.[21]

We find in the early Scriptures, particularly in parabolic speech referring to the punishment of evil, references that clearly imply a continuity of the responsible agent-self. One account tells of a man who had lived an immoral life and was reborn in the realm of waste and woe. Brought before Yama the lord of death, he is told by Yama that his evil deeds were not done by relatives, friends or any others. "By yourself alone was it done. It is just you that will experience the fruit thereof."[22]

> But what he doth, by act or word or thought:
> That is the thing he owns; that takes he hence;
> That dogs his steps like shadow in pursuit.[23]

In the *Dhammapada* we read: "The wicked man burns by his own deeds," and "By oneself the evil is done, by oneself one suffers; by oneself evil is left undone, by oneself one is purified."[24]

The Scriptures affirm the responsibility of the self to subdue the selfish self, difficult to subdue though it may be. In the *Dhammapada*, "one's own self is difficult to subdue," but "Self is lord of self, who else could be the lord? With self well subdued, a man finds a lord such as few can find." A man is urged to guard himself (against evil). He reaches the "untrodden country" (*Nirvāṇa*) by riding on his own well-tamed self.[25]

The Buddha is recorded to have said to King Prasenajit of Kośala that he who "would know the self as dear and kind"

[20] *Sanyutta-Nikāya,* III, 109-116; BKS, III, 93-99.

[21] *Visuddhi-Magga* XVII; Warren, *op. cit.,* pp. 238-240. For a discussion of the problem of identity and continuity of self see Herbert Fingarette, *The Self in Transformation,* pp. 180ff.

[22] *Anguttara-Nikāya,* I, 138-141; BGS, I, 121-125.

[23] *Sanyutta-Nikāya,* I, 93; BKS, I, 118.

[24] *Dhammapada* 136, 165; SBE, X, 37, 46.

[25] *Dhammapada* 159-160, 315, 323; SBE, X, 45, 76, 78.

should keep from evil conduct. Those whose conduct is virtuous find the self in fact a dear friend.[26] Because self is the lord of self and its refuge, the noble monk should rouse himself, examine himself, "thus self-protected and attentive will you live happily, O Bhikshu! . . . curb yourself as the merchant curbs a noble horse."[27] In the context of consideration of the self we find such exhortation to strenuous exercise of will made with reference to many kinds of positive action. We note that not seizing the temporal makes a monk "easy to speak to." "He is a reconciler of those who are at variance. . . . Concord is his pleasure, concord his delight, concord his joy, concord is the motive of his speech. . . . Whatever speech is gentle, pleasing to the ear, affectionate, going to the heart, urbane, pleasant to the multitude—such speech does he utter."[28]

The self, then, is the acting and responsible agent for achievement of the goal. It is not the goal proper. As we have noted, the self is nowhere equated with *Nirvāṇa* nor with *Dharma.* The consistent assumption, however, of the early texts is that the self as responsible agent possesses the freedom to walk the way that leads to the cutting of the karmic causal chain and to attainment of the Deathless. The self, though not partaking of eternal substance, is held to be able to act decisively and effectively in the existential situation of man. In this context the integrated self becomes a part of the larger goal and we understand the reason for the Buddha's injunction to seek the self, for instance, to the young men whom he met on his first return to Magadha from Benares.[29]

The integrated self is not only no longer subject to the chain of causation in its power to compel rebirth. When a man has abandoned craving, ill will and delusion he realizes the "profit both of self and others."[30] Such a man has a new mode of being that though identified specifically with neither infinite consciousness nor eternal substance participates in a higher plane of Reality that is bliss and happiness, the Deathless.

[26] *Sanyutta-Nikāya,* I, 71; BKS, I, 97-98.
[27] *Dhammapada* 379-380; SBE, X, 88-89.
[28] *Majjhima-Nikāya,* I, 97, 288; MLS, I, 128, 347.
[29] *Vinaya-Piṭaka, Mahāvagga,* I, 14; BD, part IV, pp. 31-32.
[30] *Anguttara-Nikāya,* I, 156-158; BGS, I, 140-141.

Ontologically, the Buddha preferred to understand man in this mode not in terms of static being but of activity charged with value. Man is more of an axiological than an ontological reality; he becomes "teleologically productive" in the sense of creating values consonant with his true goal, *Dharma-Nirvāṇa*.

Much of the early teaching on the self is oriented to denial of its "substantial" nature, and we accordingly find little reference in this context to what we now call the problem of man-in-community. This aspect of the Buddha's anthropology, however, emerges from other passages. Man's liberation from the ties of craving and consequently from the karmic process of becoming is the responsibility of the self as responsible agent. But "bourgeois individualism" is not the goal. To the contrary, as we have seen, self-in-isolation is to be replaced by the self-at-one. The self-at-one evidently refers primarily not to the achievement of harmonious societal relationships but to "spiritual" integration on a cosmically transcendent plane. This integration, however, was clearly expected to issue in benevolent compassion toward and service of all sentient beings.

In the teaching that can with any certainty be ascribed to the Buddha, we find, to alter slightly Max Weber's words, a consistent and studious minimization of formal ties of the monk not only to society at large but even to the monastic community.[31] In the early teaching no societal tie or organizational structure is ever accorded any but religiously provisional meaning or value. But the obligation to compassion and service abides. Laymen are to revere and serve the monks, to love and serve each other. Monks are to respect and serve each other, as well as teach the laity. Senior monks are to teach and correct the junior, all are to be purified by confession, as necessary. All are to practice universal benevolence without attachment. The cosmic future of personal relationships in this context was not, for the Buddha, a proper subject for discussion, but as we have seen, annihilation was not the answer.

In a discussion with the ascetic Vacchagotta the Buddha is recorded as refusing to affirm whether the Tathāgata "is" or "is not" after death. This was going to unprofitable speculative views. The Tathāgata "freed from denotation by material

[31] Max Weber, *The Religion of India*, p. 214.

shape" is "deep, immeasurable, unfathomable as is the great ocean." The categories of phenomenal existence are not fit to describe his condition. He is no longer in process of becoming; he has become (*Brahma-bhuto*, Brahma-become).[32] We may note in this context the suggestive observation of Reinhold Niebuhr that "The self in its freedom is too great to be contained within the self in its contingent existence."[33]

The Buddha was concerned to turn the spiritual orientation of men away from the selfish self in part because of the dangers of pride latent in the notion that "I am the doer, mine is the doer," "the great 'I am' conceit."[34] But when given cosmic or metaphysical significance, the notion was for him specifically false. His understanding at this point seems not dissimilar to the biblical affirmation that only God can say "I am" in a primary, underived and independent sense.[35] The empirical self is not to be identified with that which is unmade, unborn, etc.; it belongs to the category of the causally originated.

But the thrust of the Buddha's teaching on the self ends on the note of victory, the dominant note, as we have seen, of the whole of the teaching. "The disciple will overcome the earth, and the world of Yama (death), and the world of the gods."[36] The man who loves *Dharma* is the winner.[37] The well-taught Aryan disciple turns from body, mind and consciousness, seeing that "for life in these conditions there is no hereafter." There is naught of the self therein.[38] The self, however, liberated from grasping, integrated with the "One," finds itself in a new dimension of Reality that is Deathless. For the Buddha there lay before the self as responsible agent a destiny that could best be termed bliss. This was indeed a high view of man as of his destiny.

[32] *Majjhima-Nikāya,* I, 484-488; MLS, II, 162-167. *Anguttara-Nikāya,* I, 248-249; BGS, I, 227-228.

[33] Paul Ramsey, *Reinhold Niebuhr*, Charles W. Kegley and Robert W. Bretal, ed., pp. 85-86.

[34] *Vinaya-Piṭaka, Mahāvagga,* I, 3; BD, part IV, p. 5.

[35] Cf. Exod. 3:14; John 8:58.

[36] *Dhammapada* 45; SBE, X, 16.

[37] *Sutta-Nipāta* 91; WCEB, p. 16.

[38] *Sanyutta-Nikāya,* III, 20-25; BKS, III, 20-24. Cf. *Dīgha-Nikāya,* I, 46; DB, part I, p. 54.

2

The Buddha's teaching on the self inevitably brings to mind possible comparison with the studies of modern depth psychology. We have noted the views of C. G. Jung regarding different levels of the self. To repeat briefly, Jung taught that most men live at the level of self that he, with Freud, termed ego. They also experience occasional unaccountable uprushes from the unconscious. Human maturity, however, Jung saw as being achieved by the integration of these two levels whereby a new center of personality emerges, differing in nature from the ego-center. He called this new center of personality integration the *self*. The achievement, however, of this new center of personality he believed to be the discovery in experience of an immortal reality in man that is "total, timeless man," a reality termed by others as the super-conscious.[39]

The Buddha, as we have seen, refrained from ascribing the terms deathless or permanent to the self at any level. But in spite of the differences of the centuries and cultural milieus, we seem justified in assigning the modern term integration, with its associations from depth psychology, to the nongrasping self-at-one that he taught as the true Self of man.

We do not find in the early texts any word precisely equivalent to the modern term "unconscious," but, as we have seen, integration of the self was envisaged as achieved in a process that transcends all levels of consciousness. It would not seem an erroneous conclusion, therefore, to assume that for the Buddha self-integration involved correlation with what we have come to call the unconscious depths of the psyche. The wider dimensions of the higher Self in the teaching of the Buddha remind us, we may add, of the understanding of *memoria* in Augustine. Etienne Gilson has shown that Augustine included within the meaning of the word the reality indicated by our modern terms "unconscious" or "subconscious" together with the additional faculty—possessed by this

[39] C. G. Jung, *Psychology of the Transference, Collected Works,* XVI, 311. This concept is similar to that of the return to the original Self as taught in the Zen tradition. Cf. D. T. Suzuki, *An Introduction to Zen Buddhism,* pp. 42, 46-47. See also P. Teilhard de Chardin, *The Phenomenon of Man,* pp. 262-263.

dimension—of openness to wider ranges of reality, in particular serving as the point of creative encounter with the illuminating presence of the transcendent God. Like the Buddha, Augustine's understanding of this aspect of the self points to a reality-realm that is beyond words, concepts or reflective-discriminating consciousness. He perceived an intimation within the soul to know itself as it really is, beyond the covering (*glutinum*) of sensations that obscure the deeper reality.[40]

The publication of Jung's autobiography has revealed far more fully the religious dimensions of his thought, and his scientific writings that deal with personality integration must now properly be read in this light. In the Buddha's case, the centrality of the role of *Nirvāṇa,* as he conceived it, in his teaching reveals the profoundly religious orientation of his anthropological understanding. He was concerned not merely with psychological technique but primarily with the true destiny of man in the Deathless. Furthermore, the integral role he assigned to ethical conduct in the fulfillment of this destiny reveals his posture toward truth. For the Buddha, to use the phrase of a contemporary writer, "truth could only be found through transformation." Theories of the self were of little value; the important thing was to purify and transform the self unto its real destiny. For the Buddha bliss, peace and happiness were inherent in this destiny, but as to its metaphysical nature, he felt that to attempt to define or describe it with words was to "go too far."

3

Evaluation of this anthropological understanding from the standpoint of Christian faith is admittedly not easy, in terms of traditional Christian theological categories perhaps impossible. We may begin, however, by observing that its ethical goals are almost without exception consonant with the highest

[40] Étienne Gilson, *The Christian Philosophy of Saint Augustine*, pp. 100, 299 (n. 110). Augustine, *De Trinitate* X, 3, 5.

Christian ideals and worthy of close study looking toward emulation. Let us note just two possible exceptions to this statement.

One ethical teaching in the early Scriptures that occasions criticism from the standpoint of biblical affirmations regarding the original goodness of the physical creation is that which directs the cultivation of loathing for all things physical as a part of the program of (monastic) spiritual development. We have seen, however, that much, perhaps the whole, of this teaching may be the result of later developments in Buddhist monastic communities, even as we recall the presence of some variation of understanding and practice on this point in the New Testament and considerably more in the history of the church.

Another difficulty is presented by the teaching, addressed in the text to a monk, that he should refrain from critical words—and presumably any physical action—even if nuns were struck by others with the hand, a stick, a clod of earth, or given a blow with a weapon. Even though he were to view this kind of assault "face to face," he should train himself so as to be able to say, "Neither will my mind become perverted, nor will I utter an evil speech, but kindly and compassionate will I dwell with a mind of friendliness and void of hatred."[41] The Buddha himself appears to have been similarly silent when Kapilavastu was conquered by the Kośalans and members of his own Śākya clan were massacred. This teaching, however, seems strictly confined to monastics, although it reveals the extent of formal withdrawal from participation in "secular" activity expected of Buddhist monks. There is no record of the Buddha's ever directing laymen, in particular those in positions of political or military authority, to refrain from protecting the weak against wanton violence. We have noted as a major theme of the teaching injunctions to alertness of mind and related spiritual activity of a positive kind, but it is understandable that the intent of the incident just cited was sometimes interpreted as advocating passivity in the face of evil.

We are compelled to say therefore that what constitutes by far the dominant ethical teaching of the early texts must be

[41] *Majjhima-Nikāya*, I, 123-124; MLS, I, 159-160.

considered in accord with biblical teaching as regards both individual and corporate conduct. The goal of transformation of the selfish and separate self, whether as monk, householder or king, is consistently seen in terms that constitute also for Christians the purification and ennobling of human life.

In attempting to understand and evaluate the teaching of the Buddha on the self, we need to remind ourselves, then, that we are dealing not only with concepts but also with practice. Understanding is unto transformation, as in Christian terms faith—or truth—is unto goodness. The integration of self envisaged in the self-at-one seems to point to an ethico-spiritual event that, viewed in its human aspect, is closely akin to that suggested by the passage in Revelation 3:20, where are recorded the words of the Lord to the church in Laodicea: "Behold, I stand at the door and knock; if any man hears my voice and opens the door, I will come in to him and eat with him and he with me."

We find in this passage a personal call from the Divine and an appeal to a personal divine-human relationship. But the content of the call envisages the opening up of the barriers that separate the egocentric self of empirical man from his true destiny. The man who responds to this appeal allows the Lord to cross the boundaries of his isolation. The Lord who speaks the word anticipates the most intimate of personal relationships after crossing the threshold and entering the home (self), but the self in its old sense of separate, closed self-centeredness ceases to exist. This old self is no true self, it is not the proper destiny of man, it is not "satisfactory" nor worthy of preservation as such. The true self is found only where the barriers of egocentricity are let down in the presence of the ultimately Real, the Eternal.

This is to say that the nature of biblically based conversion to God in Christ and of Buddhist conversion of self to *Dharma-Nirvāṇa* is strikingly similar in terms of religio-psychological orientation, in spite of some differences in ontological understanding. In both cases the specificity of the old self has been transcended to find the new in a cosmic context radically reperceived. We have noted the role of renunciation in the teaching of Jesus the Christ as in that of Gautama the Buddha. Jesus taught that a man was to deny himself to follow him.[42] Paul stressed the death of self, even daily, as the way to life. As such, "it is no longer I who live, but Christ who lives in me."[43] The Buddha's teaching of the conquest of self seems to have envisaged as radical an ethico-spiritual transformation of the self as is to be perceived in the New Testament.

We cannot but be moved, I feel, by the spiritual understanding revealed in this early Buddhist teaching. In consequence of our faith in the God who is "Father Almighty, Creator of heaven and earth," present and at work through his Spirit in the whole of his creation, we are compelled not only to consider with the profoundest respect and appreciation the nature of the conversion of self envisaged in the teaching of the Buddha. We are also under the happy compulsion to consider the extent of the role of the Holy Spirit in his life as well as in his teaching. Teaching of this spiritual understanding and practice of this ethical quality cannot properly be held alien to the work of him who is good and Father everlasting.[44] Even more, they seem, even though at points perhaps imperfectly, expressive of that work in their own time and place.

[42] Matt. 16:24-25 (Mark 8:34-35; Luke 9:23).
[43] Rom. 8:2, 5, 10, 13; I Cor. 15:31; II Cor. 6:9; Gal. 2:19-20.
[44] Mark 10:18 (Matt. 19:17; Luke 18:19).

VII

TOWARD THEOLOGICAL INTERPRETATION

Several fragmentary attempts have been made in the previous chapters to achieve some kind of religious understanding and theological evaluation of the life and teaching of the Buddha from the standpoint of Christian faith. We come now to the place where we may attempt something more like a synthesis of these efforts on the basis of a brief historical survey of previous endeavors of the kind in the Judaeo-Christian tradition. Perhaps we should begin, however, by taking note of the context of contemporary Christian thought relative to these problems.

One of the most widely accepted assumptions of contemporary theological thinking seems to be the affirmation that God is present and at work in the secular world of men as well as in the traditionally sacred or religious. Following Dietrich Bonhoeffer perhaps no single idea has so captured the imagination of especially younger theologians in the West. It is not always seen, however, that acknowledgment of this fact has the most direct bearing upon evaluation of the religions of the world.[1] Once the Spirit of God is seen to be "free" to act independently of the ecclesial structures and ecclesiastically related personages of the Judaeo-Christian tradition, he appears free to work and to have worked in widely disparate areas, including the "non-Christian" religions. As we shall see, this understanding has been lacking in and alien to much of the older Christian orthodoxy, Catholic or Protestant. It has, however, now become one of the primary problem-considerations of contemporary theological thought. The authentic significance of this development emerges with even greater force as we see its relationship to the wider spiritual experience of men in this age.

Statements concerning the emergence of "one world" in our time, the world as a "global village" and the like, are sometimes overdrawn or too facile. But there can be no doubt that all men are being drawn into new experiences of interrelationship by factors wherein we may assign recent developments in technology and mass media of communication by no means the only role. We seem to be living in a day when previously largely disparate streams of historical experience are being drawn into one world history. There are those who see this phenomenon as more than an increase in socio-economic, political or cultural contacts across the world. Some see also a "convergence of the historical processes of different religions" with the result of a "sense of participation in each other's on-going religious history."[2] This is in effect to affirm that "all spiritual traditions are dimensions of each other and that at this point of history individuals throughout the world are becoming heir to the spiritual heritage of mankind."[3]

These are admittedly heady thoughts in terms of even the recent part of Western, especially orthodox Christian, man. But behind them and at least partly contributory to their emer-

[1] Cf. Paul Verghese, "Syncretism and the Quest for Interiority," *The Christian Century*, LXXXVII, 51 (December 23, 1970), 1529-1530.

[2] S. J. Samartha, "More Than an Encounter of Commitments," *International Review of Missions*, LIX, 236 (October, 1970), 394, 401-402.

[3] Ewert Cousins, "The Trinity and World Religions," *Journal of Ecumenical Studies*, VII, 3 (Summer, 1970), 497.

gence lie an increasing amount of solid theological work and the rediscovery or reformulation of ancient perspectives of faith. These perspectives include a "renewed understanding of the universality of God's work," seeing by theological necessity that God is and has been at work in the whole world and among all men. The expectation is of an increasingly "extended understanding of the universality and fullness of Christ" far beyond the previously largely tacit but nonetheless real theological confinement of his manifestations to "places" of explicit Christian faith. There is growing aspiration to discover and realize more fully "all that is involved in Christ, the Son and the Word of God."[4] Renewed emphasis is being given to the work of Christ through the Spirit in creation, past and present, and to the necessary connection between the orders of creation and of redemption.[5] Because God through his Son and Spirit has been graciously present and at work in all human societies and religious traditions, however broken and imperfect, even distorted, particular manifestations in human life may be, Christians are increasingly able to participate with theological understanding in the emerging spiritual awareness of contemporary mankind.

Part of this awareness is to sense not only that all men live in one world, the creation of one God, but that in some measure all draw from the same spiritual and moral source and, albeit in different ways, aspire to a common fulfillment. On the basis of this understanding it becomes both theologically meaningful and, *in potentia,* religiously and ethically helpful to inquire more widely and deeply into previously divergent traditions of human experience of the ultimate mys-

[4] See the aide-mémoire issued in consequence of the consultation involving a group of Buddhists, Christians, Hindus and Muslims held at Ajaltoun, Lebanon, in March, 1970 under the auspices of the World Council of Churches ("Christians in Dialogue with Men of Other Faiths," *International Review of Missions,* LIX, 236 [October, 1970], 383, 385, 391). Cf. David Jenkins, "Commitment and Openness," *International Review of Missions,* LIX, 236, 411; Troy Organ, "A Cosmological Christology," *The Christian Century,* LXXXVIII, 44 (November 3, 1971), 1293-1295.

[5] Col. 1:16-17; Isa. 46:4. It was a central element of the Greek theological tradition to see "creation as a Trinitarian act: from the Father, through the Son and in the Spirit." For this reason the major Greek theologians were able to be aware of the action of the persons of the Trinity in the universe and history (Cousins, *op. cit.,* pp. 488-489). Cf. Hans Urs von Balthasar, *A Theology of History,* pp. 49-75.

tery that, we believe, surrounds, permeates and yet transcends our mortal lot.

This very brief account may be of some help in understanding why the Roman Catholic theologian Raymond Panikkar has affirmed that the meeting of religions is the *kairos* of our time.[6] In the case of the Catholic Church this meeting is occurring in the context of a new respect for the religious experience of men in other traditions, and in effect the church "has abandoned officially an exclusive claim to religious values for the first time in history."[7] In the case of the Protestant churches we note a call from an important regional body for a new sensitivity to the Spirit to discern "Christ's work since history began in all our societies and spiritual 'worlds.' "[8]

We find that noted theologians, Catholic, Protestant, and to some extent Eastern Orthodox, are giving the most serious attention to the dogmatic aspects of problems related to understanding and evaluating the religions of the world.[9] Ecumenism is regaining its original meaning of "universal" so as to include dialogue with religious traditions other than the

[6] Raymond Panikkar, "Toward an Ecumenical Theandric Spirituality," *Journal of Ecumenical Studies,* V, 3 (Summer, 1968), 527-528. Cf. Raymond Panikkar, "Faith and Belief: On the Multireligious Experience (An Objectified Autobiographical Fragment)," *Anglican Theological Review,* LIII, 4 (October, 1971), 219-237; Jacques-Albert Cuttat, "Expérience Chrétienne et Spiritualité Orientale," *La Mystique et Les Mystiques,* pp. 825-827.

[7] Adrianus de Groot, "The Mission after Vatican II," *Concilium,* XXXVI, 174. Cf. Peter Schreiner, "Roman Catholic Theology and non-Christian Religion," *Journal of Ecumenical Studies,* VI, 3 (Summer, 1969), 376-399.

[8] Statement from the East Asia Christian Conference of July, 1970 (*International Review of Missions,* LIX, 236 [October, 1970], 428).

[9] E.g. Kenneth Cragg, *Christianity in World Perspective;* Jacques-Albert Cuttat, *The Encounter of Religions;* Charles Davis, *Christ and the World Religions;* Nels F. S. Ferré, *The Universal Word;* Hendrik Kraemer, *Why Christianity of All Religions?*; Hans Küng, *Freedom Today;* D. T. Niles, *Buddhism and the Claims of Christ*; Raymond Panikkar, *The Unknown Christ of Hinduism*; Wolfhart Pannenberg, *Basic Questions in Theology,* II; Karl Rahner, *Das Christentum und die nichtchristlichen Religionen;* Wilfred Cantwell Smith, *The Faith of Other Men;* John V. Taylor, *The Primal Vision;* M. M. Thomas, *The Acknowledged Christ of the Indian Renaissance;* Paul Tillich, *Christianity and the Encounter of the World Religions,* and many others. Paul Tillich stated in the last public lecture he gave before his death in 1965 that his hope for the future of theology was to move beyond the compass of his *Systematic Theology* into a long and intensive "interpenetration of systematic theological study and religious historical studies." A similar aspiration is reported of D. T. Niles before his death in 1970.

Christian.[10] This phenomenon is all the more remarkable because until the last decade or two exponents of the orthodox theological tradition, Catholic or Protestant, hardly ever mentioned other religions except disparagingly and on the basis of little knowledge.

Reasons for the phenomenon are many, some of which we have already briefly sketched. Before we turn, however, to a consideration of pertinent material in the Bible and the early church, it may be helpful if we take note of a few of the elements and steps in the background of the very great change involved. In the wider intellectual history of the West a significant change of attitude toward the cultures of the non-Western world emerged in leading spirits of the Enlightenment of the eighteenth century. We find, for example, a new and different appreciation of Islam in Gotthold Lessing's *Nathan der Weise,* which represented the three religions of Christianity, Islam and Judaism in a parable of three brothers. Earlier, in 1705 the Dutch scholar Hadrianus Relandus had published a two-volume work *De religione Mohammedanica libri duo,* the first scientifically objective representation of Islam to appear in Europe. The wider perspectives furnished by the northward movement of the Renaissance and the voyages of exploration contributed to this understanding even as the wars of religion of the previous century had led numbers of sensitive Europeans to more critical appraisals of the claims of institutional Christianity. Another factor that served to broaden men's cultural sympathies was the relatively wide diffusion of the *Lettres curieuses et édifiantes* sent back to Europe by Roman Catholic missionaries in China during the late seventeenth and early eighteenth centuries. These letters created such enthusiasm for Chinese culture among educated Europeans as to effect distinctly new styles in architecture, painting, furniture, earthenware ("chinaware"), etc. Voltaire expressed himself as favoring Chinese civilization in contrast with "Christian Europe." The Jesuit missionary theologians in Peking made use of the Logos theology of the early Greek fathers to

[10] Klaus Klostermaier, "Hindu-Christian Dialogue," *Journal of Ecumenical Studies,* V, 3 (Summer, 1968), 527-528.

develop the doctrine of "natural" revelation and knowledge of the divine law among men outside the institutional means of salvation provided by the Roman Catholic Church, as Francis Xavier had begun to do more tentatively in Japan. Both directly and indirectly they contributed to the new evaluation of world religions that began to emerge among educated Europeans in the eighteenth century.

Subsequent to these events came the discovery and translation of Sanskrit, Pāli and then Chinese, Tibetan and other Asian religious texts. The work of pioneers like A. H. Anquetil-Duperron, F. Max Müller and C. A. F. Rhys Davids contributed enormously to the expansion of horizons and enrichment of the intellectual life of Europe and the Americas as well as to the renewal of appreciation among Asians for their own religious and larger cultural heritage. Among the pioneers themselves and also among their readers were men of deep Christian faith who made some attempts, especially from the latter part of the nineteenth century, to understand the meaning of these materials, as of the contemporary manifestation of the religious traditions, in terms of Christian faith and theology. Attempts more successful than most were those of J. N. Farquhar, Nathan Söderblom and Karl Ludwig Reichelt.[11] Liberal theologians in both Europe and North America, among whom may be cited William Temple, Ernst Troeltsch and William Ernest Hocking, contributed to the development of changed or enlarged Christian views. One manifestation of this development emerged in the Jerusalem Conference in 1928 of the International Missionary Council, in the background of which the theological contributions of Asian Christians must also be taken into account.

On the whole, however, these developments had relatively little effect on the older orthodoxy, Protestant or Catholic. The rise of the movement of Dialectical or Crisis Theology under the leadership of Karl Barth, Emil Brunner and others served rather to stiffen the position of orthodoxy vis-à-vis religious traditions other than the Christian even as it contrib-

[11] J. N. Farquhar, *The Crown of Hinduism*; Nathan Söderblom, *The Living God*; Karl Ludwig Reichelt, *Truth and Tradition in Chinese Buddhism*. As an attempt not so successful may be cited Sir M. Monier-Williams, *Buddhism*.

uted a new theological sophistication and girded the churches of Europe for confrontation with the ideological and practical horrors of German National Socialism. In the specific context of missiology and more direct theological confrontation with other religions, this movement found its greatest exponent in the life and writings of Hendrik Kraemer, its most dramatic moments in the 1938 meeting of the International Missionary Council at Tambaram, Madras, India.[12]

The post-World War II years, however, have revealed new and unexpected developments in this area. For one thing, the extent and frightfulness of the war itself as well as the deeds perpetrated in the name of National Socialism shook Western civilization to its depths and caused a crisis in self-understanding of which we are only beginning to see the effects with some clarity. The perhaps thirteen million lives lost through purges, imprisonment and other measures employed against civilians in the Soviet Union during the 1920's and '30's have also contributed significantly to this crisis. One effect of all these events has been the loss, or at least the weakening, of centuries-long attitudes of Western cultural and racial as well as religious superiority toward the other peoples of the earth.[13] This effect first became noticeable among sensitive intellectuals but is now very widespread among the youth of all nations in the West, although older attitudes seem as yet to have changed but little among certain of the less educated segments of the populations.

Another factor contributing to the present situation of changing attitudes is the contemporary knowledge explosion, especially as this has derived from mass communications media and mass travel. Westerners and of course Western Christians

[12] Kraemer's position was clearly expressed in his book written for the Tambaram meeting, *The Christian Message in a Non-Christian World.* We find only nonsubstantive changes in his later books, *Religion and the Christian Faith, World Cultures and World Religions,* and *Why Christianity of All Religions?* Ernst Benz has written of the "frightening isolation" into which much Christian thought fell as a result of the "unfounded claims of dialectical theology" (*Ideen zu einer Theologie der Religionsgeschichte,* p. 36). Cf. his "Ideas for a Theology of the History of Religion," in Gerald H. Anderson, ed., *The Theology of the Christian Mission,* pp. 135-147. A key section for the thought of Karl Barth on this theme is *Die Kirchliche Dogmatik,* vol. I, part 2, pp. 356-397.

[13] Cf. John R. Hale, *Age of Exploration,* p. 17.

are able not only to read about other religious traditions; they can meet their adherents both at home and abroad. Evaluations and attitudes based on the older ignorance are therefore no longer viable among the knowledgeable in our midst. Christian theological interpretation of other religions that is free from presuppositions of cultural or religious superiority and based upon fuller and more exact knowledge has become an intellectual necessity of our time.

1

DEVELOPMENTS IN THE HISTORY OF THE CHURCH

Obviously, motives for a theological inquiry of this kind may vary. For some it may serve primarily as a useful tool for evangelization. I shall state frankly at this point that my own understanding of motives that may properly lead to this kind of study do not exclude that of preparation for religious dialogue such as may end in change of the formal religious affiliation of either—or both—of the partners in the dialogue. Nevertheless, inquiry intended to serve solely or even primarily as a tool for evangelization is, in my judgment, unsuited to the demands of our time and unworthy of the Christian spirit. We shall consider below why this motive taken alone is unsuited and unworthy.

Another motive for inquiry and the kind of dialogue that has become meaningful for many in recent years is that which looks to the establishment of mutual human understanding and fellowship and to service in behalf of each other. On this basis men of different faiths may work together in various concrete service projects that contribute to the welfare of mankind. This motivation has been given notable expression in the encyclical letter of Pope Paul VI, *Ecclesiam Suam,* and in the "Declaration on the Relationship of the Church to Non-Christian Religions" of *The Documents of Vatican II.*

A further motive, which also appears in the documents just cited, is that study and dialogue among representatives of different religious traditions may contribute to a continuing learning experience for all concerned. Men may seek not only mutual understanding and cooperation but also mutual criticism, for authentic communication presupposes the freedom to criticize in love. This kind of learning experience may also contribute to deeper insight into the truth and meaning of the participants' own traditions. For Christian theology this possibility has now become a reality and one of the most fruitful sources of both critical self-understanding and creative rethinking that our time offers.[14]

One consequence of this new posture and activity has been therefore to reperceive, in a more existential way, the meaning of the doctrines of divine creation and providence, as well as to rethink, as we have seen, the role of the Trinity in the whole world and in all history, with reference especially to the concept of the solidarity of all mankind. The Stoics regarded mankind as a single family, and in the New Testament the perspective that sees humanity as a whole is everywhere present. The Noachian covenant, moreover, was intended to comprise the whole of mankind, and the great literary prophets of Israel included, at least in eschatological perspective, the nations within the range of their concern.

In the post-Constantinian history of the West, Christian theologians continued to reaffirm the ancient teaching of universal divine creation and providence, but until recent years the bulk of European and American Christians seem to have considered the God and Father of Jesus Christ as essentially the patron deity of Western peoples and his salvific work as practically confined to those who were called Christian. The mainstreams of both Protestant and Catholic orthodoxy were characterized by notions of explicit Christian faith and membership in the visible church as indispensable to eternal salvation. It is a strange fact, as W. A. Visser 't Hooft observed, that the church and its theologians have been slower than humanistic philosophers in the West to recognize and affirm the

[14] A particularly perceptive and imaginative example of this kind of theological activity is Raymond Panikkar's "Toward an Ecumenical Theandric Spirituality," *Journal of Ecumenical Studies,* V, 3, 522-534, or his later article, "Advaita and Bhakti: Love and Identity in a Hindu-Christian Dialogue," *Journal of Ecumenical Studies,* VII, 2 (Spring, 1970). Cf. Ewert Cousins, "The Trinity and World Religions," *Journal of Ecumenical Studies,* VII, 3, 476-498.

solidarity of all men.[15] It is even stranger that for so long the Christian community failed to sense the wider soteriological significance of the Fatherhood of God.

Another consequence of recent theological studies has been a rediscovery of the wider perspectives of many of the early, especially the Greek, Church Fathers. It is with this material that we may begin to lay the foundations of our theological inquiry. The school of religious and cultural rejection represented by Tatian and Tertullian is seen to be only one and, in the first three centuries, evidently the less typical theological position. Tertullian's famous question, "What is there in common between Athens and Jerusalem, between the Academy and the Church?" by no means represented the primary Christian tradition of the time.[16] Indicative of this fact is that both Tertullian and Tatian ended their careers as members of ascetic groups separated from the "great" Catholic Church.

In the postapostolic period the question came to be asked, Did acceptance of Jesus Christ as Lord, as the supreme and normative revelation of the living God, require the complete rejection of the wisdom of this world? Did committal to what Paul called the folly of the cross mean that the cultural and religious heritage of Hellenism had no truth or value and must be summarily rejected?[17] Or were pagan culture and learning, including the religious insights of philosophers, in some way, at least in part, in accord with the wisdom and purposes of God and to be affirmed, even claimed, by those who had

[15] W. A. Visser 't Hooft, *No Other Name,* p. 114. Cf. *The Finality of Jesus Christ in the Age of Universal History,* WCC Bulletin, Division of Studies, VIII, 2 (Autumn, 1962), 4-5.

[16] Tertullian, *De Praescriptione Haereticorum* 7.9; *Corpus Christianorum, Series Latina,* pars 1, p. 193. Tertullian, of course, like all other early Christian writers, affirmed the universal presence and rule of God in the world (*Ad Nationes* 2.8). Another aspect of this complex figure is revealed in his work "On Prayer," in which he acknowledges the effectiveness of prayer in ancient times apart from the "form" of Christ and affirms that all creation, even cattle and wild beasts, prays authentically, each in its own way. The birds soar up to the sky in the morning and in place of hands spread their wings in the shape of a cross and say something that seems like prayer (*De Oratione* 29; *Corpus Scriptorum Ecclesiasticorum Latinorum,* XX, 199-200).

[17] I Cor. 1:18-2:16. The problem thus stated should be distinguished from the special area of relations with the Roman state and, in particular, worship of the emperor. See C. N. Cochrane, *Christianity and Classical Culture,* passim.

committed themselves to the one God through Jesus Christ? Both views were to be found in the church from the beginning and both could claim apostolic precedent.[18]

The general and persistent posture of the early church toward the religious worship and practice of Hellenistic paganism, particularly in its popular manifestations, was highly critical. We find Lactantius writing in the year 313 that the first step in Christian proclamation is "to perceive the religions which are false, and to cast aside the impious worship of gods made by human hands."[19] Origen, writing against Celsus around 250, described standard instruction of catechumens as including efforts to instill a disregard for idols and all images.[20]

One of the most important, however, of the theological traditions of the early church was that which took the Johannine doctrine of the Logos and attempted to expound it in such a way as to appreciate and affirm certain elements of Hellenistic culture. This activity was a particular expression of the general patristic concern to affirm both the fact of divine providence and grace from the beginning of human history and their "pedagogical" role in the divine economy of salvation prior to the coming of the Christ. Notable among the representatives of this tradition were Justin Martyr, Theophilus of Antioch, Athenagoras, Clement of Alexandria and Origen.

Origen (ca. 185-253/4) was the most learned biblical scholar and theologian in the early church. His position of discriminating evaluation of non-Christian culture is seen in his statement that philosophy "is neither at variance to the law of God at all points, nor in harmony with it in all."[21] His understanding of the wider work of God in the world was that every wise man, to the extent that he is wise, participates in Christ, for Christ is wisdom. He held that the church existed from the foundation of the world, or even before, that she was in all the saints from

[18] Cf. John Foster, *After the Apostles*, p. 100; *Clement of Rome*, 7, 5-7; 20, 11, Cyril C. Richardson, ed., *Early Christian Fathers*, pp. 47, 54.

[19] Lactantius, *De Ira Dei* 2; J. P. Migne, *Patrologia Latina*, vol. VII, col. 82.

[20] Origen, *Contra Celsum* 3.15; Migne, *Patrologia Graeca*, vol. XI, col. 940.

[21] Quoted in Foster, *op. cit.*, p. 102. Origen believed in the pre-existence of souls and held reincarnation to be "a very plausible doctrine" (Henry Chadwick, *Early Christian Thought and the Classical Tradition*, p. 115).

the beginning of time.[22] The idea of the Logos, as divine Reason and as the teacher of all mankind, is central to the thought of Origen's predecessor at Alexandria, Clement, the first Christian who may properly be called a scholar in the technical sense of the term (ca. 150-215). Clement specified the first-begotten Son, the Fellow-counselor of God, as the true teacher of the Egyptians, the Indians, the Babylonians and the Persians and affirmed many different covenants of God with men.[23]

The classic formulation, however, of the patristic doctrine of the Logos is to be found in Justin Martyr (ca. 100-165). The obvious intent of Justin and other Christian writers of like mind was that, to use the words of A. C. Bouquet, of "relating the work and person of Jesus Christ to the larger world of Mediterranean thought and of defining His position in relation to other religious teachers."[24] We may therefore appropriately consider the main lines of Justin's thought on this theme.

Justin taught that although the divine Logos appeared in fullness only in Jesus Christ, a "seed" of the Logos was scattered among the whole of mankind long before his manifestation in Jesus of Nazareth. Every human being possesses in his reason a seed (*σπέρμα*) of the Logos. Not only the patriarchs and prophets of the Old Testament, but also pagan philosophers bore a germinal seed (Λόγος σπερμάτικος) of the Logos in their souls. Justin was by no means uncritical of the pagan tradition as a whole; for him it was full of debased practices and its religion essentially corrupt. But he held that those who have lived according to the Logos are Christians,

[22] Origin, *Comm. in Ioan.*, I, 39; Migne, *Patrologia Graeca,* vol. XIV, col. 90 *Comm. in Canticum Cantic.*, II, 62; Migne, *Patrologia Graeca,* vol. XIII, col. 134 Cf. Gregory Thaumaturgus, *In Originem Oratio Panegyrica* XIII; Migne, *Patrologia Graeca,* vol. X, col. 1088.

[23] Clement, *Stromateis* 1.5.16; Claude Mondésert and Marcel Caster, *Les Stromates,* I, 65-69, 108. Clement, *Stromateis* 6, 7; Migne, *Patrologia Graeca,* vol IX, col. 280-288. Cf. *Protrepticus,* VI, 68, 72; Claude Mondésert, *Le Protreptique* pp. 133, 137. Cf. *Protrepticus,* VII, 74; *Le Proteptique,* p. 140. See John E. L. Oulton and Henry Chadwick, *Alexandrian Christianity,* pp. 96-97, where the universal scope of Clement's thought is clearly revealed.

[24] A. C. Bouquet, *The Christian Faith and Non-Christian Religions,* p. 138. Cf. Bouquet's "Revelation and the Divine Logos," Gerald H. Anderson, ed., *The Theology of the Christian Mission,* pp. 183-198. See also Étienne Cornelis, *Valeurs Chrétiennes des Religions Non Chrétiennes,* pp. 67-74.

even though they may have been considered atheists by their contemporaries. He cited as examples Socrates, Heraclitus and others of like spirit among pre-Christian Greeks.[25] Justin's use of the figure of a seed implanted in the human reason suggests in some passages, we may note, a view akin to Stoic impersonal divine immanence, in others a more dynamic and personalistic acitivity.

Justin boldly affirmed that whatever men in any place have nobly spoken is a part of the Christian heritage (*ὅσα οὖν παρὰ πᾶσι καλῶς εἴρηται, ἡμων τῶν Χριστιανῶν ἐστί*). Furthermore, all men who have written, through the seed of the Logos implanted in them, had at least a dim glimpse of the truth.[26] Everything that the philosophers and lawgivers discovered and expressed rightly, they did through their discovery and contemplation of some aspect of the Logos. Their knowledge of the Logos was not complete and hence they often fell into contradictions. Socrates was the most zealous of these, although his knowledge of the Logos was imperfect. Yet the Logos is in every man.[27]

Theophilus of Antioch (fl. ca. 180), to cite one more example among the Greeks, in his apologetical work *Ad Autolycum* strove energetically to demonstrate the greater antiquity as well as moral and religious superiority of Christian faith in its biblical roots over the Greek religious tradition. In the very midst of his argumentation, however, he showed a lively awareness of the whole world of mankind existing under God. Furthermore, he stressed the agreement of things said by Greek poets, philosophers and even the Sibylline oracle with elements of Christian faith. They said things, he asserted, concerning the unity of God, divine righteousness, judgment, punishment and providence that are essentially one with Christian understanding.[28] The framework of this understanding was that of the Logos whom the Father of all, whenever he wishes, sends to a place (as distinguished from the Father, who

[25] Justin Martyr, *The First Apology* 46; T. B. Falls, *Saint Justin Martyr,* p. 83.

[26] Justin Martyr, *The Second Apology* 13; Falls, *op. cit.,* pp. 133-134. Cf. Seneca, *Ad Lucilium Epistulae Morales,* Richard M. Gummere, ed., I, 106.

[27] Justin Martyr, *The Second Apology* 10; Falls, *op. cit.,* pp. 129-130.

[28] Theophilus Antiochenus, *Ad Autolycum,* II, 32, 36-38; Migne, *Patrologia Graeca,* vol. VI, col. 1105, 1109-1120.

may not be confined to a particular place) where he becomes present and is heard and seen.[29]

Among the earliest Latin Christian writers, Minucius Felix, a contemporary of Tertullian, followed essentially the same tradition of understanding as Justin. In his charming dialogue *Octavius,* written in elegant Ciceronian Latin in probably the first decade of the third century, he affirmed that the early Greek philosopher Thales, who taught that God is the mind that formed all things from water, was given this insight by God himself. Furthermore this insight is completely (*penitus*) consonant with the thought of Christians. Minucius found himself in similar agreement with concepts of deity held by Anaximenes and Diogenes of Apollonia. Citing also the views of a number of other thinkers, he asserted that these views, in particular Plato's, are almost the same as the understanding of Christians.[30]

This is not the place for a detailed study of patristic thought on this theme, but the essential point, I believe, is clear. A major stream of early Christian thought was concerned, in the context of faith in the triune God, to maintain the biblical affirmation of the universal creation and providence of God so as to affirm the revelatory and salvific work of God among all men in all times and places.

This cosmopolitan comprehensiveness of thought began to weaken noticeably in the Latin-speaking areas of the Mediterranean world with the breakup of the Roman Empire in the West. Oddly ambivalent elements appear in the thought of a man as great as Augustine. He saw God as the Creator and Controller of the universe, of all things animate and inanimate. He affirmed that the Christian religion constitutes "the simple way for the liberation of souls, for souls can be saved by no way but this." And outside the church no one receives or retains final salvation (*salutem beatitudinis*). Yet he wrote that this way, the reality that is now denoted by the name of Christian religion, had never been lacking to the human race at any period of its history.[31] He taught that unbaptized babies

[29] *Ad Autolycum,* II, 22; Migne, *Patrologia Graeca,* vol. VI, col. 1088.

[30] Minucius Felix, *Octavius* 19; Migne, *Patrologia Latina,* vol. III, col. 304-309.

[31] Augustine, *Retractiones,* I, 12, 3; *Corpus Scriptorum Ecclesiasticorum Latinorum,* XXXVI, 58-59. *De Civitate Dei,* V, 21; XII, 28; X, 32; *Corpus Scriptorum*

are condemned to hell but also affirmed that if Greek philosophers, especially Platonists, had said things that by some chance are true and conformable to our faith (*si qua forte vera et fidei nostrae accommodata*), we should not fear them but claim them for our use as if from unjust possessors.[32] We confront a barbarism in full force, however, in Fulgentius of Ruspe (467-533), a disciple of Augustine, who taught not only that all unbaptized children but even those who die in their mother's womb are eternally damned. He held that all pagans, Jews, heretics and schismatics who die outside the visible (*praesentem*) Catholic Church will go into the everlasting fire prepared for the devil and his angels.[33]

This understanding came to constitute the almost completely unchallenged pattern of thought in the church throughout the early and late Middle Ages. The appearance of Islam was an important factor in hindering in the East further development of the universal understanding of the history of salvation propounded by the early Christian apologists and the Alexandrian theologians. John of Damascus (d. ca. 752) and most later scholastics considered Islam to be a Christian heresy, as earlier theologians had viewed Manichaeism. But the emergence of Islam as an aggressive military and political as well as religious rival of Christendom evidently made it psychologically impossible for most Christians to consider its religious claims with any significant degree of objectivity or fairness. The Fourth Lateran Council in 1215 affirmed in the fullest literal sense the formula of Cyprian that outside the

Ecclesiasticorum Latinorum, vol. XL, 1, pp. 265-257, 613-614, 503-510. In his *Contra Faustum* 19.2 Augustine wrote, "dubitandum non est, et Gentes suos habere prophetas. Necnon et veritatem habere prophetas suos, tam idem Paulus significat, quam etiam Iesus" (Migne, *Patrologia Latina,* vol. XLII, col. 348).

[32] Augustine, *De Doctrina Christiana,* II, 40.60; *Corpus Scriptorum Christianorum, Series Latina,* XXXII, 73. *Opus Imperfectum,* III, 199; Migne, *Patrologia Latina,* vol. XLV, col. 1333. *Sermo CCCXIV,* 3-4; *Patrologia Latina,* vol. XXXVIII, col. 1337. Cf. George Dyer, *Limbo,* pp. 14-17.

[33] Fulgentius, *De Fide,* I, 27, 38; Migne, *Patrologia Latina,* vol. LXV, col. 701, 704. Cf. Philip Schaff, *History of the Christian Church,* III, 866. Indicative of the general medieval tendency to qualify rigid Augustinian views of predestination is the position of Prosperus of Aquitaine (fl. 450), who also reflected the earlier patristic breadth of sympathy with his explicit concept of general divine grace given to all men. *De Vocatione Omnium Gentium,* II, 4-5, 29, 31; Migne, *Patrologia Latina,* vol. LI, col. 690-691, 715-716.

church there is no salvation, although, it should be noted, at the time of Cyprian himself the church of Rome had opposed Cyprian and his party in their interpretation of the formula. Cyprian had insisted that baptism administered by heretics is invalid and that the martyrdom of those not in communion with the Catholic Church is of no value.[34] The Cyprianic formula was affirmed, again in the most unqualified literal sense, by Pope Boniface VIII in his bull *Unam Sanctam* issued in 1302.[35] The Council of Ferrara and Florence (1438-1439) made this position even more explicit by the declaration that "all pagans, Jews, heretics and schismatics have forfeited eternal life and are destined to everlasting fire."[36]

These views in effect conceived of the God and Father of Jesus Christ as essentially the patron deity of Western peoples and his salvific work as practically confined to persons explicitly Christian. We are now able to see that this understanding was in no small measure due to the geographical and cultural isolation of western Christendom from the rest of the world after the breakdown of the Roman Empire in the West. One has the feeling that certain elements in the thought of Augustine and his Christian contemporaries were appreciably affected by their experience of a crumbling empire and narrowing cultural horizons in the context of alliance between church and state. Not until Abelard (1079-1142) do we find a forthright questioning of Augustine's teaching that unbaptized children suffer in hell. Abelard's primary concern was to turn the punishment of such children into a privative separation from God rather than a positive suffering of the pains of fire; his view was not intended to speak to the condition of non-Christians. Yet when Peter Lombard (1100?-1160) took up Abelard's concept, which later became known through the term "limbo" coined by Albertus Magnus, it spread through-

[34] Cyprian, *De catholicae ecclesiae unitate* 6; *Corpus Scriptorum Ecclesiasticorum Latinorum*, vol. III, pars I, pp. 214-215. Cyprian does not use the formula in this passage but develops the thought with rigor: "Habere non potest Deum patrem, qui ecclesiam non habet matrem." The phrase "salus extra ecclesiam non est" occurs in *Epistulae LXXIII*, 21; *Corpus Scriptorum Ecclesiasticorum*, vol. III, pars II, p. 795.

[35] Henry Bettenson, *Documents of the Christian Church*, pp. 161-163.

[36] Cf. Karl Adam, *The Spirit of Catholicism*, pp. 172, 175.

out the universities of Europe using the Latin language.[37] It marked the reemergence of a certain cultural independence and a more "humane" spirit.

Thomas Aquinas (1225-1274) may properly be considered as at once the greatest mind and most representative theological figure of the high Middle Ages. He accepted and developed the concept of "limbo" but otherwise affirmed the prevailing belief that outside the formal structure of the Roman church and its sacraments there is no salvation. He recognized, however, the possibility of the salvation of Gentiles in the past through implicit faith in divine providence.[38] We see in Dante essentially the same theological position but with a broader and deeper sympathy for classical culture and thereby for classical man that became one of the characteristic marks of the early Renaissance. We may note in this context that the dominant attitude toward Christian heretics in the late Middle Ages was less tolerant than that toward members of other religions, although as yet few Europeans apart from Spain and Sicily had existential contacts with non-Christian persons or cultures.

Some sense of the wider world of men of course existed in the Middle Ages in particular as a result of the Crusades, the development of Venetian trade and the aforesaid contacts in Spain and Sicily. This awareness, however, developed into something far more existential and related to explicit knowledge through the voyages of exploration. This remarkable movement in the history of mankind, so pregnant with consequences for the West—and the world—may be said to have begun with Henry the Navigator of Portugal in the first half of the fifteenth century and bore such notable fruit through Christopher Columbus, Vasco da Gama, Ferdinand Magellan and many others. As a consequence of these events new perspectives emerged, and we note in Roman Catholic theologians of the sixteenth century such as Bellarmine and Suarez,

[37] Cf. Dyer, *op. cit.*, pp. 39-60.

[38] St. Thomas Aquinas, *Summa Theologica*, pt. III, q. 61, art. 1; pt II-II, q. 2, art. 7, pp. 2352, 1185. Cf. *Quaestiones Disputatae, De Veritate*, q. 14, art. 11, pp. 301-304. Bonaventura was able through his use of the concept of "appropriations" to allow certain authentic knowledge of God among the Greek philosophers (Cousins, *op. cit.*, p. 490).

and affirmed by the Council of Trent, concepts unknown to medieval scholasticism. In particular, the affirmation was made that baptism (and thereby salvation) could be received not only, as by Christians, with water (*in re*) but by desire (*in voto*).[39] A process was thus initiated that at first enabled men to make important qualifications to the Cyprianic formula. It has now come around full circle to the end of reaffirming the less rigorous position of the church of Rome of the time of Cyprian and enabling modern Catholics to participate once again in the spiritual and cultural cosmopolitanism of the early church at its highest levels.

Another factor of very great importance in creating wider understanding of the world and of mankind was the restoration of knowledge of Greek culture in Western Europe. Nicholas of Cusa (1401-1464) was a key figure in this work, but a further consequence of his trip to Constantinople in 1437 was that he returned with the vision of reconciling Christianity with Islam, almost on the eve of the Council of Florence! In his book *De Pace Fidei,* written in 1453, he anticipated the position of the eighteenth century Enlightenment by stating that there is in fact only one religion, the cult of those who live according to the principles of wisdom. The worship even of the gods of pagan polytheism witnesses to the one God, and the divine Logos affirms the essential concord and unity of the great religions.[40] Although by no means representative of contemporary orthodoxy, other humanists of the fifteenth and sixteenth centuries began to concern themselves with the problem of Christian evaluation of the other religious traditions on the basis of different perspectives from those of the medieval church. Besides Nicholas of Cusa (Cues on the Moselle River) we may note the names of Pico della Mirandola, Erasmus and Francisco de Vitoria among a number of kindred spirits.[41] Through their studies of the great writers of antiquity they came to appreciate in a new way particularly the ethical concerns of the "noblest intellects of Greece and Rome." Early Renaissance humanism had a strong moral pur-

[39] Cf. Hans Küng, *Freedom Today*, p. 119.

[40] *De pace fidei* 10-12, 16-18, 68; *Nikolaus von Kues Werke,* Paul Wilpert, ed., I, 341-342, 344, 366.

[41] Cf. Heinz Robert Schlette, *Towards a Theology of Religions,* pp. 23-24.

pose and found much in Homer and Plato, Cicero, Virgil, Seneca and Plutarch that accorded with its own sense of Christian morality.

A distinguished example of a more "humane" view of the religious situation of the non-Christian world was the Spanish Jesuit, like Nicholas of Cusa a high prelate of the church, Juan Cardinal de Lugo (1583-1660). De Lugo held that "God gives light, sufficient for its salvation, to every soul that attains to the use of reason in this life . . . the human soul, in all times and places, has a certain natural affinity for, and need of, truth . . . the various philosophical schools and religious bodies throughout mankind all contain and hand down, amid various degrees of human error and distortion, *some* truth, some gleams and elements of divine truth . . . the soul that in good faith seeks God, His truth and love, concentrates its attention, under the influence of grace, upon those elements of truth, be they many or few, which are offered to it in the sacred books and religious schools and assemblies of the Church, Sect, or Philosophy in which it has been brought up. It feeds upon these elements, the others are simply passed by; and divine grace, under cover of these elements, feeds and saves this soul."[42]

It should be noted that Cardinal de Lugo presupposed the work of divine grace in all men; he did not ascribe men's knowledge of truth and their responsible action in accordance therewith solely to their discernment of the "natural law." The formulation, however, of the doctrine of natural law in Thomistic-Aristotelian theology was characterized by an optimistic conception of nature, and this outlook, nourished by certain of the ideas of Christian humanists and later by the more tolerant perspectives of the Enlightenment, helped to keep the humane tradition of world understanding alive in the Roman Catholic Church. The views of contemporary Catholics like Karl Rahner, Heinz Robert Schlette, Hans Küng, Raymond Panikkar and Klaus Klostermaier are in the direct line of this tradition, even as they represent a reemergence of the perspectives of the early church.

42 This quotation constitutes the summary of de Lugo's views given by Friedrich von Hügel, *Essays and Addresses on the Philosophy of Religion*, p. 252.

The working of the process, however, has been slow and often painful. We note that the great apostle to the Indies, Francis Xavier, also believed that unbaptized persons go to hell and derived no little of his motivation to missionary service from this conviction. Possibly first in Japan, however, Xavier came to grapple more directly with the problem of whether divine injustice was inherent in the notion that men are committed to hell even though they have no chance to hear the gospel and worship God with explicitly Christian faith. He and his co-workers, therefore, began to explain to Japanese questioners who were concerned over the fate of their ancestors that the Creator of all peoples had taught them his moral law directly through their minds and consciences.[43]

The major Protestant Reformers held views little different from Xavier's regarding the salvation of the heathen, but for a variety of reasons, which we cannot discuss here, largely failed to follow out missionary imperatives implicit in their theology. We note, however, that the early Reformer Zwingli acknowledged the work of the Spirit of God beyond the formal "boundaries" of the Christian church. Certain early Anabaptist and Spiritual writers appear to have had similar views. Balthasar Hubmaier wrote that "God gives power and capacity to all men in so far as they themselves desire it." Sebastian Franck wrote in his letter to John Campanus: "God is no respecter of persons but instead is to the Greeks as to the barbarian and the Turk, to the lord as to the servant, so long as they retain the light which has shined upon them and gives their heart an eternal glow."[44]

The knowledge of the wider world that came to Europe as a result of the voyages of exploration penetrated more slowly into the lands north of the Alps. This knowledge, however, coupled with the long-working north- and westward movement of the Renaissance and the vast effects of the Reformation itself, clearly constituted an important part of the historical factors contributing to the great religious movement in Protestant lands that was called Pietism on the continent, evangelicalism or revivalism in English-speaking countries.

[43] Georg Schurhammer and Joseph Wicki, *Epistolae S. Francisci Xaverii Aliaque eius Scripta*, II, 266. Cf. Okada Akio, *Kirishitan Bateren*, pp. 44-45.

[44] G. H. Williams, *Spiritual and Anabaptist Writers*, pp. 129, 150.

An important consequence of this great movement was that belief was taken seriously in a new and explicit way. If faith in God through Jesus Christ was understood, on the basis of the experience of the Reformation, to be the sole means of salvation, the further consequence that "unbelief must necessarily entail damnation" was according to the still largely unquestioned tradition of medieval Christendom. For the major part of the movement damnation meant separation from God in hell for all eternity. But differently from the mainstream of early Protestant orthodoxy, men of Pietist conviction were led by their belief in the horrifying fate of "those without Christ," as this category was then understood, into a new awareness and lively concern for the peoples of Asia, Africa, the Americas and the islands of the southern seas.[45] Through their Christian faith they understood God himself to have compassion and a boundless desire for the salvation of all men, and their own missionary activity they held to be a specific consequence of that compassionate concern. The Moravians even had the modern—and ancient—conviction that Jesus Christ, through the Holy Spirit, had long been present and at work in the whole world to create disciples for his church.

Thus while important elements of Pietist and Evangelical faith were uncritically in accord with the medieval theological tradition, their perspectives contributed in time to more adequate theological understanding of the wider presence and work of God in the world of his creation. If missionaries of this tradition were in their own persons expressive of the divine concern, their personal experiences led the more perceptive into an awareness of wider manifestations of that concern. Specifically, some came to see signs of the divine presence and work in traditionally non-Christian lands in both past and present. They saw that apart from some such awareness they were in danger of depicting the God and Father of Jesus Christ

[45] Cf. H. J. Margull, "The Awakening of Protestant Missions," *History's Lessons for Tomorrow's Missions*, pp. 142-146. A significant exception to prevailing views is found in George Fox and the Society of Friends, who follow in the tradition of the "spiritual writers" of the Reformation period. Fox came to believe that every man receives from the Lord an inner light, which if faithfully followed will lead to a direct and saving knowledge of God (Rufus M. Jones, *The Journal of George Fox*, pp. 100-101).

as a tribal deity. They began to perceive increasingly the need for Christian converts to understand the spiritual and ethical tradition of their own peoples in a positive as well as critical way. It was important for men in these lands to know that God and Christ and church belonged in some way also to their past as to their present and future. Out of these soul-searching and often agonizing reappraisals of faith have come the theological perspectives that have made possible the rethinking and revaluation of the religions of the world that now play such an important role in the contemporary theological scene. It is as a participant in this tradition that I wish to attempt theological understanding of the life and teaching of the Buddha.

2

BIBLICAL PERSPECTIVES

The earlier and larger portion of this work has been written largely within the framework of the discipline of the history of religions. This discipline itself properly includes hermeneutics, that is, the interpretation of religious experience and its cultic and societal expressions. In the tradition of Joachim Wach and Gerardus van der Leeuw the goal of the discipline has been to seek understanding, not the mere accumulation of encyclopedic facts. Wach even urged scholars in the field to make value judgments, that is, appraisals of religious quality. This tradition, however, has tended to refrain from the use of metaphysical or theological dimensions in its search for understanding.[46]

Other scholars, however, feel that studies of religion that confine themselves to descriptive statements of phenomena historiographically reported, even though considered in terms of "qualitative" value, are unwarrantedly truncated. Most adherents of the religions of mankind consider the transcendental, sacred or "other" aspects of their faith-practice to be indis-

[46] Cf. Joseph M. Kitagawa, ed., *The History of Religions*, passim; G. van der Leeuw, *Religion in Essence and Manifestation*, II, 645-646, 671-695.

pensably central, and in consequence the study of religions cannot remain aloof from concern with questions of meaning and value that go beyond the stage of historical phenomena evaluated primarily in a "humanistic" context. Friedrich Heiler, for one, held that religion properly possesses orientation toward transcendent Reality and that its "essence" (*Wesen*) involves the communion of man with this Reality.[47] I do not wish to enter into a discussion of the problem of the "essence" of religion, but I believe that Heiler is right in insisting upon an extension of scholarly concern into the area of the transcendent. Furthermore, no man concerns himself with such matters in a vacuum. He must operate from his own position of spiritual understanding. I believe, therefore, that there is a place, even within the context of the discipline of the history of religions, for consideration of the religions of mankind from a clearly acknowledged position of faith and theological understanding.

My intent, accordingly, in this concluding essay is to attempt a preliminary evaluation of the life and teachings of the Buddha from the specific vantage point of Christian faith, using the primary criteria of evaluation generally presupposed in this faith, the person and teachings of Jesus the Christ as witnessed to by the New Testament and given structure by the Old. This is specifically to try to find religious meaning and value in the life and teachings of the Buddha as these may be discerned in the light of the criteria accepted. It also means to inquire as to the potential significance of the phenomena in terms of what in Christian tradition is called salvation history. Put in another way, the question may be asked, In what sense and to what extent can the presence and work of God the Father of Jesus Christ be discerned in the phenomena under consideration? In terms of our understanding of the necessary relationship of the work of the triune God in creation and in redemption, affirmation of the divine presence and work means work with revelatory and salvific intent. We are therefore to look for the signs of the saving as well as revelatory work of God in his creation, in this case in the life and

[47] Friedrich Heiler, *Erscheinungsformen und Wesen der Religion*, p. 564.

teachings of the Buddha, using the criteria of their manifestation in the Christ event.[48]

There are those who may regard questions of this kind as not only exceedingly difficult but spiritually presumptuous. But if we are required, for our spiritual sanity, to ask them, with both critical and affirmative intent, of Christianity seen as an empirical movement in human history, the historical and theological imperatives of our time compel us to ask them also of other religious traditions. The larger context, however, from which these imperatives emerge, enables us, I believe, to ask these questions with a freedom and specificity beyond that which most of our forefathers were able to do.

We may properly begin, I feel, with a brief recapitulation of the biblical witness as this is germane to our problem. This witness, we may note again, is focused on the understanding of God as the transcendent Creator of heaven and earth and all things therein, including man. The other primary point of the biblical ellipse of divine work is seen in the concept of universal divine providence, which we shall consider with emphasis upon its revelatory and salvific aspects. This is to see the history of salvation not as universal in the sense of a universally guaranteed salvation, but as touching all men in all times and places.

The theological perspective that includes the entire world and the whole of mankind within its ken and therefore encompasses the whole into some kind of integral relationship to God is found throughout the Bible. The book of Genesis begins with God's creation of the world and of man (Adam), not with the Israelites. It is man who is made in the image of God (Gen. 1:26-27). According to the priestly tradition, Yahweh established a covenant with Noah so as to include "every living creature of all flesh that is upon the earth" (Gen. 9:16). We may note that the later rabbinic tradition acknowledged on the basis of the Noachian covenant the existence of a universal divine rule with positive religious significance for the nations.

[48] We may recall that Paul in Rom. 1:19 affirms that what is known of God by all men he revealed to them. And Paul Tillich has rightly emphasized that we can never separate revelation and salvation (*The Future of Religions*, p. 81). The theological legitimacy of this kind of work from the standpoint of a particular tradition of faith is forthrightly asserted by Wolfhart Pannenberg, *Basic Questions in Theology*, II, 65-118 (*n.b.* p. 70).

The covenant with Abraham was understood as subsisting within this larger structure of relationships, and its particularity or narrower ethnic scope was effected only for a universal restorative purpose, that "by you all the families of the earth will bless themselves" (Gen. 12:3).

At least from the beginning of the period of the literary prophets Israel clearly regarded Yahweh as Creator and Lord of the universe and therefore Lord of the nations as well as of Israel. The Old Testament consistently assumes that the nations have some knowledge of Yahweh and his ethical demands, even as they are under his lordship and within his concern. In the day of the Lord men and nations are to be judged by their ethical performance, in accordance with their knowledge.[49] The unique personal knowledge of Yahweh and his will ascribed by the prophets to Israel carried a corresponding responsibility.[50] A further affirmation is made that Yahweh uses the nations in both his saving and punitive activity toward Israel.[51] We find in the Old Testament numerous references to "just Gentiles": Abel, Enoch, Noah, Daniel (as in Ezek. 14:14), Job, Melchizedek, Lot, the Queen of Sheba.[52] Among these are prophetic figures, such as Balaam and Job, as well as the priest-king Melchizedek.[53] Other men and women from among the nations are depicted with approval in the Old Testament.[54] Men of the nations are recorded as truly worshiping the Lord.[55] In the Wisdom books we note a recognition of the value of the wisdom of the nations.[56] The "anointed guardian cherub" assigned by the Lord God to the king of Tyre in Ezekiel 28:14-16 seems to represent a specific instance of the prophetic understanding of divine providence at work among the nations. This constitutes one form of the

[49] Mal. 3:18; Jer. 7:3-4; Ezek. 16:44-58; Zech. 1:15; 7:8-9; Zeph. 1:3, 9, 18.

[50] Hos. 13:4; Isa. 51:7; Amos 3:2. Cf. Jer. 7:30-34; Hos. 7:12; Mic. 3:1-4; Mal. 2:8-9.

[51] Isa. 44:28; 45:1-5. Cf. Isa. 41:25; 28:11; Dan. 9:26; Hab. 1:5-6, 12; Jer. 25:9; Ezek. 5:6-8. We note in II Kings 5:1 that Yahweh is credited with giving military victory to Syria through the valorous Syrian general Naaman.

[52] Cf. Jean Daniélou, *Holy Pagans of the Old Testament*, passim.

[53] Num. 22:1-25; Gen. 14:18-20; Ps. 110:4.

[54] Gen. 38:1-30; Exod. 2:5-10; 18:1-27; Josh. 2:1-21; Ruth.

[55] Exod. 18:10-12; Jon. 1:16.

[56] Jer. 49:7; Obad. 8. Cf. I Kings 4:30-31. See C. F. Fritsch, *The Interpreter's Bible*, IV, 767, 947.

concept in late Judaism by which an angel was assigned to each nation to signify, in personified guise, the divine presence and vocation appertaining to each. Similar is *First Clement* (29:2).

With regard more specifically to evaluation of the religious beliefs and practices of the nations, we find in the Old Testament more than one theological position. The ferocity of Deuteronomy 7:2, 5 is representative of one view, of which Elijah's recorded killing of four hundred and fifty prophets of Baal is a notable historical example (I Kings 18:40). In general, however, we find more discriminating appraisals, although idols are consistently regarded, especially by the later prophets, as nothing, as a delusion. The widening historical experience of Israel brought widened views; acquaintance with the Persian Empire beginning with Cyrus brought Israel for the first time into contact with ethical monotheism of a high level outside of itself, that of Zoroastrianism. Here the Jews met with religion of a different ethical and spiritual quality from what their ancestors had known in the worship of the Baalim and Ashtaroth. In Malachi we find the suggestion that Yahweh is worshiped throughout the world under the guise of every man's worship (Mal. 1:5, 11, 14; cf. Isa. 28:11). A basic theme of the book of Jonah is the universal concern of Yahweh as the background for its depiction of the responsibility of Israel. In this context we understand that the election of Israel was for service, not for privilege.[57] Nowhere in the Old Testament do we find the notion that God's salvation, a term whose meaning developed considerably during the Old Testament period, is denied the nations because they are not of Israel.[58]

In the New Testament we see that the Logos was sent to the whole created universe (τὰ ἴδια, John 1:11).[59] God's love for

[57] H. H. Rowley, *The Biblical Doctrine of Election*, p. 52. Cf. I. Pet. 2:9.

[58] Statements like Isa. 60:2 are more descriptive of Israel's commission than of eschatological judgment. The foreigners (*ben-hannēkhār*) of Isa. 56:3, 6, who do not reside in Palestine—to be distinguished from the *gēr*, or resident aliens—may refer to others than circumcised proselytes.

[59] The AV translation of τὰ ἴδια in John 1:11 as "his own" and therefore to be naturally understood by readers as identical in meaning with "his own" (οἱ ἴδιοι—his own people) in the second part of the verse is most unfortunate. The RSV "his own home" is little better. The Jerusalem Bible's "his own domain" more properly gives the meaning of the Greek, which by the use of the neuter plural was evidently intended to denote the whole of creation.

the world is seen as the basic premise of his action (John 3:16), as a reality prior to the singling out of Israelites or Christians. We do not have space to consider in detail the teaching of Jesus with regard to the nations, but we may note one or two items that give us a key to the main lines of the biblical account. In Luke 12:47-48 we find the clearest exposition of the prophetic conviction that the judgments of God relate primarily to the ethical quality of men's deeds and that higher knowledge brings higher responsibility. The saying of Jesus in this passage, that the servant who knew but did not act in accordance with his master's will shall be more severely treated than he who so acted but did not know, expresses what H. J. Cadbury called the principle of proportionate duty.[60] The particularity of election cited in the Bible and the diversity of personal endowments given men are both properly to be understood by means of this principle, which seems basic to the whole of Jesus' teaching and practice.

The context of Jesus' assertion to his disciples of God's fatherly concern, that the very hairs of their head are all numbered (Matt. 10:30), implies that the affirmation applies to all men. For even in the case of sparrows, "not one of them is forgotten before God" (Luke 12:6), nor will one fall to the ground apart from the Father's will (Matt. 10:29). The heavenly Father "makes his sun rise on the evil and on the good, and sends rain on the just and the unjust" (Matt. 5:45). Jesus was clearly free of nationalistic or ethnic feelings of hatred against either Samaritans or Romans and specifically rejected all notions of arbitrary divine vengeance, eschatological or present, upon the nations.[61] Luke cites statements of Jesus that were particularly phrased to show God's concern for those outside historic Israel (Luke 4:26-27).

Problems of literary and historical criticism inevitably come to the fore when we note that specific criticism of Gentile religious mores ascribed to Jesus is found in Matthew alone in the Synoptic Gospels.[62] There is reason to believe, however, that Jesus considered the Jews to have been granted certain spiritual endowments beyond those given the nations, but the

[60] H. J. Cadbury, *Jesus: What Manner of Man?*, p. 23. Cf. Luke 12:48.

[61] Cf. Matt. 19:30; 20:16; Mark 10:31; Luke 13:30; Matt. 12:41-42; 11:21-24; Luke 9:51-56.

[62] Matt. 6:7, 32 (John 4:22). But cf. Matt. 11:21-24.

clear thrust of his message was that they would for that reason be held to account all the more severely.[63] And special notice should be taken of his appreciation of the religious faith and ethical conduct of certain Gentiles.[64] Indeed, we read that "he that is not against us is for us" (Mark 9:40; cf. John 10:16). And not he who proclaims the "name" or even performs miracles but he who does the will of the Father shall enter the kingdom (Matt. 7:21-23; 25:14-46; cf. I Cor. 13; Luke 13:22-30; 10:25-37).

Turning to the book of Acts we note the statement of Peter in the house of Cornelius, the Roman centurion, that "truly I perceive that God shows no partiality, but in every nation any one who fears him and does what is right is acceptable to him" (10:34-35; cf. Luke 2:14). Peter's words as recorded in Acts 4:12 are properly understood in the larger context constituted by his affirmation before Cornelius. This affirmation was evidently intended by the author of Acts to appear as a corrective of 4:12 ("And there is salvation in no one else, for there is no other name under heaven given among men by which we must be saved"). Not only does it appear later in the narration of events; it is cited as the result of Peter's experience of what he believed to be divine revelation correcting his former understanding. A few chapters later we find Paul at Lystra of Lycaonia asserting a view (14:15-17) essentially similar to that of Peter's corrected understanding.

In the famous address of Paul to the Athenians recorded in Acts 17:16-34 we find that Paul was critical of idol worship and assumed that he must instruct his hearers more particularly as to who and what God really is and what he had done in Jesus Christ. But he boldly asserted the solidarity of all men, that the whole of the Greek past as well as the Hebrew had been under the providential care and within the purposes of God. Furthermore, he asserted that not only had the Greeks been zealous in their religious devotion, even in their ignorance they had worshiped the one, true God. In his earlier message at Lystra Paul specifically affirmed that God had not left himself without witness throughout the entire range of the history of mankind before Christ.

[63] Cf. Luke 13:28-29; Matt. 8:11-12; 5:20; 10:15; 11:21, 23.

[64] Matt. 8:5-13 (Luke 7:1-12; John 4:46-54); Luke 10:30-37; 17:11-19.

The *locus classicus* for Paul's treatment of the place of the nations in the economy of God is the first three chapters of Romans. His contention in Romans 1:19-32 is that the fact of God, his nature as eternal power and deity, is knowable to all men through his creation. But Paul does not say that this knowledge is attained by the exercise of human reason alone, for "God has shown it to them" (Rom. 1:19). He further contends that God's law or basic moral requirements are written in the consciences of the Gentiles (Rom. 2:15). And the main thrust of Romans 2 is a Pauline exposition of what again we may call the principle of proportionate duty. Israel's election and related "advantages" are real (Rom. 2:17-18). But if Israel is unfaithful to God and disobedient to his law, the whole structure of advantage is demolished, for God shows no partiality (Rom. 2:25, 11). "He will render to every man according to his works" (Rom. 2:6); he is the God of the Gentiles as well as of the Jews (Rom. 3:29). Paul shares the view of other New Testament writers that the Mosaic law itself was communicated through the intermediation of angels (Gal. 3:19; Acts 7:53; Heb. 2:2). In light of the concept in late Judaism of the divinely assigned role of angels among the nations, this view may have constituted the predominant apostolic understanding of the mode of divine working among the nations as well as within Israel. Perhaps we see Paul at his most mature and mellow point of growth in his letter from prison to the church in Philippi, in which he urges the Christians there to be open to all truth and goodness wherever found (Phil. 4:8). We note universal perspectives in Col. 1:12-20; 2:9-10; Eph. 1:22-23; 4:9-10.

We do not have space to pursue this biblical inquiry in more detail, but we may confidently affirm an essential unity in both Old and New Testaments with regard to the following points. Israel and the nations are equally the creation of God, equally the object of his love and concern. Differences, however, are held to obtain in the mode and degree of divine revelation to men. In particular, the people of Israel and then the "people of God" in the new aeon, the Christian church, are believed to participate in a unique covenantal relationship with the God of all men. This relationship, however, is for service, not for privilege, that the "people of God" may serve as special instruments for the fulfillment of his purposes toward all mankind. This service is properly performed in the context of awareness of the ancient (Noachian) divine covenant with all men. All men have some light, revealed to them by God himself, and the judgments of the Eternal are proportioned to the degree of the true light men have received and to the ethical quality of their response. The central message of the prologue of the gospel of John is of a universal divine acting and speaking, for the Logos is "the true light that enlightens every man" (John 1:9; cf. 1:4, 16; 10:16; I John 2:2; 4:7, 16).[65]

3

CLARIFICATION OF CRITERIA

The primary purpose of the preceding theological and biblical excursus has been to establish that the best theological thought of the early church concurred with the central witness of the Scriptures to affirm that God is one and the Creator of the whole universe, that his providential and fatherly care extend to the whole of his creation and that through all three persons of the Trinity he is and always has been working with both revelatory and salvific intent among all men.[66]

If then in the context of biblical faith and of early and recurring streams of Christian theology we affirm without hesitation the presence and work of the Spirit of God at all times and in all places of his creation, a further and more difficult question may be asked. This is the question whether and to what extent a particular person or movement within the freedom and ambiguities of human history may be said to manifest such moral and spiritual qualities as to reflect or

[65] John 14:17 should properly be interpreted in the larger context seen in John 1:9. Raymond Panikkar, following Jean Daniélou, uses the term "Cosmic Covenant" to denote the universal scope of the Noachian covenant (*The Unknown Christ of Hinduism,* pp. 58-59). Regarding the Johannine literature see J. Edgar Bruns, *The Christian Buddhism of St. John.*

[66] Cf. Kenneth Cragg's "The neighbourhood of man is constituted in the Saviourhood of God" (*Christianity in World Perspective,* p. 16).

manifest with a certain perceptible distinctiveness the presence and work of the God whom, through Christian faith, we acknowledge as the Father proclaimed and revealed through Jesus of Nazareth, the Christ. Beset with difficulties though this kind of question may be, we now proceed to ask it of Gautama the Buddha. We shall do so on the basis of the historical studies in the first section of this work and use the criteria of judgment and theological principles affirmed above. We may properly, however, first attempt to give further specificity and sharpness to the criteria to be employed.

We noted in considering the life of the Buddha the criterion that he is recorded as offering in answer to a question as to how to distinguish between true and false teachers. His reply was in effect that men should judge for themselves and their criterion of judgment should be whether the teachings "when performed and undertaken" lead to moral loss and sorrow or the reverse, to the ethical disintegration of a man or to his moral and spiritual development. This is to say that the criterion of religious authenticity for the Buddha was quality of ethical content and its fruit in life.

This mode of evaluation seems remarkably similar to that of the Christ, who—in spite of Matthew's evident use of the material to serve his own contemporary purposes—was assuredly the author of the criterion that men are known by their fruits of conduct. This is the primary means by which his followers are to test the religious authenticity of men. Names and particular professions of faith do not appear to have primary meaning in such a context.[67]

Another biblical passage that is meaningful in this context is the following: "He who receives a righteous man because he is a righteous man shall receive a righteous man's reward" (Matt. 10:41). Some scholars hold that the writer of Matthew wished the term "righteous man" to be understood as "tested and honored Christians."[68] But if the saying comes from Jesus, as

[67] Matt. 7:15-23; 11:9; 12:33-35; Luke 6:43-45. Cf. Matt. 25:31-46; John 14:11. This criterion was the one which Jeremiah employed as primary in his evaluation of the contemporary "false prophets" in Judah (Jer. 23:14-22). Cf. Alfred Guillaume, *Prophecy and Divination*, pp. 349, 353; *Didachē*, 11, 8-12, Kirsopp Lake, tr., *The Apostolic Fathers*, I, 327.

[68] Cf. *The Interpreter's Bible*, VII, 377.

is very likely, we may confidently affirm that he thought with wider reference, as is suggested by his praise of the Roman centurion: "not even in Israel have I found such faith" (Matt. 8:10). The import of the prior verse, then, is that reward is cosmically assured to him who acknowledges and receives an ethically good man just because he is a good man. The followers of Jesus are presumably expected to recognize, appreciate and appropriately accept a good man wherever he may be.

The testimony of all the evidence is that Gautama the Buddha was such a man. The early texts of Buddhism are unanimous in affirming that men and women of every class among his contemporaries regarded him as a man of singularly noble conduct and concern for others. We find some opposition to certain of his teachings, criticism of his style of life as too easy, perhaps some distaste for his person, but no accusation of serious moral fault has come down to us. We note again the statement recorded of Peter in the book of Acts: "in every nation any one who fears him [God] and does what is right is acceptable to him."[69] If the Buddha did not fear God in the personalized way in which he was known in Israel, he respected *Karma,* which is just, revered *Dharma,* which is lovely, and aspired to *Nirvāṇa,* which is bliss and deathless Reality. And even Israel would not question his having done "what is right." This interpretation, I believe, leads inescapably to the conclusion that in some authentic way the Buddha was, and is, "acceptable" to God. If acceptable to the God of the biblical tradition, can he properly be altogether alien to believers in this God?

Our context of thought, let us recall, is the biblical faith that God is One, the Creator and Sustainer of the universe. His providence is universal, to the extent that the number of the hairs of men's heads is known to him, not a sparrow is forgotten before him. The emergence in human history, therefore, of a man of the ethical life-quality and spiritual perception of the Buddha cannot be imagined as apart from the presence and work of God in the world. This is not to say that the life and teaching of the Buddha are entirely or perfectly

[69] Acts 10:35. Cf. James 1:27.

representative of the work of God. I suggest only that they may be so in important part. Let us consider more concretely how this may be.

4

BASIC EVALUATIONS

The teaching of the Buddha consists of two main themes: an analysis of the empirical situation of man, which he found basically unsatisfying, and the way of deliverance from this situation into a condition of life completely satisfying. The first of the Four Noble Truths denoted the universality of suffering, in the sense of basic dis-ease, in phenomenal existence as such. In the Second Noble Truth the Buddha affirmed the root cause of this suffering to lie in the craving of sentient beings for that which does not satisfy, a craving that is the result of a misplaced sense of values. The Buddha included within the category of that which does not and cannot satisfy the whole of phenomenal existence as the latter is commonly understood. He held therefore that neither the whole of phenomenal existence nor any part of it is worthy of craving or attachment in an ultimate or religious sense, and to grasp after it as if it were so worthy is radically to misunderstand its value and is primarily responsible for the cosmically as well as personally unsatisfying situation of empirical man.

The Buddha saw the whole of phenomenal existence, all "form and name," as participating in a process of endless change, and an axiom of his thought was that the Real is changeless.[70] Anything and everything that changes—the Buddha perceived process change largely in the sense of deterioration and disintegration—must therefore by definition be "unreal." The Buddha was too much of a practical realist to regard the physical universe as *māyā*, or illusion, but he saw it as specifically other than the truly or ultimately Real and Dependable. The entire realm of phenomenal existence for the

[70] Cf. James 1:17.

Buddha, then, in terms of its fitness to minister to the ultimate needs and destiny of man, was neither satisfying, dependable nor truly real. This is clearly an example of what has come to be called a desacralized religious view of the world such as was held by the most creative figures of the "Axial Period," as this latter term was used by Karl Jaspers to denote the activity of formative religious personages appearing in India, China, Persia, Israel and Greece between 800 and 200 B.C.[71]

Biblical teaching regarding the phenomenal universe is that it is the creation of God, who alone is ultimate and independent Reality. It is, therefore, at essential points other than God, specifically contingent, dependent and not independently or ultimately real.[72] Any attempt to offer to the whole or any part of the created universe—material, physical or spiritual—the kind of ultimate devotion or commitment that is owed only to God the Bible calls idolatry, which is for the Bible the essence of sin, the distortion of right personal relationships, the misplacement of ultimate values. Also, while the Bible teaches that the creation in itself is "good" (Gen. 1:31), it affirms with equal if not greater emphasis, as in the myth of the "Fall," that the situation of empirical man is full of suffering as a consequence of his yielding to the temptation to choose the universe, or its parts, before God.[73] Christian exaltation of the Christ, it should be noted, is properly in the context of Jesus' representative character, which always points and is subordinate to the Father.[74]

We may say therefore that the Buddha is at one with the witness of the Bible in affirming that man's proper relationship

[71] Karl Jaspers, *The Origin and Goal of History*, pp. 1-21. A. C. Bouquet prefers to extend the period to about A.D. 300 and, in the case of Egypt, to before 800 B.C. (*The Christian Faith and Non-Christian Religions*, pp. 47, 56, 405).

[72] Cf. Karl Rahner and Herbert Vorgrimler, *Theological Dictionary*, pp. 90-100.

[73] In the context of biblical thought sin as rebellion or rejection of God generally takes the religious or quasi-religious form of exalting that which is not God, including oneself or one's own will, to the place of God. Viewed negatively, according to Reinhold Niebuhr, the distinctively Christian doctrine of sin sees its origin to lie in "man's willful refusal to acknowledge the finite and determinate character of his existence" (*The Nature and Destiny of Man*, I, 177). Cf. Matt. 6:24 (Matt. 6:19-21): "No one can serve two masters"; I Cor. 10:14.

[74] Cf. Mark 10:18 (Matt. 19:17; Luke 18:19); Phil. 2:7-8; I Cor. 15:28. For a suggestive treatment of the theme see Dorothee Sölle, *Christ the Representative*, pp. 67-71, 101-152.

to the phenomenal universe is *not* to give it ultimate value or devotion and that a primary cause of the suffering and inadequacy experienced by men lies in their giving it or any of its parts such value.

This kinship of affirmation, however, regarding the proper relationship of man to phenomenal existence should not be understood to imply a complete similarity in ethos of evaluation. We noted passages in early Buddhist Scriptures that emphasize meditation on the loathsomeness of the physical as a proper spiritual exercise. While this particular emphasis may have originated in the later monastic communities and not with the Buddha, its role in the later tradition cannot be denied. Over against this emphasis, however, we noted other passages in the early texts that make more positive affirmations, especially as to the high possibilities available to men in this life. Going beyond the formal purview of this book, we may mention that the early Mahāyāna Buddhist thinkers, as well as later Zen and Pure Land representatives, made what we now call anti-monastic, anti-ascetic protests against certain developments within Buddhist monasticism in the name and, as they evidently believed, in the spirit of the Buddha.

The Bible, moreover, is not without strongly negative statements regarding the empirical world. Jesus is recorded as once having addressed his hearers, presumably his disciples, as you "who are evil" (Matt. 7:11). Paul saw the whole of creation as subjected to futility and groaning in travail until now (Rom. 8:20, 22). Peter quoted Isaiah to the effect that "All flesh is like grass and all its glory like the flower of grass" (I Pet. 1:14). James wrote: "What is your life? For you are a mist that appears for a little time and then vanishes" (James 4:14; cf. 1:10-11; 5:2-3). The biblical writers, however, while fully recognizing these profound inadequacies in the empirical situation, go on to make the bold affirmation, however difficult to justify evidentially, that, as the psalmist put it, "The earth is the Lord's and the fulness thereof, the world and those who dwell therein" (Ps. 24:1; cf. 50:12; I Cor. 10:26). Furthermore, the biblical perspective looks for the redemption of the whole of creation, for the transformation of the physical universe as well as of the spiritual; it believes that creation has been subjected to its present futility and frustration precisely in that hope (Rom. 8:20; cf. Rev. 21:1). And even now God is believed somehow to be in control of the whole, setting limits to evil, maintaining the process of just judgment and working to save and transform the whole.[75]

To give a summation of the Buddha's position, then, we may say that there is reason to question whether certain extremely negative views of phenomenal existence found in the early texts fairly represent the Buddha's own understanding. Other passages indicate that he was primarily concerned to show that phenomenal existence is not ultimately real, permanent or dependable, not that it is loathsome or evil. The ultimate aspiration of man ought to be directed toward that which is "lovely," the fount of bliss, the Deathless, and under the aegis of this orientation the life of man on earth is properly to be led.

In this context of understanding the Buddha saw *Karma,* which is just, operating as the integrative principle of all existence, which was thus seen as ordered if not permanent in "name and form." He perceived as operative and accessible within this order, although not to be identified with it, the reality of *Dharma.* For the Buddha *Dharma,* the "lovely," the right and the good, was not only an ideal, that which ought to be done. He seems to have regarded it as a force that "makes for righteousness" within the world, operative, like a stream, with an inner dynamism and direction as well as ethical quality of its own. *Dharma* appears as the way to the goal (of *Nirvāṇa*), as not only the ideal means but also the dynamic Power by participation in which men are helped to achieve the goal. It may not be amiss to speak of *Dharma* as performing the role of a "gracious Presence" within the world.

Thus while the Buddha saw the whole of phenomenal existence as lacking permanence, true reality or ultimate dependability within itself and even its integrative principle of *Karma* as an imprisoning order from which man's true destiny was to be liberated, it was the "place" where the "redeeming" power of *Dharma* may be plunged into, where *Nirvāṇa* may be

[75] Cf. Isa. 40:22-44; Matt. 7:2; I Cor. 10:13; Gal. 6:7.

aspired to and attained.[76] Once the goal was won, neither the inadequacies of this world nor the evils of one's past, which were still seen as in some sense karmically operative, had any longer the power spiritually to hurt or "demoralize" him. The evil therefore lay more in the grasping of man than in phenomenal existence as such. We may properly see in this understanding, moreover, the origin of recurrent emergence within historical Buddhism, both northern and southern, of varied kinds of protest and reform of overly negative views of phenomenal existence. The Buddha apparently saw no overriding purpose at work in the world with intent to transform phenomenal existence as such, to create "a new heaven and a new earth," but it was the place where much good can be found, much that is "pleasant," and above all here the ultimate solution to the dilemma of man can be realized, here his true destiny achieved. This is therefore an understanding of the world, or phenomenal existence, basically akin to biblical affirmations, at least with reference to the availability "therein" of the fullest possibilities for the moral and spiritual transformation of man, as for the attainment of a fundamental aspect of his ultimate destiny.

5

FOCI OF UNDERSTANDING

The Third Noble Truth was the stopping of suffering. Basic to this affirmation was the conviction that solution of the universal human dilemma is possible while still remaining within the conditions of temporal existence. We have already anticipated this point by our discussion of the role of *Dharma* in the section just preceding. The point of affirmation, however, was that of solution—frequently termed liberation or victory in the texts—the proclamation of a veritable "gospel." The Bud-

[76] For a suggestive interpretation of the reticence of the Buddha in defining *Nirvāna* see H. D. Lewis, "Philosophy in the Meeting of East and West," in *The Study of Religions*, pp. 179-180.

dha taught *Dharma* as the way and power of deliverance from the human dilemma, a way and power available to men in phenomenal existence. Although he evidently used the term "*Dharma*-men" to refer to those who lived according to the power-quality of *Dharma,* he resolutely refused to identify *Dharma* in an essential way with phenomenal existence or any formal aspect of it, nation, class or societal institution. The formulation of the concept of nonattachment is a doctrinal expression of this fact. Yet a man may choose and plunge into the stream of *Dharma* in this life.

We have discussed the relationship of *Dharma* to *Nirvāṇa* and seen the former as the way to the goal but in its quality as in its dynamism somehow "representative" of *Nirvāṇa* in phenomenal existence. That the relationship was integral seems to have been a universal assumption of primitive Buddhism. A further point to consider in the context of the Third Noble Truth is that of the relationship of *Dharma* to *Karma. Karma*, as we have seen, is a primary element in the dilemma of man, for according to the operation of *Karma* man reaps in proportion as he sows. *Karma* itself, however, is not the evil; the evil is wrongly placed desire. Indeed, *Karma* plays a role similar to the law in the thought of Paul, who insisted that the law, which in the rigor of its working is the instrument of sinful man's spiritual imprisonment and moral impotence, is in itself by no means evil or sin; rather it is "holy and just and good." It was sin that worked death through what is good, through the operation of the law.[77] The Buddha never spoke of *Karma* itself as good, but he did not call it evil or unjust.[78] Like the law for Paul the rigorous justice of its operation constituted the formal framework of the human dilemma, man's imprisonment in the chain of his own deeds and his consequent suffering.

[77] Rom. 7:5-7, 12-13.

[78] Winston L. King has suggested that the four elements of *Dharma, Karma, Nirvāna* and the Buddha constitute a "reality-complex," or "reality-structure," that provides a "God-substitute" or fulfils a "God-function" in Buddhism (*Buddhism and Christianity,* p. 38). These four elements are integral to the larger world view of Buddhism and indeed perform functions similar to those of God and his Christ according to Christian faith. In Buddhism, however, the four elements are not comparably the object of religious devotion, in primitive Buddhism not the Buddha, and in all Buddhist history not *Karma.*

The focus of the entire message of the Buddha lies then in the Third Noble Truth, the proclamation of the possibility of the deliverance of man from his imprisonment. This is to say that the integrative principle of phenomenal existence, the process of causal sequence, can be stopped and its direction reversed. Furthermore, by reversing the turn of the wheel of causation not only may the cause of suffering be stopped but a chain of sequence in a new direction begun that issues in blessings present and eternal. This is a claim of astounding proportions and its cosmic implications must not be overlooked.[79]

The process once reversed constituted what was called the building of "good *Karma*," a process of ethically good conduct, mental as well as physical, properly ending in the attainment of *Nirvāṇa.* But the point of turning was the real issue. For the Buddha and primitive Buddhism this point appears to have been a focus of human consciousness and will. That is, it was believed that a human being is free and capable by decisive acts of will of effecting a change in his basic orientation of self and thereby in his relationship to the whole karmic process.

We have noted that the Buddha frequently urged his hearers to the energetic use of will, and it has been inferred by some interpreters that the Buddha meant by this teaching not only human effort to change man's moral and spiritual orientation but that in effect by such effort one changes cosmic process itself, at least insofar as it relates to oneself. To my knowledge, this problem was not discussed in such terms by the Buddha, but as we have seen from our consideration of *Dharma,* there is reason to believe that for the Buddha more than "self-help" was involved in the process of change.

We noted that *Dharma,* operating as a kind of "Emmanuel" factor, the available "Presence" in phenomenal existence of certain forces representative of the "Other," of *Nirvāṇa*, functions with a dynamism as well as direction and quality of its own. *Dharma* for the Buddha was not merely an ideal description of the right way to the goal. It was evidently also the "force that makes for righteousness" in phenomenal existence.

[79] Winston L. King speaks in this context of a "loophole in the apparent mechanical determination of Karma" (*ibid.*, p. 44).

It was the stream into which men plunged, the stream that bore its own direction and carried men on to the goal. Rather than a program merely of self-help and focus on self-will, for the Buddha the methodology of salvation, or liberation, lay significantly in participation, participation in Reality that both ontologically and ethically was other than the "dark stream" of empirical existence in karmic imprisonment.

The Buddha clearly assumed the fact of human freedom, specifically freedom of the will sufficient to change the basic orientation of the self from self-centeredness toward the direction of the goal of *Nirvāṇa*, which is also the self-at-one. But the salvific process, which was evidently presumed to take some time, involved participation in *Dharma,* seen as a Reality both present and available. Furthermore, the recorded emphasis of the Buddha upon sustained friendship or intimacy with *Dharma* as the "lovely" not only reveals much of his daily interior life. The texts also affirm that such friendship is more effective than anything else in removing the hindrances and abetting the achievements of the religious life that leads to the authentic goal, the true destiny of man. The Buddha's affirmation of the possibility of cosmic liberation must be considered in the light of this understanding.

6

THE PROBLEM OF PERSONALISM

It is generally held that neither the Buddha nor any other representative figure in primitive Buddhism ever spoke of *Dharma* or *Nirvāṇa* in personal terms. That is, the reversal of the direction of karmic process and the availability of a helpful "Force" with thrust in the direction of ethical goodness and endless bliss did not entail the establishment of interpersonal relationships between men and the "Other" nor presume the possibility of "revelation." We may define revelation at this point as properly consisting of intelligible communication and a measure of self-disclosure from the Divine (or "Other") to the human. It presupposes consciousness in both the human and the Divine in the sense of awareness of self and others, who however united in some aspects of solidarity are yet at significant points other; it implies possession by the Divine of both wish and means to effect mutually intelligible communication with men.

I do not wish specifically to deny this widely held thesis, but I feel that some questioning or qualification may be in order. We noted in the first section ascription of a "quasi-personal" aspect to *Nirvāṇa*, because men were invited to "come and see" it as manifest evidently in certain men as in their teaching. Even more significant, however, is the friendship or intimacy with the "lovely" taught, and evidently experienced, by the Buddha. Obviously a sustained as well as intimate relationship was meant, whether this can be called interpersonal or not. The Buddha clearly practiced as well as taught a religious life characterized in a primary way by such a rich and deep spiritual relationship. The coolness of *Nirvāṇa* was not expected to make life cold or lonely. Furthermore, we have seen that the Buddha taught and practiced concerned and responsible interpersonal relationships among men. In fact, such conduct was an integral and necessary part of the life of "*Dharma*-men."

We may say, therefore, that we should not overstress the apparently "impersonal" aspects of either *Dharma* or *Nirvāṇa,* as might be inferred from some elements of the teaching. The apparent absence of "revelation" was evidently "compensated for" by the achievement of "insight" through the practice of meditation in the context of "faith" and strenuous intellectual and moral discipline. Perhaps it is beyond the power of the human mind to be certain and a question to be resolved only through interpretations issuing from faith whether in certain cases a man receives truth through revelation or insight or both. In any case, we can suggest that later ascriptions of a distinctly personal element to the "Other" in the faith of the Mahāyāna may represent a truer faithfulness to the understanding and practice of the Buddha than has generally been realized.

The theological question can now be asked, I believe, whether the Buddha's understanding of the quality and function of *Dharma* can have specific meaning in terms of Christian theology and, if so, whether it may specifically represent the presence and work of the Spirit of God as known in the context of Christian faith.

Obviously any answer must be offered with the modesty becoming to all who are aware of the mystery that enfolds all ultimate aspects of human life and the universe. But upon consideration of the ethical quality consistently ascribed by the Buddha to *Dharma* and of the nature of the relationship thereto that he both taught and practiced, I myself am led to the conclusion that the Buddha was indeed in contact with aspects of the Reality that Jesus termed the kingdom of God, even though I also wish to affirm, on the basis of Christian faith, that unique and fuller aspects of the same kingdom were manifested through the person and work of Jesus the Christ. This is also to say that we may detect in this particular part of the teaching and practice of the Buddha the presence and work of the same God who wrought so wondrously in the history of Israel.[80]

7

SELF AND THE "CRITICAL" ROLE OF THE BUDDHA

The Buddhist teaching of the non-self (*anātman*) is a paradoxical doctrinal exposition of two basic affirmations. One is that the self of empirical man (including his consciousness), as well as the whole of phenomenal existence, is ontologically neither ultimate nor eternal.[81] It is not ultimate and unchanging Reality and therefore is not the proper "refuge" or goal of man in his existential need. It represents, in spite of the strong Buddhist emphasis upon meditation, a religious orientation

[80] Ewert Cousins suggests that the medieval concept of "appropriations" is a theological technique that can be useful in understanding the relationship between the Spirit of God and authentic contact by non-Christians with an essential aspect of the divine nature (*op. cit.*, pp. 490-491).

[81] This affirmation, it will be recalled, was made in the context of the proto-Sāṅkhya teaching of the eternality of separate selves and the Brahmanic tendency to absolutize religious rites and societal structures.

away from the self to the "Other." The Buddhist Scriptures record numerous instances of directions to meditation upon specific themes, but meditation was clearly expected also to move beyond intellectuality and the empirical self to participation in deeper levels of reality.

The second affirmation is that the self as empirically known exists in spiritual bondage that must be broken by a "denial" of the self. This is because the self as empirically known is not only ontologically not worthy of "ultimate concern" but is characterized by selfish self-centeredness, self-assertiveness, separate isolation. As we have seen, however, the self as responsible agent is urged to turn its primary life-orientation from the selfish, separate self and its roots in attachment to phenomenal existence to the "Other," which is "lovely." In so doing it finds its true Self, which is the self-at-one. As the early texts affirm, this is self become Brahma, the Sublime. Such a person is a great self, he dwells in the immeasurable.[82] This is not annihilation of the self but to find "life" at the level of a higher Self that, with all that belongs to it, actually exists even though it is incomprehensible in terms of empirical existence.[83] The teaching ascribed to the Buddha clearly affirmed therefore the possibility even in this life of integration of the self at a "deeper"–or "higher"–level of reality wherein man can live in unselfish (unattached) happiness, joy and peace with himself and all that is about him. The early texts do not precisely teach that there is no self, only that particular elements of phenomenal existence are not-self and that man finds his true refuge in none of these.

Several additional points may properly be noted at this juncture. One is that the "conversion" of self that is envisaged in this teaching does not seem to be "confined" to integration merely with higher or expanded aspects of self, even though the word be written as Self. This integration is clearly one aspect of the whole, and the higher Self seems also to partake of a higher order of reality. But the goal *par excellence* of primitive Buddhism was *Nirvāṇa*, and, as we have seen,

[82] *Anguttara-Nikāya*, II, 207; BGS, II, 221. *Anguttara-Nikāya*, I, 249; BGS, I, 228.
[83] *Majjhima-Nikāya*, I, 138; MLS, I, 177.

cosmic—in the sense of other than phenomenal existence—aspects consistently inhere in the understanding of its "nature." Conversion was not only a psychological experience but even more a cosmic event, with participation in the Deathless, the Unchanging, the One. The teaching envisaged integration of self into an integrated goal, which was more than the self or even the Self. As we have seen, the primary thrust of the teaching of the Buddha was orientation from the many to the One.

Another point to be emphasized is the ethical quality characteristic both of the way and of the goal in the primitive teaching. Ethical qualities that, from the standpoint of Christian faith, seem to contribute to the purification and ennobling of human life were consistently ascribed both to *Dharma* and to *Nirvāṇa*, in particular as the latter were seen to be manifest in the lives of those who had reached the goal.

As we noted in our earlier consideration of the self, in the primitive Buddhist understanding of the conversion of self to *Dharma-Nirvāṇa* there are certain basic similarities with that of biblically perceived conversion to God in Jesus Christ. As God is one, *Nirvāṇa* is one. Similarly to the Buddha's sense of the self of empirical man as in bondage, Paul wrote of the natural man as "captive to the law of sin which dwells in my members" (Rom. 7:23). In a manner clearly akin to the Buddha's call to rejection of the unworthy self, Jesus taught that a man must deny himself to follow the Christ, and that whoever would lose his life for the sake of the Christ will find it (Matt. 16:24-25; Mark 8:34-35; Luke 9:23). The true self is found only where the barriers of egocentricity are let down in the presence of the ultimately Real, the Eternal (Rev. 3:20).

This teaching became life and practice in the case of both the Buddha and the Christ. We have noted the victory over self recorded of the Buddha in the early texts, his consistent courtesy toward others, his self-restraint and freedom from self-assertiveness, his benevolence freed from both craving and despair. The primary event, however, denotive of this spiritual victory was the decision—and its lifelong implementation—to turn from mere self-realization to serve the needs of his fellow men.

The selflessness of the Christ emerges clearly from the Gospel narratives, so as to make Dietrich Bonhoeffer's phrase, "the man for others," a singularly apt description. But may we not see in the event of the cross the supreme focal act of the spirit that prayed primarily for others, and for himself "not my will, but thine, be done" (Luke 22:42)? The cross was the supreme victory over the self, over all selfishness, self-centeredness, self-aggrandizement, over the self as separate from God, as alienated from his will. Because the victory was perfect, God was able to confirm it with the resurrection and use it as his ultimate instrument for the liberation of the world.

The conclusion to which, I feel, we are inevitably drawn is that also in the case of the Buddha's teaching and practice of the "denial" of the self, we sense the work of the same impelling Spirit who wrought in Jesus the Christ. The likenesses of both structural content and fruits in life allow us, I believe, no other conclusion.

I should like to add one final point of concern to this particular recital, the "critical" role of the Buddha. If we accept Paul Tillich's structure of three forms—the mystical, the prophetic and the secular—by which the divine revelatory process subjects to criticism the manifestations in life of the "particular revelatory experiences" of men, we may assert, I believe, that the Buddha's ministry expressed itself in each one of these forms.[84]

Over against the professionally religious, the Brāhman caste, the Buddha was in a sense a layman. In contrast with their emphasis upon formal rites, he stressed the primacy of life-transforming inner experience. Differently from their focus upon the *ex opere operato* efficacy of religious ceremonies he emphasized the vital importance of the ethical quality of life.

The Buddha was not a social reformer of modern kind, nor a prophet like Nathan before David. His understanding of the need for detachment from all aspects of phenomenal existence led him to a certain reserve toward men and events that, as we have seen, was yet by no means to be equated with either

[84] Cf. Tillich, *The Future of Religions*, p. 81.

indifference or lack of active concern. But this very detachment was one facet of a radical spiritual independence toward the personages and structures of his social milieu.

The Buddha was honored and supported by the most powerful rulers of the Ganges river basin, King Bimbisāra of Magadha and King Prasenajit of Kośala. We find, however, that he conducted himself with independent dignity and grave courtesy before them, as well as before men of every rank. The Buddha's free posture toward these and other rājas, as we noted in specific instances in our study, as well as the main purport of his teaching, reveals his freedom from any concept of the sacral king.[85] We see him, for instance, criticizing Prasenajit for his prejudice against women, but in the case of the murder of Bimbisāra by his son, or the later slaughter of his own clan of the Śākyas, we find no evidence of direct confrontation or public denunciation of those guilty of these crimes. To account for this posture, we may suggest, in addition to his reserved life style, his evidently firm conviction that the working of karmic retribution was sufficient in itself and possibly his awareness that in the particular context of the events a public word would be of no practical use.

Yet if the Buddha did not declaim in public places against these or other social evils, such as the caste system, we find in his teaching and the composition of the order of monks a radical rejection of both principle and practice of caste with regard to the spiritual potential of men. He admitted men of the lowest classes into his order and taught the honoring of workmen. His criticism of the Brāhmans, moreover, was at points scathing, and we find in this area the primary focus of the Buddha's "critical" role as recorded in the Pāli texts.

One of the probably early poetic sayings ascribed to the Buddha forthrightly affirms that he who is a true Brāhman keeps himself from evil, trusts not in ritual potencies, is pure, self-controlled; he joins right living to his Vedic knowledge.[86] In the *Dhammapada* we note repeated emphasis that a man

[85] Cf. Günter Lanczkowski, "Das Heilsziel des Nirvana in der Lehr des Buddhas," *Asien Missioniert im Abendland,* Kurt Hutten and Siegfried von Kortzfleisch, eds., p. 135.

[86] *Vinaya-Piṭaka, Mahāvagga,* I, 1, 3; BD, IV, 3-4. Cf. *Anguttara-Nikāya,* I, 166; BGS, I, 150.

does not become a Brāhman by his birth or family, nor by self-mortification, but by truth and righteousness.

> What is the use of matted hair, O fool!
> What of the raiment of goat-skins?
> Within thee there is ravening,
> but the outside thou makest clean.[87]

We find passages expressing in the strongest terms the worthlessness of the sacrifice of animals and the sacred fire.[88] The Buddha is recorded as saying that sacrifice involving the destruction of animal life he could not praise; only the sacrifice of worldly means for others, sacrifices free from cruelty and for the profit of many can the Buddha praise.[89]

The Buddha is also recorded as criticizing the Brāhmans for the exclusive secrecy characteristic of their methods of teaching. As we noted, he accommodated his teaching to what he believed were the varying capacities as well as needs of his hearers, but his final claim was that he held back nothing essential. The origins of later esoteric Buddhism would seem to lie more in Brahmanic Hinduism than in the practice of the Buddha himself. His openness to all men to the extent that they could receive seems very similar to the teaching and practice of the Christ.[90] Likewise his posture in rejecting the extremes of either asceticism or indulgence for the Middle Way of balanced control of both the inner and outer man was similar to Jesus' practice of moderation between the severity of John the Baptizer and the laxness of the Sadducees.[91]

In sum, the "critical" role of the Buddha did not constitute a total rejection of the claims and content of Brahmanism as such. Indeed, we noted that there is no record of the Buddha's teaching his disciples, monastic or lay, to refrain from participation in any of the traditional, local religious rites or practices. He appears to have included within his world view the

[87] *Dhammapada,* XXVI, 391-394; SBE, X, 91. In this passage I have put the word "matted" in place of the "platted" of F. Max Müller's translation.

[88] *Dhammapada,* VIII, 106-107; SBE, X, 32.

[89] *Anguttara-Nikāya,* II, 42-43; BGS, II, 49-51.

[90] Cf. Mark 4:11-12 (Matt. 13:10-15; Luke 8:9-10).

[91] Cf. Mark 2:15-22; Luke 7:31-35.

gods and goddesses, heavens and hells, of popular religion, although his teaching transcended and subordinated them. Apart from his apparently profound dissatisfaction with the practice of animal sacrifice, his primary criticism seems to have been directed toward Brahmanic failures to practice, inwardly as well as outwardly, what the tradition at its best required. Chapter twenty-six of the *Dhammapada* is in effect a recasting of what a Brāhman should be on the basis of the Buddha's insights into the true meaning of the tradition.

We note that Jesus similarly offered no major criticism of Greek or Roman religion in itself, apart from the brief observations cited above from Matthew (6:7, 32; but cf. 11:21-24).[92] Nor did he reject the formal structures of traditional Jewish practice as such. His teaching and practice looked toward a life style that included yet purified and transcended the old. Perhaps his parables of the new patch and the old garment and of new wine and old wineskins (Mark 2:21-22) were intended to mean that forms and structures were also due to change, but he evidently viewed the process as involving a certain continuity with the old.

8

AN ORIENTAL SUMMATION

The comparisons attempted above have not been intended to establish likenesses as if in the framework of thought of the older "comparison of religions." My intent has been rather to detect in the life and teaching of the Buddha that which, in terms of Christian theological and biblical evaluative procedures, seems to have positive significance as indications of divine presence and work and therefore of divine action in salvation history. This is not to equate either the persons or the religious roles of the Buddha and the Christ. It is rather to see them both as a part of a larger pattern of religious reference and meaning. Specifically, it means that Christians can no

[92] John 4:22 is possibly to be included in this category.

longer consider the life and teaching of the Buddha nor the history of the movement that is called Buddhism as without specific meaning and value in terms of salvation history. This is also to say, I believe, that the Christian missionary imperative must needs be carried out henceforth on the basis of a recognition of this premise-fact.

A concrete summation of these observations may perhaps be found in the thought of the Japanese Christian Kamegai Ryōun. Kamegai was born in the Hokuriku district of western Japan, the heartland of Pure Land Buddhism. His father was priest of a True (*Shin*) Pure Land temple that Rennyo (1415-1499) was said to have founded. He received a first-rate education, including studies in Buddhist philosophy at the then Tokyo Imperial University, and after brief service as a teacher became chief priest of his father's temple. As a result of his studies, wide range of contacts and long search for truth, he became a Christian and a pastor near the place where he had served as a Buddhist priest.

After thirty years of service as a Christian pastor, Kamegai published in 1951 an account of his life and thought in a book of rare beauty and spiritual sensitivity. As a distillation of long and loving meditation on the events of his life, particularly the religious significance of his early background and training, the meaning of Christian faith in the context of Oriental life and history, the book created a sensation in Japan and has gone through many subsequent editions.

Kamegai writes with warmest appreciation of the zeal, the joy in faith and the earnest desire to hold faith firmly that he found in many of the parishioners of his father's temple. He has none of the scorn that some converts show for the views and practices of their former allegiance. He remembers the joy that men, women and children experienced as a result of their faith in the grace of Amida (Amitābha), the Bodhisattva who had become the Buddha of infinite Light and Life and the supreme Object of devotion for Pure Land Buddhists; theirs was a life of thanksgiving and practical morality. In thinking of the effect of their faith upon these people, upon his parents, and upon himself he cannot but conclude that the grace of the living God whom he came to know in a new way in Jesus Christ was truly present and at work in the lives of these people, and, specifically, in the loving care and training he himself had received from his parents.[93]

Kamegai came to be dissatisfied with the form of Amida faith that he knew in his own experience and environment. He longed for some specific, historical manifestation of Amida by which he could know that Amida was more than human ideal or mythological symbol. He felt that adoring recitation of the name of Amida (*Nembutsu*) as it was practiced was more affirmation of faith than prayer and yearned for the privilege of personal communication with the Author of life. He felt that the *Shin* tradition in general lacked adequate ethical guidance. As he came to know the Christian faith, he hoped for a while that he could be both Buddhist and Christian believer at the same time. He finally came, however, to make the decision of utter committal to God in Jesus Christ. He felt that this step required him to give up his position as priest of the temple and to make formal and public profession of Christian faith.

This renunciation, however, did not mean for Kamegai a rejection of the people who are Buddhists nor a denial *in toto* of the "divine significance" of the Buddhism of his heritage. His new faith rather confirmed his long appreciation of the religious worth and cosmic significance of the faith-lives of these people. They were not beyond the pale of the love and active concern of the God and Father of Jesus Christ, the Creator of heaven and earth, the Lord of history. The Spirit of Jesus Christ was at work among them before the first Christian missionaries came, and the history and experience of his people until that time were not without meaning in the divine economy of salvation.

Kamegai came to conclude that Jesus Christ is not the destroyer of Buddhism, rather he is its builder, its fulfiller, its completer.[94] Whether Shinran, Dōgen (Zen), or Nichiren, to cite some of the creative figures of Japanese Buddhism, we find in Christ the words and reality of mercy, knowledge and power to which these men aspired. These aspirations, therefore, were not basically misplaced. Furthermore, these men

[93] Kamegai Ryōun, *Bukkyō kara Kirisuto e*, pp. 2-10.
[94] *Ibid.*, p. 117.

not only sought, they also found. Kamegai came to believe that Jesus' word with regard to the Old Testament, "Think not that I have come to abolish the law and the prophets; I have come not to abolish them but to fulfil them" (Matt. 5:17), can be applied with comparable significance also to Buddhism. This is to say that Jesus Christ brings to fulfillment that which is authentically of God in the teaching and spirit of Buddhism.

Kamegai saw similar possibilities of interpretation also of other religious traditions in Japanese history: Tenrikyō faith in the one God who loves the ill and serves the needs of mankind, Konkōkyō faith in the God who hears and heeds the prayers of men; these faiths are also in some measure to be recognized as authentically representative of the presence and work of God and can find fulfillment in Jesus the Christ.[95] Similarly, the benevolence, courtesy, knowledge and faith taught by Confucius in China are of the same provenance and have the same potentiality of fulfillment.[96]

Kamegai's interpretive position is that which has been called the concept of fulfillment and is only one of a number that have emerged in the Christian world within the past century or more. It is significant that this position has been particularly helpful to Oriental Christians who have been compelled both by their new faith and the existential reality of their religious and cultural heritage to strive to find meaning in the past of their people from the standpoint of the history of salvation.[97]

In Japan many of the leaders of early Protestantism endeavored to combine appreciation with careful criticism as they reflected on the religious past of their nation. Kozaki Hiromichi saw Christianity as the fulfillment of the basic spirit of the teaching of Confucius, although he strongly criticized the role of Neo-Confucianism as a bulwark of the rigidly class-structured, feudalistic patterns of traditional Japanese society. Ebina Danjō had a similarly high view of the best of

[95] Both of these religions manifest a strongly theistic orientation. Cf. H. Neill McFarland, *The Rush Hour of the Gods*, p. 59. For a contemporary, equally open Roman Catholic interpretation of Zen see Augustin Hideshi Kishi, *Spiritual Consciousness in Zen from a Thomistic Theological Point of View*, pp. 113-116.

[96] Kamegai, *op. cit.*, p. 118.

[97] An important attempt to summarize these efforts in India in the early part of the twentieth century is J. N. Farquhar's *The Crown of Hinduism*.

Confucianism. Uemura Masahisa, the pioneer leader of Presbyterian-Reformed Christianity in Japan, saw *Bushidō* (the Way of the Warrior) as a singular gift of God to Japan and a veritable Old Testament. He believed that the Christian doctrine of the redemptive sacrifice of Christ for the world is particularly possible of comprehension for men reared in that tradition.[98] He objected to the overweening pride and class consciousness that it frequently begot and felt that it had lost the notion of authentic humanity that he found in the gospel. But it had meaning and validity as preparation under God.[99]

The concept of fulfillment is not as widely held now as it was earlier in this century, partly because it has meaning primarily only for Christians. To non-Christians it smacks of notions of superiority and religious imperialism. Another reason for present dissatisfaction with the concept, even among Christians, is ·hat it takes no account of the possibility of meaning and value in other religious traditions as continuing realities in human history. Furthermore, properly understood, the theory means that Jesus Christ, not Christianity as an empirical movement in history, is the fulfillment of the religions. This fulfillment, moreover, is to be perfectly and visibly realized only as an eschatological reality, at the edge or end of history. At that time the Lord will fulfil Christianity as well as the other religions; in the meantime Christianity and the church share in the imperfections and inadequacies of all human experience, as do the other religious traditions of mankind.

The abiding value of the fulfillment theory, however, lies in its service toward opening the eyes of Western man to the reality of the presence and salvific work of God in the whole world and among all mankind. The God of biblical faith has come to be seen once more as the Creator of all, the Lord of all history, not only of Israel and the Western world, the God and Father of all men. The concept of fulfillment may be seen

[98] A concept of vicarious suffering is an old and persistent feature also of folk religion in Japan. Cf. Joseph M. Kitagawa, *Religion in Japanese History*, pp. 319-321.

[99] Dohi Akio, "Nihon ni okeru Fukuin no Dochaku," *Fukuin to Sekai*, XXI, 10 (October, 1966), 10-13. Nitobe Inazō saw the seeds of the kingdom of God as having blossomed in *Bushidō* (*Bushido, The Soul of Japan*, p. 128).

therefore as one theological expression of the emergence of Western man from tribalism and cultural isolation.[100] It acknowledges that the previous life experiences of the peoples of Asia (or of Africa, the Americas and the islands of the seas) have not been apart from the salvific and revelatory work as well as the providence of God. From this point of view the meaning and the value of both the Buddha and Buddhism in salvation history is very great, indeed. The sense that the Buddha had of the ethical quality of Ultimate Reality as it impinges upon men in *Dharma,* his conviction that empirical man by participation therein and by way of selfless, ethical living may be transformed and attain authentic selfhood in *Nirvāṇa*, the faith of the Mahāyāna in the personal and compassionate nature of the Ultimate, the grateful devotion of the Pure Land schools to Amitābha as the one gracious divine Figure, the committal of Zen to ethical conversion and sympathetic appreciation of both small and great—these are signs, I believe, of the work of the God whom we see in Jesus Christ.

9

CONCLUDING POSTSCRIPT

I am keenly aware that the above constitutes but a highly imperfect sketch of an attempt to give a theological interpretation of the life and teachings of the Buddha, not to speak of Buddhism as a whole. I have, for instance, made no reference to problems involved in the interpretation of Buddhist, especially Mahāyāna, philosophy with its many and varied attempts to understand the nature of Ultimate Reality and its relationship to phenomenal existence. I have said little of the missiological implications of this kind of an approach to an understanding of the religions of the world, although my own interest in the subject derives primarily from concerns of faith

[100] The biblical parable of the pearl of great price can be taken as pointing to a concept of fulfillment. The merchant in the parable was a professional, seeking pearls, and he presumably already had pearls, perhaps good ones. But for "the one pearl of great value" he was willing to sell all that he had (Matt. 13:45-46).

that I see as necessarily including the missiological. As we noted above, in recent years attempts have been made by a number of well-known theologians to grapple especially with the dogmatic aspects of the problem of the religions. The present effort is intended as a small contribution to the work of applying this kind of dogmatic thinking to the case of a specific religious tradition, in this instance a focus on the life and teachings of the Buddha.

In conclusion it may be in order to offer the following recapitulation as hopefully a pointer toward a solution of our problems both theological and missiological. I hold it to be a necessity of Christian faith and theology to accept Jesus the Christ as our standard of truth and value. Acceptance of him in any authentic sense of course is dependent upon our knowing him. And we know him by his "name" through the Scriptures, the inspiration-guidance of his Holy Spirit and the fellowship of his church (including its tradition). Through the mutual interworking of these three factors Christian people come to know their Lord and his will and thereby acquire the criteria by which they may measure all truth and quality of spirit or life.[101] The "possession" of these criteria, however, cannot properly mean that all else apart from the criteria is of negligible value or meaning. Indeed, the biblical doctrines of divine creation of the universe and of universal divine love and providence, with their revelatory and salvific implications, specifically forbid such a conclusion. A major problem of contemporary Christian theology is therefore to understand the historic religions of the world in such a way as to be faithful both to these doctrines and to a biblically derived understanding of the church and its mission. The related problem of missiology is to recognize truth and value in the other religious traditions of mankind without falling into disobedience to the divine commission to proclaim the gospel to the whole creation and to plant the church as the eschatological community that points to the consummation of history in the Lord Christ.

Perhaps a tentative theological answer to this dilemma may be found in some form of a concept of eschatologically signifi-

[101] Cf. Richard H. Drummond, "Authority in the Church: An Ecumenical Inquiry," *The Journal of Bible and Religion,* XXXIV, 4 (October, 1966), 339-341.

cant "convergence" of heretofore largely distinct or disparate foci or streams of divine revelatory and salvific activity in human history. According to this notion the historic Christian church is but one of several such foci, and among these foci we may properly include other religious traditions as potentially having some meaning and value in the sense of both divine presence and working and human participation in the divine revelatory and salvific activity. As Christians—which is to say with appreciative love and the humility of a heart ready to learn as well as with boldness to teach—we are privileged to evaluate the quality and degree of the meaning and value of these religious traditions according to the criteria we have been given. Admittedly this is no easy task, especially since, as Karl Rahner has said, we have heretofore looked too ineptly and with too little love at the "non-Christian" religions to discern traces of divine grace.[102]

We are of course likewise privileged—and obligated—to perform a similar evaluative task with reference to empirical Christianity. The consequences of this latter task may lead us to a sobering and penitent humility, very possibly to the conclusion that in certain places and among certain of its "faithful" the Christian church has by no means manifested the purest or highest form of divine presence and activity in its age. But the church knows the "name" of the Lord and Savior of all men and, when true to itself, recognizes and heeds his voice. The church is called to proclaim the true name and person even though it finds no eschatological ultimacy in its own institutional forms and sees the structures of its life to be but one of the "converging" foci of divine presence and activity in human history.[103]

The way of the church in life and mission will therefore not be triumphal but modest and, as needful, penitent, a *via crucis* of unassuming witness and service that looks not to its own temporal aggrandizement but to the glorification of the name

[102] Karl Rahner, "Das Christentum und die nichtchristlichen Religionen," *Schriften zur Theologie*, V, 153.

[103] This concept of eschatological convergence can be seen as a concrete application of the thought of P. Teilhard de Chardin. Cf. his *The Phenomenon of Man*, pp. 262-263; *The Future of Man*, pp. 89-96, 120-123. Cf. Pannenberg, *op. cit.*, II, 92-96; Nels F. S. Ferré, *The Universal Word*, pp. 170-171, passim.

of the one, true God and his Christ. The church looks forward to the convergence and manifestation in transformed glory of all the strands of divine activity, of which it is but one. Yet the Lord who will effect this transformation is the Lord whose name it knows. In service of the purposes of this Lord the church finds its own self and life but not, for now, its glory. The glory will be known only at the time of the consummation, which is also the time of full convergence. The glory will be shared with others who "will come from east and west, and from north and south, and sit at table in the kingdom of God."

APPENDIX I

PROBLEMS OF TEXT AND CANON

Gautama (Pāli: Gotama) the Buddha, like Jesus the Christ, wrote nothing.[1] In the immemorial fashion of the Indian *guru*, he taught his disciples and others who would hear by word of mouth alone. This is in part at least because at that time India possessed, so far as is known, no technique for writing on materials other than rock. In the historical-critical investigation of the primary documents of Christian faith, the time gap of perhaps fifty to sixty years between the date of Jesus' death and the appearance of the Gospel narratives in their present form has caused, especially since the middle of the nineteenth century, varying degrees of uncertainty in the wider Christian community as well as among scholars.[2] According to Sinhalese Buddhist tradition, however, at least four hundred years

[1] The early Indian tradition in general held that religious teaching was too sacred to be communicated other than verbally.

[2] Rudolf Bultmann, *The Historical Jesus and the Kerygmatic Christ*, pp. 25-26.

elapsed before the canonical form of the Buddha's teaching was written down, that is, in the reign of King Vattagāmani (89-77 B.C.).

The original language by means of which Buddhist doctrine was first spread and which the Buddha himself probably employed for most of his own teaching was Māgadhī, the Sanskritic dialect in use in the most important area of primitive Buddhism.[3] We have seen that possibly the Buddha's mother tongue, the language of the Śākyas, was of the linguistically quite different Tibetan-Burman family, but the bulk of his public teaching was evidently in a Sanskritic dialect. The oldest documents of Buddhist literature, the stone-engraved edicts of the great Mauryan emperor Aśoka (273-232 B.C.) are written in Kośalan, a sister dialect of Māgadhī. Much of the transmission of the teaching by verbal means in the early centuries was by means of the related Prākrit dialect, and the whole was finally reduced to writing in Pāli by the Theravāda school and in Sanskrit by the Sarvāstivādin school.[4] Pāli is also related to Sanskrit, but its origin as a language is obscure, since no group of people is known to have spoken it as a native tongue. Ananda Coomaraswamy suggests that it was artificially created in Ceylon about 80 B.C. (or 29-17 B.C.) as a literary development of Māgadhī to serve as a vehicle fit for writing the Scriptures. There is, however, a stronger scholarly consensus that the basis of Pāli, in the main, is a western or west-central Middle Indian dialect.[5]

The Scriptures record the names of eighteen different schools that developed during the four centuries of verbal transmission. There were some differences in detail and the arrangement of material in use in the different schools, but apparently there was only one canon. What divergences existed lie chiefly in what we should call legendary matter.[6] Modern scholars often refer to the Pāli and Sanskrit literatures as separate canons, and in fact they constitute the respective canons for the main contemporary divisions of Buddhism, the

[3] Edward J. Thomas, *The Life of the Buddha as Legend and History*, p. xix.

[4] *Ibid.*, p. vii.

[5] Ananda Coomaraswamy, *Buddha and the Gospel of Buddhism*, p. 263. Franklin Edgerton, *Buddhist Hybrid Sanskrit Grammar and Dictionary*, I, 1-3.

[6] Thomas, *op. cit.*, p. viii.

southern or Theravāda and the northern or Mahāyāna. In this sense there was a plurality of canons in use among the early schools as each developed its own tradition of recension and transmission.[7] It is noteworthy, however, that the special doctrines developed by the different schools are not reflected in their transmission of the content of one canon itself, and the divergences in the latter are of secondary significance.

Western scholars have tended to favor the Pāli Scriptures, but recent discoveries of Chinese and Tibetan documents translated from Sanskrit originals make it certain that other schools had recensions as fully developed as the Pāli. Although the Pāli and the Sanskrit are the only two recensions of the one canon—the products primarily of two schools—that have come down to us, there is no intrinsic reason to regard the Pāli as superior to the Sanskrit.

Western scholarly prejudice against Sanskrit Buddhist literature, or Buddhist Hybrid-Sanskrit as Franklin Edgerton preferred to call the bulk of it, is revealed in Henry Clarke Warren's observation that "Sanskrit literature is a chaos; Pāli, a cosmos."[8] Nevertheless, it is now recognized that the Chinese *Agamas* (Pāli: *Nikāya*—the documents belonging to the *Sutta Piṭaka,* one of the three Baskets of the Law, in particular the one containing what purports to be the teaching of the Buddha) are translations of Sanskrit originals at least as old as most of the Pāli canon.[9] Also, in recent years more and more portions of the Sanskrit Scriptures in their original form have been discovered. The Chinese and Tibetan Buddhist Scriptures belong to the Mahāyāna tradition and contain much later material, especially that which records the distinctive positions of that tradition. But they also contain almost the whole of the Pāli canon as well, and, together with the recently discovered Sanskrit works, make it clear that there was a fundamental doctrinal agreement in the earlier schools.[10]

Thus we can say that there was originally only one canon, of which the Pāli is but one version, and it is now possible to form a consistent view of the Sarvāstivāda or Mahāyāna tex-

[7] *Ibid.,* p. xxiii.
[8] Henry Clarke Warren, *Buddhism in Translations,* p. xix.
[9] Christmas Humphreys, *Buddhism,* p. 233.
[10] Thomas, *op. cit.,* p. xxiii.

tual tradition and compare it with the Pāli in such a way as to come fairly close to the original written texts. Since the divergences are found to lie primarily in what is called legendary matter, the consequence is that we are able to form a relatively consistent and authentic account of primitive Buddhism.[11] This account, however, must be recognized as largely the result of Western scholarly efforts to abstract historical from legendary material. And as Karl Jaspers has observed, in the process of excision of legendary material there are no conclusive criteria by which to determine how far the excision should go.[12]

It is quite another matter, of course, to evaluate the fidelity to historical event or reality of the very substantial quantity of material in the one canon which purports to be the teaching or acts of the Buddha and which clearly does not belong to the category of the legendary. The extant texts represent the result of a process of transmission which includes the possibility of revision or "interpretation" to a greater or less degree. The consensus of modern critical scholarship is that the early monastic communities, in order to serve their institutional and/or "theological" needs, instituted some changes in the traditions, particularly in the form of additions.

Nevertheless, we are by no means, as I am suggesting, without strong clues as to the proper use of the material which has come down to us. As Beatrice Lane Suzuki has written, the only way to trace the original teaching of the Buddha amidst legendary and interpretive accretions is to examine carefully and scientifically the pertinent literature, including the *Vinaya*, and endeavor to pick up the consistent thread which in fact runs through it.[13] The continuing efforts of buddhologists have led to what seem more balanced and assured results than prevailed a half century or more ago. For example, no reputable scholar any longer presumes to dismiss the Buddha

[11] *Ibid.*, pp. vi, viii.

[12] Karl Jaspers, *The Great Philosophers*, p. 32.

[13] Beatrice Lane Suzuki, *Mahayana Buddhism*, p. 4. This book by the wife of the Zen Buddhist scholar and philosopher D. T. Suzuki may be properly regarded as also representative of the thought of the latter. He furnished the lengthy introduction, and we may safely assume that the contents proper received his careful scrutiny. Cf. Sukumar Dutt, *The Buddha and Five After-Centuries*, pp. 3-16.

as a solar myth. And in spite of difficulties encountered in treating accounts which sometimes include stupendous miracles and divine interventions, or which simply seem "out of character," at least the principal aspects of the life and teaching of the Buddha emerge, I believe, with considerable clarity.[14]

[14] Cf. André Bareau, *Bouddha*, p. 15; *Die Religionen Indiens*, III, 11; Richard H. Robinson, *The Buddhist Religion, An Historical Introduction*, pp. 13, 18-19.

APPENDIX II

DEFINING HISTORY AND RELIGION

In the preface I proposed functional definitions for two key words used in this work. They are history and religion. I should like at this point to expand briefly on both definitions.

I defined history as "the study and descriptive statement of the human past." This definition is intended to presuppose the possibility of authentic human knowledge, even though as historical knowledge its content constitutes no more than probabilities of greater or less degree. I make this epistemological assumption without proof, partly because I do not think it can be proved and partly because a serious attempt to discuss the problem philosophically would carry us beyond the purview of this work.

History by my definition is primarily concerned with human experiences and actions. Other phenomena, such as of nature, are introduced generally only insofar as they impinge upon human life. In the case of what is called religious experience, the testimony of witnesses may refer to dimensions of reality which transcend the human in the sense of not being accessible to the methodologies of the scientific study of history which focus upon the empirically and historically knowable. Historical study as such, however, will not pass judgment on the truth or reality of such dimensions.

Religion I defined as "that dimension of human life which refers to ultimate meaning, value and/or reality insofar as these are apprehended by the person or persons concerned." In this sense religion has clearly been a very significant element of human life throughout all known history. In fact, as Robert B. Baird has aptly put it, "the religious question is probably the most significant *historical* question that one can ask."[1] Almost all human beings appear to have had "ultimate concerns." Historically they have assigned high importance both individually and in community to religious or ultimate dimensions in their lives and to their particular faiths and related practices. No study or descriptive account of human life that pretends to be inclusive or fairly representative can therefore omit this aspect of human experience. Religion as a manifestation of ultimate concerns in human experience and activity is a legitimate, indeed necessary, subject of historical investigation.

Historians then can legitimately investigate and describe the phenomena that are called religious insofar as these are accessible to their methodologies. But, as we have noted previously in this work, the study of religion in history, ancient or more recent, is not adequately or satisfactorily made in exclusive confinement to these methodologies. The time comes when man in his heart wishes to ask normative questions, that is, questions regarding the nature and the truth of that which is ultimate for him and for others. These are not questions properly to be asked in the context of the procedures of historical investigation, but they cry out to be asked–and answered–at some time. My contention is that they may be asked–and answers attempted–in association with historical investigation if they are identifiably distinguished for what they are, normative or theological questions.

The term "ultimate" means that the meaning, value or reality under concern is, compared with aught else, of supreme

[1] Robert D. Baird, *Category Formation and the History of Religions,* p. 52. I have been greatly helped by this book and find myself generally in agreement with the author's conclusions.

importance. There is by implication an ordered hierarchy of meaning, value and reality in a religious world view. Human beings differ in the range as well as quality of their apprehension. But the ultimate will be at the apex of that hierarchy. It may not, from the point of view of others, always be sublime, but for the person or persons concerned it is supreme, the superlative.

For most persons in known human history, moreover, consciousness of ultimacy has included, among other things, affirmation of the existence of being, beings or other realities beyond the human and aspiration toward proper (as humanly perceived) and helpful relationships with these. The term "beyond" denotes that which transcends the empirically or historically human, as the latter is "pre-religiously" apprehended. The question of the nature and truth of these transhistorical beings or realities must remain outside the range of historical investigation *per se.* But, as I contend, this question may be asked in another context of inquiry, the normative or theological, which is, presumably, specifically oriented and equipped to deal with it. Theological statements, however, must be supported or verified by data and reasoning appropriate to their kind, even as historical descriptions require verification through historical materials and consonant explanations.

If religion, as historically perceived, is constituted by human consciousness and practice, a further consequence emerges. There is no need to seek for the "essence" of religion, as if the word itself denoted metaphysical reality. In human religious awareness and practice the relational referents posited may, as we have seen, be perceived as metaphysical (transhistorical) realities and believed to possess some "essence" of substance and/or quality. They may be designated, as by Rudolf Otto, as the *numinosum* or *mysterium tremendum,* thereby denoting a preternaturally awesome, fearful and mysterious quality. But religion in human history, as human practice, cannot be demonstrated to have a discernible "essence" or identity in and of itself that subsists in all its varied manifestations. Perhaps no single definition could adequately include or account for all manifestations that have been called religious. I content myself therefore with the reaffirmation of my original functional definition as non-pretentious and yet hopefully representative of a significant proportion of these manifestations.

Because religion, as an historical phenomenon, is constituted by human awareness and practice, the word can be used, I affirm, of what Paul Tillich called quasi-religions. In this category may be included Marxism, Fascism, humanism, secularism, scientism and other forms of ideological understanding and commitment. The ascription of ultimacy which I cite as centrally characteristic of the religious dimension of human life may be ideationally obscured in these activities but yet significantly operative in practice. Participants in these movements may practically and in their consciousness ascribe ultimate meaning, value and even reality to the objects of their commitment quite as unreservedly as any practicer of an historical religion.

The nature of the consequences in human life, however, of religious activities of this latter kind constitute for me one weighty reason why I believe I must go on to ask normative questions of truth and quality in religion. This I do of course not as an historian of religion but as a religious man and a theologian. And if I do so, I am under compulsion, I feel, to distinguish and identify when and where I am operating on this level rather than on another. Furthermore, verification of this activity must be acceptable in terms of the appropriate discipline, that is, of theology, as the verification of historical work is effected through the materials and methodology of history.[2] I covet responses from my peers on both of these levels.

To summarize, then, religion studied as history means a focus on man, his consciousnesses, his relationships and practices, insofar as these are seen to have ultimate referents. Religion considered from a theological or faith perspective involves consideration of the truth and reality of the ultimacy in question.

A final word may be in order to justify the use of the word religion in the plural. Some historians of religion have objected

[2] Cf. Baird, *op. cit.*, p. 42.

to the plural number, particularly as manifested in the "subordinate categories" of Hinduism, Buddhism, Judaism, etc.[3] The primary objection seems to be not only that the terms are contentually imprecise but that there are in fact radical differences within the categories, differences which at times exceed those commonly held to obtain among them.

This objection is not without force, I feel. But if such terms as Hinduism or Islam continue to be employed by participants within a tradition—as distinguished from appellatives assigned from without—employed as significantly denotive of self-identity, it would seem pedantic and perhaps presumptuous to reject them. Even though, as in the case of Hinduism, the name be of relatively recent provenance, if it is sufficiently denotive of authentic self-awareness to be used by a substantial number of representative spokesmen from the tradition itself, we are hardly in a position to gainsay them. As historians of religion we are permitted to point out generic or qualitative differences within a tradition insofar as the data support us. At the same time it would generally not be wise to assume that the participants themselves are not already aware of these alleged differences. It would seem that the "accidents" of history and geography, at times as much as if not more than contentual likenesses, serve to create what Ludwig Wittgenstein called "family resemblance."

[3] E.g., Wilfred Cantwell Smith, *The Meaning and End of Religion*, pp. 128-132. Smith wishes to replace the terms "religion" and "religious" with "faith" or "faiths" of men. Unfortunately the word "faith" is as imprecise and problematic in usage as "religion."

BIBLIOGRAPHY

Adam, Karl. *The Spirit of Catholicism.* New York: Doubleday, 1962.

Altizer, Thomas J. J. *Oriental Mysticism and Biblical Eschatology.* Philadelphia: Westminster, 1961.

Anderson, Gerald H. *The Theology of the Christian Mission.* New York: McGraw-Hill, 1961.

Anguttara-Nikāya I; *The Book of the Gradual Sayings,* vol. I, F. L. Woodward, tr. London: Luzac, 1951.

Anguttara-Nikāya II; *The Book of the Gradual Sayings,* vol. II, F. L. Woodward, tr. London: Luzac, 1952.

Anguttara-Nikāya III; *The Book of the Gradual Sayings,* vol. III, E. M. Hare, tr. London: Luzac, 1952.

Anguttara-Nikāya IV; *The Book of the Gradual Sayings,* vol. IV. E. M. Hare, tr. London: Luzac, 1955.

Anguttara-Nikāya V; *The Book of the Gradual Sayings,* vol. V, F. L. Woodward, tr. London: Luzac, 1955.

The Apostolic Fathers, vol. I, Kirsopp Lake, tr. Cambridge, Mass.: Harvard University, 1945.

Appleton, George. *On the Eightfold Path.* London: SCM, 1961.

Aquinas, Thomas. *De Veritate; Quaestiones Disputatae.* Roma: Marietti, 1949.

———. *Summa Theologica.* New York: Benziger, 1942.

Arndt, W. F. and F. W. Gingrich. *A Greek-English Lexicon of the New Testament and Other Early Christian Literature.* Chicago: University of Chicago, 1957.

Augustine. *Contra Faustum;* J. P. Migne, *Patrologia Latina,* vol. XLII. Paris: J. P. Migne, 1886.

———. *De Civitate Dei; Corpus Scriptorum Ecclesiasticorum,* vol. XL. New York: Johnson, 1962.

———. *De Doctrina Christiana; Corpus Christianorum, Series Latina,* vol. XXXII, pars IV, 1. Turnhout, Belgium: Brepols, 1962.

———. *De Trinitate; Corpus Christianorum,* vol. L. Turnhout, Belgium: Brepols, 1968.

———. *Opus Imperfectum Contra Julianum;* J. P. Migne, *Patrologia Latina,* vol. XLV. Paris: J. P. Migne, 1865.

———. *Retractiones; Corpus Scriptorum Ecclesiasticorum Latinorum,* vol. XXXVI. New York: Johnson, 1963.

———. *Sermo CCCXIV;* J. P. Migne, *Patrologia Latina,* vol. XXXVIII. Paris: J. P. Migne, 1865.

Baird, Robert D. *Category Formation and the History of Religions.* The Hague: Mouton, 1971.

Balthasar, Hans Urs von. *A Theology of History.* New York: Sheed and Ward, 1963.

Bareau, André. *Bouddha.* Paris: Éditions Seghers, 1962.

———. *Die Religionen Indiens,* vol. III, C. M. Schroeder, ed. Stuttgart: Kohlhammer Verlag, 1964.

Barth, Karl. *Die Kirchliche Dogmatik,* vol. I, pt. 2. Zollikon-Zürich: Evangelischer Verlag A. G., 1945.

Beal, Samuel. *Travels of Fah-Hian and Sung-Yun.* London: Gupta, 1964.

Benz, Ernst. *Ideen zu einer Theologie der Religionsgeschichte.* Mainz: Verlag der Akademie der Wissenschaften und der Literatur, 1961.

———. "Ideas for a Theology of the History of Religion," in Anderson, Gerald H., ed., *The Theology of the Christian Mission.*

Bettenson, Henry. *Documents of the Christian Church.* New York: Oxford University Press, 1947.

Bolle, Kees W., "The History of Religions and Christian Theology," *Anglican Theological Review,* vol. LIII, no. 4 (October, 1971).

The Book of the Discipline (*Vinaya-Piṭaka* I), vol. I, I. B. Horner, tr. (*Sacred Books of the Buddhists,* vol. X). London: Luzac, 1949.

The Book of the Discipline (*Vinaya-Piṭaka, Mahāvagga*), vol. IV, I. B. Horner, tr. (*Sacred Books of the Buddhists,* vol. XIV). London: Luzac, 1962.

The Book of the Discipline (*Vinaya-Piṭaka, Cullavagga*), vol. V, I. B. Horner, tr. (*Sacred Books of the Buddhists,* vol. XX). London: Luzac, 1963.

The Book of the Gradual Sayings (*Anguttara-Nikāya* I), vol. I, F. L. Woodward, tr. London: Luzac, 1951.

The Book of the Gradual Sayings (*Anguttara-Nikāya* II), vol. II, F. L. Woodward, tr. London: Luzac, 1952.

The Book of the Gradual Sayings (*Anguttara-Nikāya* III), vol. III, E. M. Hare, tr. London: Luzac, 1952.

The Book of the Gradual Sayings (*Anguttara-Nikāya* IV), vol. IV, E. M. Hare, tr. London: Luzac, 1955.

The Book of the Gradual Sayings (*Anguttara-Nikāya* V), vol. V, F. L. Woodward, tr. London: Luzac, 1955.

The Book of the Kindred Sayings (*Sanyutta-Nikāya* I), pt. I, C. A. F. Rhys Davids, tr. London: Luzac, 1950.

The Book of the Kindred Sayings (*Sanyutta-Nikāya* II), pt. II. C. A. F. Rhys Davids, tr. London: Luzac, 1952.

The Book of the Kindred Sayings (*Sanyutta-Nikāya* III), pt. III, F. L. Woodward, tr. London: Luzac, 1954.

The Book of the Kindred Sayings (*Sanyutta-Nikāya* IV), pt. IV, F. L. Woodward, tr. London: Luzac, 1956.

The Book of the Kindred Sayings (*Sanyutta-Nikāya* V), pt. V, F. L. Woodward, tr. London: Luzac, 1965.

Bouquet, A. C. *The Christian Faith and Non-Christian Religions.* New York: Harper, 1958.

————. "Revelation and the Divine Logos," in Anderson, Gerald H., ed., *The Theology of the Christian Mission.*

Bright, John. *The Kingdom of God.* New York: Abingdon, 1953.

Brown, W. Norman. *Man in the Universe, Some Cultural Continuities in India.* Berkeley: University of California, 1966.

Bruns, J. Edgar. *The Christian Buddhism of St. John.* New York: Paulist, 1971.

Buddhacarita; Sacred Books of the East, vol. XLIX, E. B. Cowell, tr. Oxford: Clarendon, 1894.

Buddhadāsa Indapañño. *Buddha Dhamma for Students.* Bangkok, Thailand, M. P., 1966.

————. *Christianity and Buddhism.* Bangkok, Thailand: Karn Pim Pranakorn Partnership, 1968.

Buddhaghosa, in Henry Clarke Warren, *Buddhism in Translations.* New York: Atheneum, 1963.

Bultmann, Rudolf. *The Historical Jesus and the Kerygmatic Christ.* New York: Abingdon, 1964.

————. *Kerygma und Mythos,* vol. I. Hamburg: Bartsch, 1951.

Buttrick, George A. *The Parables of Jesus.* New York: Harper, 1928.

Cadbury, H. J. *Jesus: What Manner of Man?* New York: Macmillan, 1947.

Chadwick, Henry. *Early Christian Thought and the Classical Tradition.* New York: Oxford University Press, 1966.

"Christians in Dialogue with Men of Other Faiths," *International Review of Missions,* vol. LIX (October, 1970).

Christy, Arthur. *The Orient in American Transcendentalism.* New York: Columbia University, 1932.

Clement, *Stromateis; Les Stromates,* Claude Mondésert and Marcel Caster, eds., vol. I. Paris: Éditions du Cerf, 1951.

Cochrane, Charles Norris. *Christianity and Classical Culture.* New York: Oxford University Press, 1944.

Commentary to *Dīgha-Nikāya,* in Henry Clarke Warren, *Buddhism in Translations.* New York: Atheneum, 1963.

Conze, Edward. *Buddhist Scriptures.* Harmondsworth, Middlesex: Penguin, 1959.

————. *Buddhist Thought in India.* Ann Arbor: University of Michigan, 1967.

Coomaraswamy, Ananda. *Buddha and the Gospel of Buddhism.* Bombay: Asia Publishing House, 1956.

Cornelis, Étienne. *Valeurs Chrétiennes des Religions Non Chrétiennes.* Paris: Les Éditions du Cerf, 1965.

Cousins, Ewert, "The Trinity and World Religions," *Journal of Ecumenical Studies,* vol. VII, no. 3 (Summer, 1970).

Cragg, Kenneth. *Christianity in World Perspective.* New York: Oxford University Press, 1968.

Cuttat, Jacques-Albert. *The Encounter of Religions,* Pierre de Fontnouvelle and Evis McGrew, trs. New York: Desclée, 1960.

———. "Expérience Chrétienne et Spiritualité Orientale," in *La Mystique et Les Mystiques.* Paris: Desclée De Brouwer, 1965.

Cyprian. *De Catholicae Ecclesiae Unitate; Corpus Scriptorum Ecclesiasticorum Latinorum,* vol. III, pars I. New York: Johnson, 1965.

———. *Epistulae LXXIII; Corpus Scriptorum Ecclesiasticorum Latinorum,* vol. III, pars II. New York: Johnson, 1965.

Daniélou, Jean. *Holy Pagans of the Old Testament.* London: Longmans, Green, 1957.

Davis, Charles. *Christ and the World Religions.* New York: Herder and Herder, 1971.

Dhammapada; Sacred Books of the East, vol. X, F. Max Müller, tr. Oxford: Clarendon, 1898.

Dialogues of the Buddha (*Dīgha-Nikāya* I), pt. I, T. W. Rhys Davids, tr. (*Sacred Books of the Buddhists,* vol. II). London: Luzac, 1956.

Dialogues of the Buddha (*Dīgha-Nikāya* II), pt. II, T. W. and C. A. F. Rhys Davids, trs. (*Sacred Books of the Buddhists,* vol. III). London: Luzac, 1957.

Dialogues of the Buddha (*Dīgha-Nikāya* III), pt. III, T. W. and C. A. F. Rhys Davids, trs. (*Sacred Books of the Buddhists,* vol. IV). London: Luzac, 1965.

Dīgha-Nikāya I; *Dialogues of the Buddha,* pt. I, T. W. Rhys Davids, tr. (*Sacred Books of the Buddhists,* vol. II). London: Luzac, 1956.

Dīgha-Nikāya II; *Dialogues of the Buddha,* pt. II, T. W. and C. A. F. Rhys Davids, trs. (*Sacred Books of the Buddhists,* vol. III). London: Luzac, 1966.

Dīgha-Nikāya III; *Dialogues of the Buddha,* pt. III, T. W. and C. A. F. Rhys Davids, trs. (*Sacred Books of the Buddhists,* vol. IV). London: Luzac, 1965.

Dohi Akio, "Nihon ni okeru Fukuin no Dochaku," *Fukuin to Sekai,* vol. XXI (October, 1966).

Drummond, Richard H, "Authority in the Church: An Ecumenical Inquiry," *The Journal of Bible and Religion,* vol. XXXIV, no. 4 (October, 1966).

Dumoulin, Heinrich, "Understanding Other Religions," *The Japan Missionary Bulletin,* vol. XXV, no. 7 (August, 1971).

Dutt, Sukumar. *The Buddha and Five After-Centuries.* London: Luzac, 1957.

Dyer, George J. *Limbo: Unsettled Question.* New York: Sheed and Ward, 1964.

Early Christian Fathers, Richardson, Cyril C., ed. Philadelphia: Westminster, 1953.

Edgerton, Franklin. *The Bhagavad Gītā.* New York: Harper, 1965.

———. *Buddhist Hybrid Sanskrit Grammar and Dictionary,* vol. I. New Haven: Yale University, 1953.

Eliot, Sir Charles. *Hinduism and Buddhism,* vol. I. New York: Barnes and Noble, 1954.

Embree, Ainslie T. *The Hindu Tradition.* New York: Random House, 1960.

Evans-Wentz, W. Y. *The Tibetan Book of the Dead.* London: Oxford University Press, 1960.

Falls, T. B. *Saint Justin Martyr.* New York: Christian Heritage, 1948.

Farquhar, J. N. *The Crown of Hinduism.* London: Oxford University Press, 1915.

Ferré, Nels F. S. *The Universal Word.* Philadelphia: Westminster, 1969.

The Finality of Jesus Christ in the Age of Universal History, WCC Bulletin, Division of Studies, vol. VIII (Autumn, 1962).

Fingarette, Herbert. *The Self in Transformation.* New York: Basic Books, 1963.

Foster, John. *After the Apostles.* London: SCM, 1951.

Fritsch, C. F. *Psalms and Proverbs; Interpreter's Bible,* vol. IV. New York: Abingdon, 1955.

Fulgentius. *De Fide;* J. P. Migne, *Patrologia Latina,* vol. LXV. Paris: Garnier Frêres, 1893.

Gard, Richard A. *Buddhism.* New York: Washington Square Press, 1963.

Gilson, Étienne. *The Christian Philosophy of Saint Augustine.* New York: Random House, 1960.

Glasenapp, Helmut von. "Nachträge und Ergänzungen," in Hermann Oldenberg, *Buddha.* München: Wilhelm Goldman Verlag, 1961.

Govinda, Lama Anagarika. *The Psychological Attitude of Early Buddhist Philosophy.* London: Rider, 1969.

Gregory Thaumaturgus. *In Origenem Prosphonetica ac Panegyrica Oratio;* J. P. Migne, *Patrologia Graeca,* vol. X. Paris: J. P. Migne, 1857.

Groot, Adrianus de. "The Mission after Vatican II," *Concilium,* vol. XXXVI. New York: Paulist, 1968.

Guardini, Romano. *The Lord.* Chicago: Regnery, 1954.

Guillaume, Alfred. *Prophecy and Divination.* New York: Harper, 1938.

Hale, John R. *Age of Exploration.* New York: Time, 1970.

Hallencreutz, Carl F. *New Approaches to Men of Other Faiths.* Geneva: World Council of Churches, 1970.

Heiler, Friedrich. *Erscheinungsformen und Wesen der Religion.* Stuttgart: Kohlhammer Verlag, 1960.

Horner, I. B. *Ten Jātaka Stories.* London: Luzac, 1957.

Hügel, Friedrich von. *Essays and Addresses on the Philosophy of Religion.* London: Dent, 1921.

Humphreys, Christmas. *Buddhism.* Harmondsworth, Middlesex: Penguin, 1958.

Pope Innocent III. *De Contemptu Mundi;* J. P. Migne, *Patrologia Latina,* vol. CCXVII. Paris: Garnier Frêres, 1890.

Introduction to the *Jātaka,* in Henry Clarke Warren, *Buddhism in Translations.* New York: Atheneum, 1963.

Iwamoto Yutaka, *Bukkyō Nyūmon.* Tokyo: Chūōkōronsha, 1964.

James, William. *The Varieties of Religious Experience.* New York: The New American Library of World Literature, 1961.

Jaspers, Karl. *The Great Philosophers.* New York: Harcourt, Brace, 1962.

———. *The Origin and Goal of History.* New Haven: Yale University, 1959.

Jātaka, in Henry Clarke Warren, *Buddhism in Translations.* New York: Atheneum, 1963.

Jātakamala, in Edward Conze, *Buddhist Scriptures.* Harmondsworth, Middlesex: Penguin, 1959.

Jenkins, David, "Commitment and Openness," *International Review of Missions,* vol. LIX, no. 236 (October, 1970).

Jones, Rufus M. *The Journal of George Fox.* New York: Capricorn, 1963.

Judah, Stillson, "Indian Philosophy and the Meta-physical Movement in the United States," *Religion in Life,* vol. XXVIII, no. 3 (Summer, 1959).

Jung, Carl Gustav. *The Basic Writings of C. G. Jung,* Violet Staub de Laszlo, ed. New York: Random House, 1959.

———. *Memories, Dreams, Reflections,* Aniela Jaffé, ed. London: Collins, 1967.

———. "Psychology of the Transference," *Collected Works,* vol. XVI. New York: Pantheon, 1954.

Justin Martyr. *Saint Justin Martyr,* T. B. Falls, ed. New York: Christian Heritage, 1948.

Kamegai Ryōun. *Bukkyō kara Kirisuto e.* Tokyo: Fukuinkan Shoten, 1958.

King, Winston L. *Buddhism and Christianity.* Philadelphia: Westminster, 1962.

Kirk, G. S. and J. E. Raven. *The Presocratic Philosophers.* Cambridge: Cambridge University Press, 1960.

Kishi Augustin Hideshi. *Spiritual Consciousness in Zen from a Thomistic Theological Point of View.* Nishinomiya, Japan: Catholic Bishop's House of Osaka, 1966.

Kitagawa, Joseph M. *Religion in Japanese History.* New York: Columbia University, 1966.

———. *Religions of the East.* Philadelphia: Westminster, 1960.

———. *The History of Religions.* Chicago: University of Chicago, 1967.

Klostermaier, Klaus, "Hindu-Christian Dialogue," *Journal of Ecumenical Studies,* vol. V, no. 1 (Winter, 1968).

Kraemer, Hendrik. *The Christian Message in a Non-Christian World.* New York: International Missionary Council, 1947.

———. *Religion and the Christian Faith.* Philadelphia: Westminster, 1957.

———. *Why Christianity of All Religions?,* Hubert Hoskins, tr. Philadelphia: Westminster, 1962.

———. *World Cultures and World Religions.* Philadelphia: Westminster, 1960.

Kümmel, Werner. *Verheissung und Erfüllung.* Zürich: Zwingli-Verlag, 1956.

Küng, Hans. *Freedom Today.* New York: Sheed and Ward, 1966.

Lactantius. *De Ira Dei;* J. P. Migne, *Patrologia Latina,* vol. VII. Paris: Vraget, 1884.

Lanczkowski, Günter. "Das Heilsziel des Nirvāṇa in der Lehre des Buddhas," *Asien Missioniert im Abendland,* Kurt Hutten and Siegfried von Kortzfleisch, eds. Stuttgart: Kreuz-Verlag, 1962.

Lewis, H. D. "Philosophy in the Meeting of East and West," *The Study of Religions,* with R. L. Slater. Baltimore, Maryland: Penguin, 1969.

de Lubac, Henri. *Amida.* Paris: Éditions du Seuil, 1955.

Mahābhārata, in Ainslie T. Embree, *The Hindu Tradition.* New York: Random House, 1960.

Majjhima-Nikāya I; *The Middle Length Sayings,* vol. I, I. B. Horner, tr. London: Luzac, 1967.

Majjhima-Nikāya I; *The Middle Length Sayings,* vol. II, I. B. Horner, tr. London: Luzac, 1957.

Majjhima-Nikāya II; *The Middle Length Sayings,* vol. II, I. B. Horner, tr. London: Luzac, 1957.

Majjhima-Nikāya III; *The Middle Length Sayings,* vol. III, I. B. Horner, tr. London: Luzac, 1967.

Margull, H. J. "The Awakening of Protestant Missions," *History's Lessons for Tomorrow's Missions.* Geneva: WSCF, 1960.

Masutani Fumio. *A Comparative Study of Buddhism and Christianity.* Tokyo: CIIB Press, 1962.

McFarland, H. Neill. *The Rush Hour of the Gods.* New York: Macmillan, 1967.

The Middle Length Sayings (*Majjhima-Nikāya* I), vol. I, I. B. Horner, tr. London: Luzac, 1967.

The Middle Length Sayings (*Majjhima-Nikāya* I), vol. II, I. B. Horner, tr. London: Luzac, 1957.

The Middle Length Sayings (*Majjhima-Nikāya* II), vol. II, I. B. Horner, tr. London: Luzac, 1957.

The Middle Length Sayings (*Majjhima-Nikāya* III), vol. III, I. B. Horner, tr. London: Luzac, 1967.

Milindapañha; Milinda's Questions, vol. I, I. B. Horner, tr. (*Sacred Books of the Buddhists,* vol. XXII). London: Luzac, 1969.

Milindapañha; Milinda's Questions, vol. II, I. B. Horner, tr. (*Sacred Books of the Buddhists,* vol. XXIII). London: Luzac, 1969.

The Minor Anthologies of the Pali Canon (*Udāna*), pt. II, F. L. Woodward, tr. (*Sacred Books of the Buddhists,* vol. VIII). London: Oxford University Press, 1935.

Minucius Felix. *Octavius;* J. P. Migne, *Patrologia Latina,* vol. III. Paris: J. P. Migne, 1886.

Mondésert, Claude. *Le Protreptique.* Paris: Éditions du Cerf, 1951.

——— et Caster, Marcel. *Les Stromates,* vol. I. Paris: Éditions du Cerf, 1951.

Monier-Williams, Sir M. *Buddhism.* Varanasi: Chowkhamba Sanskrit Series Office, 1964.

Nakamura Hajime, *Gōtama Budda.* Kyōto: Hōzōkan, 1965.

———. *Shūkyō to Shakai Rinri.* Tokyo: Iwanami Shoten, 1967.

———. *The Ways of Thinking of Eastern Peoples.* Tokyo: Japanese National Commission for UNESCO, 1960.

Niebuhr, Reinhold. *The Nature and Destiny of Man,* vol. I. New York: Scribner's, 1949.

Nikhilananda, Swami. *The Upanishads.* New York: Harper, 1964.

Nikolaus von Kues Werke, Paul Wilpert, ed., vol. I. Berlin: Walter de Gruyter, 1967.

Niles, D. T. *Buddhism and the Claims of Christ.* Richmond: John Knox, 1967.

Nitobe Inazō. *Bushido, The Soul of Japan.* Los Angeles: Ohara Publications, 1969.

Okada Akio. *Kirishitan Bateren.* Tokyo: Shibundo, 1955.

Oldenberg, Hermann. *Buddha,* Helmut von Glasenapp, ed. München: Wilhelm Goldmann Verlag, 1961.

Organ, Troy, "A Cosmological Christology," *The Christian Century,* vol. LXXXVIII, no. 44 (November 3, 1971).

Origen. *Commentarius in Canticum Canticorum;* J. P. Migne, *Patrologia Graeca,* vol. XIII. Turnhout, Belgium: Brepols, n.d.

———. *Commentarius in Ioannem;* J. P. Migne, *Patrologia Graeca,* vol. XIV, Turnhout, Belgium: Brepols, n.d.

———. *Contra Celsum;* J. P. Migne, *Patrologia Graeca,* vol. XI. Paris: J. P. Migne, 1857.

Origen on First Principles, G. W. Butterworth, tr. Gloucester, Mass.: Peter Smith, 1973.

Oulton, John E. L. and Henry Chadwick. *Alexandrian Christianity* (*The Library of Christian Classics,* vol. II). Philadelphia: Westminster, 1954.

Panikkar, Raymond. *The Unknown Christ of Hinduism.* London: Darton, Longman and Todd, 1964.

———, "Advaita and Bhakti: Love and Identity in a Hindu-Christian Dialogue," *Journal of Ecumenical Studies,* vol. VII, no. 2 (Spring, 1970).

———, "Faith and Belief: On the Multireligious Experience (An Objectified Autobiographical Fragment)," *Anglican Theological Review,* vol. LIII, no. 4 (October, 1971).

———, "Toward an Ecumenical Theandric Spirituality," *Journal of Ecumenical Studies,* vol. V, no. 3 (Summer, 1968).

Pannenberg, Wolfhart. *Basic Questions in Theology,* George H. Kehm, tr., vol. II. Philadelphia: Fortress, 1971.

Phillips, Bernard, ed. *The Essentials of Zen Buddhism, An Anthology of the Writings of Daisetz T. Suzuki.* New York: Dutton, 1962.

Prosperus Aquitanus. *De Vocatione Omnium Gentium;* J. P. Migne, *Patrologia Latina,* vol. LI. Paris: J. P. Migne, 1861.

Psalms of the Early Buddhists (*Therī-gāthā*), pt. I, Mrs. Rhys Davids, tr. London: Luzac, 1964.

Psalms of the Early Buddhists (*Thera-gāthā*), pt. II, Mrs. Rhys Davids, tr. London: Luzac, 1964.

Rahner, Karl. "Das Christentum und die nichtchristlichen Religionen," *Schriften zur Theologie,* vol. V. Einsiedeln: Benziger Verlag, 1964.

——— and Herbert Vorgrimler. *Theological Dictionary.* New York: Herder and Herder, 1965.

Rahula, Walpola. *What the Buddha Taught.* Bedford, England: Gordon Fraker, 1959.

Ramsey, Paul. "Love and Law," in *Reinhold Niebuhr,* C. W. Kegley and R. W. Bretal, eds. New York: Macmillan, 1956.

Reichelt, Karl Ludwig. *Truth and Tradition in Chinese Buddhism.* Shanghai: The Commercial Press, 1927.

Robinson, Richard H. "Buddhism: in China and Japan," in *The Concise Encyclopedia of Living Faiths,* R. C. Zaehner, ed. New York: Hawthorn Books, 1959.

———. *The Buddhist Religion.* Belmont, California: Dickenson, 1970.

Rowley, H. H. *The Biblical Doctrine of Election.* London: Lutterworth, 1950.

Saddharmapundarika, in Edward Conze, *Buddhist Scriptures.* Harmondsworth, Middlesex: Penguin, 1959.

Samartha, S. J., ed. *Dialogue between Men of Living Faiths.* Geneva: World Council of Churches, 1971.

———, ed. *Living Faiths and the Ecumenical Movement.* Geneva: World Council of Churches, 1971.

———, "*More* Than an Encounter of Commitments," *International Review of Missions,* vol. LIX, no. 236 (October, 1970).

Sanyutta-Nikāya I; *The Book of the Kindred Sayings,* pt. I, C. A. F. Rhys Davids, tr. London: Luzac, 1950.

Sanyutta-Nikāya II; *The Book of the Kindred Sayings,* pt. II, Mrs. Rhys Davids, tr. London: Luzac, 1952.

Sanyutta-Nikāya III; *The Book of the Kindred Sayings,* pt. III, F. L. Woodward, tr. London: Luzac, 1954.

Sanyutta-Nikāya IV; *The Book of the Kindred Sayings,* pt. IV, F. L. Woodward, tr. London: Luzac, 1956.

Sanyutta-Nikāya V; *The Book of the Kindred Sayings,* pt. V, F. L. Woodward, tr. London: Luzac, 1965.

Schaff, Philip. *History of the Christian Church,* vol. III (*Nicene and Post-Nicene Christianity*). Grand Rapids, Michigan: Eerdmans, 1957.

Schlette, Heinz Robert. *Towards a Theology of Religions.* New York: Herder and Herder, 1966.

Schreiner, Peter, "Roman Catholic Theology and Non-Christian Religion," *Journal of Ecumenical Studies,* vol. VI, no. 3 (Summer, 1969).

Schurhammer, Georg and Joseph Wicki, eds. *Epistolae S. Francisci Xaverii Aliaque eius Scripta.* Roma: Monumenta Historica Societatis Iesu, 1945.

Seneca. *Ad Lucilium Epistulae Morales,* Richard M. Gummere, ed. Cambridge: Harvard University, 1961.

Shakespeare, William. *As You Like It; Shakespeare, the Complete Works,* G. H. Harrison, ed. New York: Harcourt, Brace, 1952.

Smith, Wilfred Cantwell. *The Faith of Other Men.* New York: Harper, 1972.

———. *The Meaning and End of Religion.* New York: New American Library, 1964.

Söderblom, Nathan. *The Living God.* Boston: Beacon, 1962.

Sölle, Dorothee. *Christ the Representative.* London: SCM, 1967.

Spiritual and Anabaptist Writers, Williams, G. H., ed. Philadelphia: Westminster, 1957.

Stcherbatsky, Fedor Ippolitovich. *Buddhist Logic.* New York: Dover, 1962.

Steinilber-Oberlin, Émile. *Les Sectes bouddhiques japonaises.* Paris: Les Éditions G. Cres et Cie., 1930.

Sumañgala-Vilāsinī, in Henry Clarke Warren, *Buddhism in Translations.* New York: Atheneum, 1963.

Suzuki, Beatrice Lane. *Mahayana Buddhism.* London: Allen and Unwin, 1959.

Suzuki, Daisetz Teitaro. *An Introduction to Zen Buddhism.* New York: Grove, 1964.

Taylor, John V. *The Primal Vision.* London: SCM, 1963.

Teilhard de Chardin, Pierre. *The Phenomenon of Man.* New York: Harper, 1959.

———. *The Future of Man.* New York: Harper, 1964.

Tertullian. *Ad Nationes; Corpus Christianorum,* vol. I, pars I. Turnhout, Belgium: Brepols, 1954.

———. *De Oratione; Corpus Scriptorum Ecclesiasticorum Latinorum*, vol. XX. Turnhout, Belgium: Brepols, 1954.

———. *De Praescriptione Haereticorum; Corpus Christianorum, Series Latina*, vol. I. Turnhout, Belgium: Brepols, 1964.

Theophilus Antiochenus. *Ad Autolycum;* J. P. Migne, *Patrologia Graeca*, vol. VI, Paris: J. P. Migne, 1857.

Thera-gāthā; Psalms of the Early Buddhists, pt. II, Mrs. Rhys Davids, tr. London: Luzac, 1964.

Therī-gāthā; Psalms of the Early Buddhists, pt. I, Mrs. Rhys Davids, tr. London: Luzac, 1964.

Thomas, Edward J. *The Life of the Buddha as Legend and History*. New York: Barnes and Noble, 1952.

Thomas, M. M. *The Acknowledged Christ of the Indian Renaissance*. London: SCM, 1969.

Tillich, Paul. *Christianity and the Encounter of the World Religions*. New York: Columbia University, 1963.

———. *The Future of Religions*. New York: Harper, 1966.

Udāna; Minor Anthologies of the Pali Canon, pt. II, F. L. Woodward, tr. (*Sacred Books of the Buddhists*, vol. VIII). London: Luzac, 1935.

van der Leeuw, G. *Religion in Essence and Manifestation*. New York: Harper, 1963.

Verghese, Paul. *The Freedom of Man*. Philadelphia: Westminister, 1972.

———, "Syncretism and the Quest for Interiority," *The Christian Century*, vol. LXXXVII, no. 51 (December 23, 1970).

Vinaya-Piṭaka; The Book of the Discipline, vol. I, I. B. Horner, tr. (*Sacred Books of the Buddhists*, vol. X). London: Luzac, 1949.

Vinaya-Piṭaka, Mahāvagga; The Book of the Discipline, vol. IV, I. B. Horner, tr. (*Sacred Books of the Buddhists*, vol. XIV). London: Luzac, 1962.

Vinaya-Piṭaka, Cullavagga; The Book of the Discipline, vol. V, I. B. Horner, tr. (*Sacred Books of the Buddhists*, vol. XX). London: Luzac, 1963.

Visser 't Hooft, W. A. *No Other Name*. Philadelphia: Westminster, 1963.

Visuddhi-Magga, in Henry Clarke Warren, *Buddhism in Translations*. New York: Atheneum, 1963.

Warren, Henry Clarke. *Buddhism in Translations*. New York: Atheneum, 1963.

Watanabe Shōkō. *Shin Shakuson Den*. Tokyo: Daihōrinkaku, 1967.

Weber, Max. *The Religion of India*. Glencoe: The Free Press, 1962.

Woven Cadences of Early Buddhists (*Sutta-Nipāta*), E. M. Hare, tr. London: Oxford University Press, 1947.

Yagi Seiichi. *Shinyaku Shisō no Tankyū*. Tokyo: Shinkyō Shuppansha, 1972.

Younger, Paul. *Introduction to Indian Religious Thought*. Philadelphia: Westminster, 1972.

Zimmer, Heinrich. *Philosophies of India*. Cleveland: World, 1961.

INDEX

Abel, 177
Abelard, 168
Abidharma (Abidhamma), 143 n. 16
Abraham, 177
Acts of the Apostles, book of, 180, 181
Addis Ababa, 12
Agama, Chinese, 55, 211
Aggregates (elements), Five, 140, 143, 195
Ajātaśatru, 59, 77, 78 n. 120
Ājīvakas, 21, 29
Ākāśa (space), 125
Albertus Magnus, 168
Ambapāli, 65
Ambattha, 58
Amida (Amitābha), 201f., 205; grace of, 201, 205; *Nembutsu* (recitation of Amida's name), 202; supreme object of devotion, 201, 205
Amitābha, *see* Amida
Anabaptists, 172
Ānanda, 58, 59, 63, 64, 74, 75, 76, 78, 81, 82, 133
Anāthapiṇḍika, 68, 69
Anātman (anatta), see Non-Self
Anaximenes, 166
Angela of Foligno, 110 n. 74
Angulimāla, 118f.
Anquetil-Duperron, A. H., 158
Anthropology, the Buddha's, 138-152; axiological rather than ontological, 146f.; centrality of *Nirvāṇa* for, 149, 188ff., 191, 196, 205; ethical concerns of, 149ff., 183f., 196, 197, 205
Appasamy, A. J., 13
Aquinas, Thomas, 169
Arhat, 43, 96, 122, 125, 143; in the world but not of it, 126
Ariga Tetsutarō, 13
Ārya, 28
Ārya Satya, see Four Noble Truths
Aryan (Brāhman), a true, 36, 99f., 110, 134, 200
Aryan (Vedic-Aryan), 21, 22, 28, 29
Ascetics, Five (first disciples), 37, 45, 46, 85, 132

Ashtaroth, 178
Asia Minor, 17
Asita, 30
Aśoka, Maurya emperor, 27
Aśvaghoṣa, 25, 135
Athenagoras, 163
Ātman (self), 19, 23, 24, 139
Augustine, 148f., 166, 167, 167 n. 31, 168; predestination, 167 n. 33; salvation and the church, 166
Avantī, 28
Avidyā (ignorance), *see* Ignorance

Baal, 178
Bareau, André, 111
Barth, Karl, 158, 159 n. 12
Barthian Theology, *see* Theology, Christian
Baskets of the Law, Three, 211
Baum, Gregory, 13
Bellarmine, 169
Benares, 45, 47, 48, 49, 53, 132, 145
Benz, Ernst, 13, 159 n. 12
Bhaṇdagāma, 80
Bhikṣu (bhikkhu), 46, 57
Bhikṣunī (nun), 63, 64
Bihar, 36
Bimbisāra, Seniya (King), 34, 51, 52, 56, 59, 66, 77, 94, 198
Bleeker, C. J., 11
Blondel, Maurice, 13
Bodh-gayā, 36, 47, 50, 51
Bodies, Three, 135
Bolle, Kees W., 11
Bonaventure: appropriations, concept of, 169 n. 38
Bonhoeffer, Dietrich, 153; Jesus as "the man for others," 197
Boniface VIII, Pope, 168; *Unam Sanctam,* 168
Book of Discipline, see Vinaya-Piṭaka
Bouquet, A. C., 12, 13, 164, 186 n. 71
Brahma (as Buddhist goal), 134, 195
Brahmā (as creator), 19
Brahmā Sahampati, 44
Brahma-bhuto, 147
Brahmajāla-Sūtra, 19
Brahmaloka, 134
Brahman (Brahmā as Ultimate Reality), 24, 139
Brāhman (member of priestly caste), 20, 21, 22, 29, 48, 52, 58, 59, 66, 69, 70, 73, 75, 76, 79, 119, 130, 197, 200
Brihadāraṇyaka Upaniṣad, 22
Brunner, Emil, 158
Buddha, Gautama the: birth and early years, 30-34; cosmology of, 199f.; daily life of, 67-77; detachment from phenomenal existence, 197f.; end of his life, 77-83; public ministry, 44-67; search and enlightenment, 34-44; social criticism, 197ff.; understanding of his mission, 52
Buddhacarita, 25
Buddhaghosa, 26, 63 n. 79, 68, 92, 103, 105, 110, 121, 143f.
Buddhas, 43, 79; Buddha of infinite Light and Life (Amitābha; Jap. Amida), 201
Buddhism: Japanese, 202; Mahāyāna, 63, 135, 138, 187, 193, 205, 210f.; Pure Land, 61, 187, 201f., 205; Sarvāstivāda, 210f.; Shin tradition, 201f.; Sinhalese tradition, 209; Theravāda, 63, 138, 139, 143, 210f.; Zen, 138, 148 n. 39, 187, 202, 203 n. 95, 205
Buddhologists, 9, 15, 212
Bultmann, Rudolf, 98 n. 33

Cadbury, H. J.: principle of proportionate duty, 179
Campanus, John, 172
Cāpa, 110 n. 74
Ceylon, 68, 210
Chakkarai, V., 13
Chāndogya Upaniṣad, 46
Chenchiah, P., 13
China, 60, 157, 186
Christianity, 157
Cicero, 171
Clement, First Letter of, 178
Clement of Alexandria, 163, 164; Logos doctrine, 164
Columbus, Christopher, 169
Commandments, Ten (Hebraic), 90
Common Law, English, 62
Confucianism, 204
Confucius, 203
Congar, Yves, 13
Coomaraswamy, Ananda, 210
Cornelius, 18
Cousins, Ewart, 13, 194 n. 80
Covenant: Abrahamic, 177; Noachian, 161, 176, 182, 182 n. 65; rabbinic tradition, 176; unique relationship for service, 181

Cragg, Kenneth, 13
Crisis (Dialectical) Theology, *see* Theology, Christian
Crusades, 169
Cunda, 81
Cyprian, 167f., 168 n. 34, 170; formula of, 167f., 170
Cyrus, 178

da Gama, Vasco, 169
Daniel, 177
Daniélou, Jean, 13; Cosmic Covenant, 182 n. 6
Dante, 169
David, King, 197
Davis, Charles, 13
"Declaration on the Relationship of the Church to Non-Christian Religions," *see* Vatican Council, Second
De Contemptu Mundi, see Innocent III, Pope
Deer Park, 45, 85, 132
della Mirandola, Pico, 170
de Lubac, Henry, 13, 123 n. 37
de Lugo, Juan (Cardinal), 171 n. 42; universality of God's salvific concern, 171
Dependent origination (or causation), 102ff., 105, 130; twelve links of, 102
Depth psychology, 148f.
De religione Mohammedanica libri duo, see Relandus, Hadrianus
Deva, 38, 40, 48, 122; gods of the ten world systems, 76
Devadatta, 59, 60, 71
Devadutt, V. E., 13
Devanandan, Paul D., 13
De Vitoria, Francisco, 170
Dhammapada, 63 n. 79, 86 n. 4, 91, 95, 96, 99, 111, 120, 121, 144
Dharma (Dhamma), 16, 35, 41, 43, 44, 45, 48, 49, 58, 63, 70, 72, 75, 78, 80, 84, 85, 88, 94, 98, 99, 105, 112, 128-137, 147, 189; Buddha and, 132f., 137, 190; as Buddha's teaching, 84ff., 94, 105, 130; Christian concept of God and, 132; Christian thought and, 136f., 193f., 205; dharmas (elements of phenomenal existence), 131f., 131 n. 7; dynamic character of, 130, 132f., 137, 188ff.; ethical character of, 129ff., 137, 188, 194, 196; etymology of, 128f.; as "Force" or "Power," 96, 121, 137, 191; as "gracious Presence," 188, 191f.; *Karma* and, 137, 188, 190 n. 78; *-Kāya,* 135; Logos concept and *Dharma:* Christian Logos concept, 137; pre-Socratic Logos concept, 131, 136; Stoic Logos concept, 136; -lord (*Dhamma-bhūta*), 132; as "lovely," 48f., 124f., 133, 135, 184, 188, 192; -men, 129, 190, 193; multiple usages of, 130, 135; *Nirvāṇa* and, 98f., 129, 133ff., 136, 139, 146, 151, 188, 190, 190 n. 78, 191f., 196; part of fourfold "reality-structure," 190 n. 78; problem of personalism, 192-194; as refuge and support, 133ff.; rolling of *Dharma*-wheel as cosmic event, 132; social life of wider India, 129f.; as stream, 123, 135, 188, 192; Tao and, 135; as Truth, 78, 79, 130, 132, 134; Wisdom Literature (Hebraic) and, 136f.
Dhyāna (meditation), 92
Diogenes of Apollonia, 166
Doctrine, exoteric and esoteric, 70 n. 96, 199
Doctrines, Judeo-Christian: creation, 161, 166; divine Law, knowledge of, 158; economy of salvation, 163, 166; election for service, 178, 181f.; grace, 163, 167 n. 33; "natural" revelation, 158, 171; providence, 161, 163, 165, 166, 169; revelation, 192ff.
Documents of Vatican II, *see* Vatican Council, Second
Dōgen, 202
Dogmatic Theology, *see* Theology, Christian
Doi Masatoshi, 13
Drang, 21
Dravidian, 24
Duḥkha (dukkha—suffering, ill), 97, 140

Early Buddhist socio-ethical values, 53-56
Ebina Danjō: theological appreciation of Confucianism, 203f.
Ecclesiam Suam, see Paul VI, Pope
Ecumenism, 156f.; and other religions, 156f.
Edgerton, Franklin, 211
Eightfold Noble Path, 46, 72, 86, 88-93, 117, 124; ethical quality of, 86, 88ff.; pure manifestation of Ultimate Reali-

ty, 92f.; unconditioned character of, 92f.
Elijah, 178
Eliot, Charles, 100
Emerson, Ralph Waldo, 88
Empirical man, condition of: and consciousness, 142; dilemma of, 102ff., 131, 139; fundamental inadequacy, 99f., 100 n. 39, 140, 185f., 194f., 196; solution to, 105, 139f., 189f., 191f., 191 n. 79
Enlightenment, 27, 35, 36, 37, 40, 41, 43, 44, 45, 47, 81 n. 127, 85, 102, 126, 132
Enlightenment (European epoch), 157, 171
Enoch, 177
ἐπιθυμία (desire), 101 n. 45
Equivocators, 19
Erasmus, 170
Eternalists, 19
Ethical conduct, category of (*śīla*) (right speech, action and living), 90
Ethical results of religious teaching, 73; of Buddha's teaching, 106f.
Evangelicalism, *see* Pietism
Extensionists, 19

Fah-Hian (Chinese Buddhist pilgrim), 60
Faith (in context of early Buddhist texts), 37
Fall, the, 186
Farmer, H. H., 12
Farquhar, J. N., 158
Fascism, 217
Felix, Minucius, 166; *Octavius*, 166
Felix, the Roman governor, 47
Ferré, Nels F. S., 13
Fire Sermon, 101
Fortuitous Originists, 20
Four Noble Truths (*Ārya Satya*), 39, 46, 70, 85, 89, 97-112, 130 n. 5, 185
Franck, Sebastian, 172
Freud, Sigmund, 148
Fulfillment, concept of, *see* Theology and non-Christian religions
Fulgentius of Ruspe, 167

Gandharva (gandhabba), 142
Ganges River (and basin), 17, 18, 20, 21, 22, 29, 34, 44, 45 n. 47, 53, 60, 65, 67, 71, 78
Gard, Richard A., 130 n. 5
Gardet, Louis, 13
Gautama, Siddhartha, *see* Buddha, Gautama the
Gautamī, Mahāprajāpatī, 28, 63
Gayā Head, 101
German National Socialism, 159
Gilson, Étienne, 148
Glutinum, 149
God, 24, 108f., 132, 136f., 151, 152, 166, 168; Creator, 166, 186, 202, 204; ethical demands of, 177, 181; ethical quality and judgment of, 179; Father of Jesus Christ, 161, 168, 173, 175, 203; patron deity of Western peoples, 161, 168, 174, 205; revelatory character of his work, 175, 176 n. 48; sovereignty of, 13, 162 n. 16, 166, 202, 204f.; transcendent, 149; Trinity active in universe and history, 155 n. 5, 161, 166, 175ff., 182ff., 207f.; as ultimate and independent Reality, 186; universality of his work, 155, 166, 175-182, 206ff.; Yahweh, 177f., 177 n. 51
Godhika (or Vakkali), 107 n. 62
Good, the, 36, 98, 100
Greece, 186
Guardian cherub, anointed, 177f.
Guardini, Romano, 15
Guru, 209

Hakuin, 96 n. 27
Hallencreutz, Carl F., 13
Heiler, Friedrich, 10, 175
Henry the Navigator, 169
Heraclitus, 131, 165
Hetairai, 65
Historians of religions, 10f., 13, 174f.
History of religions, 9-14; definition of, 15, 215; disciplines informing, 10, 11, 174f.; methodological discussion of, 26, 215ff.
Hocking, William Ernest, 13, 158
Hokuriku, 201
Homeless life, 21, 32, 35, 46, 47, 52, 53, 63, 100, 110, 111
Homer, 171
Horner, I. B., 94, 117
Humphreys, Christmas, 37

Ignorance, 102ff., 105
Impermanence *(anicca)*, 98ff., 105, 140
India, 17, 27, 28, 29, 30, 35, 44, 56, 60, 71, 83, 96, 100, 111, 186, 209
Innocent III, Pope: *De Contemptu Mundi*, 100 n. 39

International Missionary Council: Jerusalem Conference, 1928, 158; Tambaram, Madras (India) Conference, 1938, 159
Interpretive criteria, theological: ethical fruits, 183f.; God as One, Creator and Sustainer, 182-185; Jesus Christ, 175, 182-185
Ionia, 17
Ionian Greeks, 19, 20
Irenaeus, 13
Isipatana, 45, 85, 132
Islam, 157, 167
Israel, 184, 186; election to service, 178; encounter with ethical monotheism of Zoroastrianism, 178; and God's concern for others, 179, 181
Iśvara (Lord), 24

Jain, 21, 29, 35, 47, 52, 62, 71, 87
Jainism, 29, 30, 115
James, disciple and apostle: view of human condition, 187
James, William, 99 n. 34
Japan, 172, 201
Jaspers, Karl, 212; "Axial Period" of history, 186
Jātakas, 26f., 55
Jeremiah, 183 n. 67
Jesus Christ, 29, 30, 44, 66, 70 n. 96, 73, 74, 88, 107ff., 110, 126f., 151, 161, 173, 179, 186; affirmation of history, 109; attitude towards Jews and non-Jews, 179f.; Bonhoeffer's "man for others," 197; consummation of history in, 206f.; criterion for interpreting religions, 175, 206f.; ethical fruits as evaluative criterion, 183f., 197; exoteric and esoteric doctrine, 199; fulfillment of Buddhism as well as OT (Kamegai), 203; historical-eschatological perspective of, 108f.; Kingdom of God and, 127, 194, 207f.; practice of moderation, 199; role of Holy Spirit and, 152; same impelling spirit in Jesus and Buddha, 197; Son and Word of God, 152, 164; teaching of God's universal concern, 179; victory of cross over self-centered self, 197; as Wisdom, 163
Jeta Grove, 68
Jewels, Three *(Ratna), see* Refuges, Three
Jīva (individual soul), 23
Job, 177
John, Gospel according to, 182
John of Damascus, 167
John the Baptizer, 199
Jonah, book of: universal concern of Yahweh, 178
Judaism, 157, 178, 181
Judas Iscariot, 59
Jung, Carl Gustav: and Self, 118, 118 n. 16, 148f.
Justin Martyr, 163; Logos doctrine, 164f.; σπέρμα of the Logos, 164

Kairos, 156; meeting of religions as, 156
Kālāma, Ārāda, 35, 46
Kālāmas, 73
Kalyāṇa (lovely), *see Dharma; Nirvāṇa;* the lovely
Kamegai, Ryōun, 201ff.; fulfillment, concept of, 203ff.; God's concern for non-Christians, 201ff.; Jesus as fulfillment of Japanese religions as well as OT, 203; sensitivity and appreciation of, 201
Kapilavastu, 27, 28, 34, 150
Karma (action, deeds and their ethical quality), 23, 35, 39, 43, 56, 58, 87f., 95f., 96 n. 27, 119, 122, 130, 142, 144, 145, 146, 183, 192; basic integrative principle, 131, 188, 191; and *Dharma,* 137, 188, 190 n. 78; part of fourfold "reality-structure," 190 n. 78; primary aspect of man's dilemma, 131, 188f., 191; similar to Paul and the Law, 190
Kārttika (November), 82
Kasi, *see* Benares
Kaśyapa, 50, 51
Kesaputra, 73
Khodr, Georges, 13, 14
King, Winston L., 190 n. 78, 191 n. 79
Kingdom of God, 108f., 126f.; Buddha and, 194; consummation of church and creation in, 208; manifested through person and work of Jesus, 194; present reality of, 127
Kishi, Hideshi, 13, 15
Klostermaier, Klaus, 171
Koḷiyan, 54, 74
Koṇdañña, 132
Konkōkyō, 203
Kośala, 27, 60, 65, 68, 73, 118, 144, 198; language of, 210
Kozaki Hiromichi: theological appreciation of Confucius, 203

Kraemer, Hendrik, 13 n. 1, 159, 159 n. 12
Kṣatriya (warrior and administrative caste), 22, 28, 30, 59
Kümmel, Werner, 110 n. 71
Küng, Hans, 13, 171
Kuśinagara, 81, 82

Lactantius, 163
Lalita-vistara, 25
Laodicea, church in, 151
Lateran Council, Fourth: Cyprian formula, 167f.
Lessing, Gotthold, 157
Lettres curieuses et édifiantes, 157
Liberation, 22, 24, 40, 42, 51, 92, 93, 96, 97, 105, 106, 115, 122, 124, 131, 140, 146, 189; cosmic as well as psychological implications, 107, 192
Licchavis, 34, 65, 70 n. 95, 71, 77
Limbo, 168f.
Logos, concept of: Christian, 137, 157; Clement of Alexandria, 164; Johannine and early church, 163, 178, 182; Justin Martyr, 164f.; pre-Socratic, 131, 136; Stoic, 136; theology of early Greek fathers, 157f.; Theophilus of Antioch, 165f.
Lokuttara, 120, 121
Lombard, Peter, 168
Longknee, 54
Lot, 177
Lovely, the, 48f., 123-126, 133, 135, 184, 188, 192f., 195
Lumbinī Park, 27, 32

Magadha, 28, 34, 35, 49, 51, 52, 56, 59, 66, 67, 68, 76, 77, 94, 145, 198; language of, 210
Magellan, Ferdinand, 169
Mahābhārata, 129
Mahākaśyapa, 50, 59, 66
Mahā-Parinibbāna Sutta, 77, 82, 93
Mahāsanghika, 85
Mahāvagga, 85
Mahāvīra (founder of Jain tradition) (Nātaputra), 29, 30, 51, 62, 87, 115
Mahāyāna Buddhism, *see* Buddhism
Malachi, book of, 178
Mallas, 82, 83
Māluṅkyāputta, 113f.
Manichaeism, 167
Māra (the Tempter), 37, 38, 38 n. 32, 43, 80, 86, 87, 99
Marga (Path), 86
Marxism, 217
Massignon, Louis, 13
Materialists, 24
Matthew, Gospel according to, 179, 183
Maudgalyāyana, 51, 52, 59, 62, 67
Māyā (illusion), 185
Māyādevī, 28
Mbiti, John S., 13
Meditation, 20, 35, 37, 45, 52, 69, 82, 92, 96 n. 27, 117, 187, 193, 194; participation in deeper levels of reality, 195
Melchizedek, 177
Memoria, 148
Mental discipline, category of *(samādhi)* (right effort, mindfulness, and concentration), 90
Metaphysical Movement, *see* New Thought
Methodology, history of religions and theology, 9-15; metaphysical, 10, 11
Mettā (benevolence), 88
Middle Ages, 167ff.
Middle Way, 37, 46, 53, 69, 85, 85 n. 4, 86, 100, 107, 199
Milinda (Menander), 125
Milindapañha, 125
Miracles, 50, 50 n. 56
Missiology, *see* Theology and non-Christian religions
Missionaries: imperative of, 200f.; Protestant, 173f.; Roman Catholic, 157f.
Monasticism (monastic order, Buddhist), 33, 46, 48, 53, 55, 59, 69 n. 93, 77, 187
Morality of Intention, 88
Moselle River, 170
Moses, D. G., 13
Muḥammad, 70
Müller, F. Max, 158

Naaman, 177 n. 51
Nāgasena, 125
Nakamura Hajime, 18 n. 1, 47, 55
Name and form, *see* Phenomenal existence
Nathan, 197
Nathan der Weise, 157
Neill, Stephen, 13

Nembutsu, see Amida
Neo-Confucianism, 203
Neo-orthodoxy, 10
Nepal, 27
New England Transcendentalists, 88
New Testament, 88, 108, 110, 175, 178-182; ethico-spiritual transformation of self, 152; humanity as a whole, 161; relationship to OT, 181f.
New Thought (Metaphysical Movement), 88
Nichiren, 202
Nicholas of Cusa, 170, 171; *De Pace Fidei,* 170; unity of great religions, 170; vision of reconciling Christianity with Islam, 170
Nidāna-kathā, 26
Niebuhr, Reinhold, 147, 186 n. 73
Nikāya, 211
Niles, D. T., 12, 13, 156 n. 9
Nirattaṃ, see Non-Self
Niraya Hell, 119
Nirodha (cessation of suffering), 104
Nirvāṇa (Nibbāna), 16, 34, 41, 42, 43, 54, 61, 64, 80, 81 n. 127, 85, 86 n. 4, 88, 89, 91, 92, 93, 96, 98, 99, 104, 106, 109 n. 68, 111, 113-127, 131, 139, 144, 184; authentic selfhood and, 205; centrality for the Buddha's anthropology, 149, 188ff., 191, 196, 205; coolness of, 116f., 193; cosmic as well as psychological implications of, 118f., 122, 191, 196; deeper mode of human consciousness, 117f., 191; *Dharma* and, 98f., 129, 133ff., 136, 139, 146, 151, 188, 190, 190 n. 78, 191f., 196; etymology of, 115f.; friendliness and compassion, 117; independent reality, 119ff.; integrative and unitive experience of, 118; *lokuttara* (other than the world), 120f.; the lovely, 123-126, 193, 195; as One, 118 n. 17, 123, 123 n. 39, 126; as "Other," 98, 105, 109, 120, 124, 126, 139, 191, 193, 195, 196; part of fourfold "reality-structure," 190 n. 78; phenomenal existence and, 120, 139, 188f., 196; problem of personalism, 192-194; realization rather than definition, 114f., 189 n. 76; relationship to the world, 122, 188f.; soteriological necessity of, 120; stream *(sota)* suggestive of independent dynamism, 121; unconditioned character of, 121; undecaying, the undying . . . , 101, 120, 123, 139
Noah, 176, 177
Noble Truth, First (suffering or ill), 97-101; as dis-ease, 185
Noble Truth, Second (craving or thirst), 101-104; as result of misplaced values, 185
Noble Truth, Third (cessation of suffering), 104-112, 189, 191f.
Non-attachment, 34, 41, 51, 91, 106f., 126, 131
Non-Aryan, 22
Non-Eternalists, 19
Non-Self, 138-152; *attaṃ* and *nirattaṃ*, 142; becoming and, 147; empirical man and, 139f., 195f.; five aggregates, 140, 143; monistic-ontological, 138; no entity with continuity, 138, 143f., 145f., 147, 148, 195f.; spiritual orientation, 147, 149, 194ff.; three uses of "self" and, 141ff.; true self and, 139, 141, 148, 196
Nothingness, 92

Octavius, see Felix, Minucius
Old Testament, 176ff., 181; Jesus as fulfillment of, 203; relationship to NT, 181f.
Origen, 39-40 n. 34, 163f.; pre-existence of souls and reincarnation, 163 n. 21; salvific concern of God in the world, 163f.
Otto, Rudolf, 10, 216

Pāli, 210ff.
Pali Text Society, 15
Palm Grove, 51
Paññā, 93
Panikkar, Raymond, 13, 14, 156, 161 n. 14, 171; Cosmic Covenant, 182 n. 65
Pannenberg, Wolfhart, 13; relatedness of revelation and salvific concern, 176 n. 48
Parables: blind men and elephant, 73; new patch and old garment (Jesus), 200; new wine and old wineskins (Jesus), 200; pearl of great price (Jesus), 205 n. 100; poisoned arrow, 114; raft, 135; soils (Jesus), 70 n. 97
Parinirvāṇa, 42 n. 38, 106

"Participation" (spiritual), 37, 41, 120f., 120 n. 25, 124, 192, 195, 205
Pātimokkha, 61, 94
Paul, the apostle, 47, 100 n. 39, 109 n. 70, 110; address to Athenians, 180; historical-eschatological perspective, 109; Kingdom of God and, 127; *Karma* and Buddha similar to Law and, 190; natural man, 196; providence and purposes of God as universal, 180f.; revelation and man's knowledge of God, 176 n. 48, 181; view of creation, 187; " . . . whatever is true, whatever is honorable, . . ." (Phil. 4:8), 125, 181
Paul VI, Pope, 160; *Ecclesiam Suam,* 160
Pāvā, 80
Perry, Edmund, 13 n. 1
Persia, 186
Persian Empire, 178
Peter, disciple and apostle, 180, 184; view of human condition, 187
Phenomenal existence, 34, 35, 40, 41, 42, 74, 78, 93, 98, 101, 102, 106f., 110, 119, 126; biblical view, 186ff.; Buddha's detachment from, 197f.; *Dharma* and, 131f.; as flux, 98ff., 123, 185f.; as name and form *(nāma-rūpa),* 105, 185f.; *Nirvāṇa* and, 120, 139, 205; not of ultimate value, 185ff.
Philippi, church of: Paul's letter to, 181
Philippidis, Leonidas J., 13
Pietism, 172f.
Plato, 166
Platonists, 167
Pleasures (sensory), 33, 37, 39, 47, 48, 89
Plutarch, 171
Polytheism, 29
Portugal, 169
Prakrit, 210
Prāna (breath, vital principle), 23
Prasenajit, King, 65, 118, 144, 198
Pratītyasamutpāda (dependent origination), *see* Dependent origination
Pre-Aryan, 23, 24
Pre-Socratic Greek philosophers, 18
Precepts, Five, 90; Ten, 90 n. 15
Primitive Buddhism, 17, 98, 102f., 106f., 111, 122, 191, 195, 212; cosmology, 122, 199f.; language of, 210
Prophets of Israel, literary: from the eschatological perspective, 161; understanding of providence, 177f.
Proportionate duty, principle of, 179, 181
Prosperus of Aquitaine, 167 n. 33
Protestant ethic, 55
Psalms of the Sisters, 66
Punabbasu's mother, 111
Pure Land Buddhism, *see* Buddhism
Purpose in the cosmos, 109, 109 n. 68
Puruṣa (person), 23; life-monad, 139
Pythagoras, 17

Rahner, Karl, 13, 14, 171, 207
Rāhula, 31, 59
Rājagriha, 34, 51, 57, 68, 77
Rāmaputra, Udraka, 35, 46
Rammaka, 75
Rapti River, 27
Ratna, see Refuges (Jewels), Three
Real, *see* Ultimate Reality
Reality, *see* Ultimate Reality
Rebirth (transmigration, reincarnation, pre-existence of souls), 22f., 39 n. 34, 40 n. 35, 42, 81, 100, 119, 121, 122, 145, 163 n. 21
Reformation, 172f., 173 n. 45
Refuges (Jewels, *Ratna*), Three, 48, 105, 128
Reichelt, Karl Ludwig, 158
Relandus, Hadrianus: *De religione Mohammedanica libri duo,* 157
Religious authenticity and ethics, 72
Renaissance, 169ff.
Rennyo, 201
Revelation: definition of, 192ff.; and insight, 193
Revelation, the book of, 151
Rhys Davids, Mrs. Caroline Augusta Foley, 66, 158
Rhys Davids, T. W. V., 77 n. 117
Right action, 89
Right aim, 89
Right concentration, 91ff.
Right effort, 90
Right living, 89
Right mindfulness, 91
Right speech, 89
Right view, 89
Riṣi (seer), 30
Rita (principle of order), 129
Rites and sacrifices, 21, 23, 29, 38, 51, 87, 130, 194 n. 81, 197, 199f.
Roman Empire, 166, 168
Rūpa (material form), 140

Sadducees, 199
Ṣāgata, 50 n. 56
Śākya(n), 20, 27, 28, 30, 54, 59, 61, 73, 150, 198; language of, 210
Salvific concern of God, 13, 162; Abrahamic Covenant, 177; confined to Christians, 161, 168, 173; concept of fulfillment, 203-205; Francis Xavier, 172; Gentiles and, 169; historic religions and, 206f.; Juan (Cardinal) de Lugo, 171; literary prophets of Israel, 161, 164; love as motivation, 178f.; Nicholas of Cusa, 170; Noachian Covenant, 161, 176, 182, 182 n. 65; Origen, 163f.; redemption of creation and, 187f.; religions and, 14, 155, 175-182, 200-205; revelation and, 175, 176 n. 48; same impelling spirit in Jesus and Buddha, 197; Sebastian Franck, 172; theological criterion for religious understanding, 175-182; Thomas Aquinas, 169; universality of, 166, 171, 175-182, 204f.
Sama, 134
Samādhi, 93
Samaṇa, 77; *see also Śramaṇa*
Samartha, S. J., 12, 13
Saṁsāra (sphere of phenomenal change, birth and death), 22
Saṃskāra, 39, 140
Sangāmaji, 110
Saṅgha, 35, 46, 48, 62, 105
Sañjaya, 52
Sāṅkhya (one of the schools of classical Indian philosophy), 23, 131, 139, 194 n. 81
Ṣanskrit, 210f.; Buddhist Hybrid-, 211
Śāriputra (Sāraputta), 52, 59, 62, 67, 79, 143
Saundaranandakavya, 135
Schlette, Heinz Robert, 13, 171
"Seek first his kingdom . . ." (Matt. 6:33), 107
Sela, 79
Self, 118, 138-152; affirmation of, 143; -at-one, 146, 148, 151; authentic selfhood, 205; axiological reality, 146; consciousness and, 118 n. 16, 140ff., 148f.; conversion, 195f.; cosmic future of personal relationships, 146f.; ego and, 148, 196; epistemic reorientation, 151; falsity of cosmic or metaphysical significance, 147, 149, 194; higher, 118, 139, 141f., 148, 195; inadequacy of terminology based on phenomena, 143, 147; -in-isolation, 146; integrated, 145, 147, 148, 151, 195; lord of, 144f.; lower, 118, 141; morality, 144f., 146; *Nirvāṇa* and *Dharma* and, 145; not of eternal substance, 145f.; original, 148 n. 39; service of others, 196f.; spiritual orientation, 147, 191, 194f.; teleologically productive, 146, 191; three uses of, 141ff.; transformation of, 151f.; "unconscious" or "subconscious" and, 148f.
Seneca, 171
Sermon on the Mount, 127
Sheba, Queen of, 177
Shinran, 202
Sibylline Oracle, 165
Sicily, 169
Ṣīha, 70 n. 95, 71
Śīla, 93
Simeon, 30
Skandhas, Five, *see* Aggregates, Five
Smith, Wilfred C., 13, 218 n. 3
Socrates, 19, 165
Söderblom, Nathan, 10, 158
Sölle, Dorothee, 186 n. 74
Soviet Union, 159
Spae, Joseph J., 13
Spain, 169
Ṣpiritual Writers, 172, 173 n. 45
Śramaṇa (samaṇa—ascetic, generally a celibate striver after knowledge), 21, 46, 57, 111
Śrāvastī, 68
Stages of awareness, four, 38
Stages of knowledge, three, 38, 39
Stcherbatsky, F., 143 n. 16
Steinilber-Oberlin, E., 105
Stoicism, 136, 161
Stūpa, 83
Suarez, 169
Subhadra, 72, 82
Ṣuchness, 135
Śuddhodana, 27, 28, 30
Suffering, vicarious, 204 n. 98
Sujātā, 37 n. 30
Sūkara-maddava (boar's flesh or a fungoid), 81
Ṣunīta, 57, 61
Sūnya, see Void
Supernormal, psychic powers *(siddhis),* 22, 50, 50 n. 56, 51, 59, 60, 122

Sutta-Nipāta, 72, 79, 121, 123, 134
Sutta-Piṭaka, 211; moral concern rather than scholastic, 143 n. 16
Suttavibhaṅga, 63
Suzuki, Beatrice Lane, 212, 212 n. 13
Suzuki, D. T., 212 n. 13
Śvetaketu, 46
Synoptic Gospels, 179
Syria, 177 n. 51

τὰ ἴδια (John 1:11), 178, 178 n. 59
Tathāgata, 20, 43, 53, 76, 85, 114, 115, 143
Tathatā, *see* Suchness
Tatian: religious and cultural rejection outside the church, 162
Taylor, John V., 13
Teaching of the Buddha, the, 84-112; two primary themes of: (1) unsatisfying condition of empirical man, 185ff.; (2) way of deliverance, 185ff., 190f.
Thera-gāthā, 57
Teilhard de Chardin, P., 207 n. 103
Temple, William, 10, 158
Tenrikyō, 203
Terai (or Tarai), 27
Tertullian, 162 n. 16, 166; religious and cultural rejection outside the church, 162
Text and Canon, problems of, 209-212; textual criticism, 211f.
Thales, 166
Theology, Christian, 9ff., 15; Barthian, 11, 13; Crisis, 10, 158f., 159 n. 12; dogmatic, 10; specific, 11; Thomistic-Aristotelian, 171
Theology and history of religions, 10-14, 174ff.; interpretive criteria, 175, 182-185; salvation history, 175ff.
Theology and non-Christian religions: appropriations, medieval concept of, 194 n. 80; author's development of, 182-208; contemporary developments, 153-160; eschatological convergence, 206ff., 207 n. 103; fulfillment, concept of, 203ff.; function of the church, 207f.; in biblical perspective, 174-182; in church history, 160-174; interpretive criteria for, 175, 182-185, 206f.; missiological implications, 205-208; perspectives of early church fathers, 162-168; salvation history, 175ff., 200f., 205
Theophilus of Antioch, 163; *Ad Autolycum*, 165; Logos doctrine, 165f.
Theravāda Buddhism, *see* Buddhism
Thomas, M. M., 12, 13
Thomistic-Aristotelian Theology, *see* Theology, Christian
Tillich, Paul, 12, 13, 156 n. 9; "quasi-religions," 217; relatedness of revelation and salvific concern, 176 n. 48; religious historical studies and, 156 n. 9; threefold evaluative structure for "particular revelatory experiences," 197
Tokyo Imperial University, 201
Toynbee, Arnold, 13
Trent, Council of, 170
Trikāya, *see* Bodies, Three
Trinity, the, 155; active in universe and history, 155 n. 5, 161, 166, 175ff., 182ff.
Tṛṣṇā (*taṇhā*—craving or thirst), 101
Troeltsch, Ernst, 10, 158
Truth and speculation, 72f., 113, 146f.
Tuṣita heaven, 30
Tyre, 177

Udāna Sūtra, 120
Udāyin, 117
Uemura Masahisa: Bushidō (Way of the Warrior) as Japan's OT, 204
Ultimate Reality (Reality, Real), 24, 40, 41, 42, 43, 86, 89, 92, 93, 98, 106, 107, 113, 122, 130, 130 n. 5, 132, 134, 137, 139, 147, 205; changeless, 185; ethical quality of, 205
Unam Sanctam, *see* Boniface VIII, Pope
Upaka, 110 n. 74
Upāli, 59
Upaniṣads, 18, 21, 22, 23, 24, 28, 29, 32, 35, 41, 42, 46, 86, 125, 139
Upāsaka (lay follower), 47
Upāsikā (female lay follower), 47
Upavāna, 76
Uruvilvā, 36, 49, 50, 51
Uttarakuru, 98

Vaccha, 115
Vaiśakha (April-May), 82
Vaiśālī (Veśālī), 34, 35, 65, 71, 72, 78, 78 n. 119, 80
Vaiśyas (merchant caste), 29, 30, 48
Vajrian Confederacy, 54, 71, 77
Vakkali, 132f.

Vamsā, 28
van der Leeuw, Gerardus, 10, 174
van Leeuwen, Arend Th., 13 n. 1
Vatican Council, Second, 12, 13; "Declaration on the Relationship of the Church to Non-Christian Religions," 12, 160f.; Documents of, 160
Vattagāmani, King, 210
Vedānta (one of the schools of classical Indian philosophy), 139
Vedas, 21, 23, 29; *Rig-,* 139
Vedic-Brahmanism, 18, 20, 21, 23, 28, 29, 30, 38, 46, 51, 71, 129, 130, 194, 199f.; Brahmanic-Hinduism, 199
Verghese, Paul T., 13
Vicedom, Georg F., 13 n. 1
Videha, 34, 65
Vimutti, 93
Vinaya (-Piṭaka), 35, 61, 62, 85, 93, 122
Virgil, 171
Viśākha, 63 n. 79
Visser 't Hooft, W. A., 161
Void, 135
von Hügel, Friedrich, 171

Wach, Joachim, 10, 174
Warren, Max, 12
Weber, Max, 55, 146
Wheel of Life (Existence), 102f.
Wisdom, category of *(prajña, pañña)* (right view and aim), 90
Wisdom Literature (Hebraic), 136f.
Wittgenstein, Ludwig, 218
World Council of Churches, 12; Central Committee of, 12; Dialogue with Men of Living Faiths and Ideologies, subunit of Central Committee, 12; 1971 meeting of Central Committee in Addis Ababa, Ethiopia, 12; 1970 Conference in Ajaltoun, Lebanon, 155 n. 4

Xavier, Francis, 158, 172
Xenophanes, 17

Yagi Seiichi, 13
Yahweh, 177f., 177 n. 51; worshiped under guise of every man's worship, 178
Yama, 144, 147
Yamaka, 143
Yasa, 47, 48
Yaśōdharā, 31, 34
Yoga (introspective, meditative practices), 20, 23, 35; philosophy (one of the schools of classical Indian philosophy), 85, 139
Younger, Paul, 69 n. 93

Zaehner, Robert Charles, 13
Zen Buddhism, *see* Buddhism
Zimmer, Heinrich, 84
Zoroastrianism, 178
Zwingli, 172